Fastlane

STUDENT'S BOOK 1   **KEN WILSON**

International Goods
Can animals talk?
What makes you different?
Before you, who?
Shooting stars
Danger signals
I'll be there
Fit for life

Think big!
Tall stories
Taking off
East to West
Future perfect?
It's not allowed!
Natural explosions
Here is the news

PRENTICE HALL
PHOENIX ELT

New York   London   Toronto   Sydney   Tokyo   Singapore

The author wishes to thank the following people for their help in the production of this book:
Dede Wilson and the teachers and students of Westminster College, London, who piloted the material. The teachers who attended Ken and Dede's Drama Plus course at Bugac, Hungary in July 1996. Karen Jamieson and Diana Bateman for all their help, support and encouragement. The people who contributed to the *Fastlane* Interviews and Questionnaires: thank you for all your time and trouble. The actors of the English Teaching Theatre who did the recorded material: Angela Marshall, Garry Fox, Ian McShane, Lizzie Lewendon, Matthew Bates, Stuart Nurse, Wendy Parkin and Richard Vranch.

This book is dedicated to John Haycraft.

The author and publishers would like to thank the following for permission to reproduce copyright material: Faber and Faber for the extract from '*The Story of English*' by McCrum, Cran and McNeil; *The Guardian* for 'The Colony strikes back' by Victor Keegan (12 December 1994) and the review of the film *Wyatt Earp* by Phillip French (11 September 1994); Reed Books for the extract on Donald Campbell from '*1,000 Great Lives*' by Plantagenet Somerset Fry © Hamlyn Books and for the extract on the ape from '*The Animal Encyclopedia*'; National Geographic Society for the extract on volcanoes (12 December 1992); Sidgwick and Jackson for the extract from '*Is That It?*' by Bob Geldof.

While every effort has been made to trace the owners of copyright material in this book, there have been cases where the publishers have been unable to locate the sources. We would be grateful to hear from anyone who recognises their copyright material and is unacknowledged.

The publishers are grateful to the following for permission to reproduce photographs and other material: Action Images: p. 56; Action Press p. 120 (BL); Airwear Ltd Dr Martens Footwear/R. Griggs Group: p. 41; Allsport: pp. 16 (B), 28, 29 (T), 39, 84 (T); BBC: pp. 5, 80 (L); Barnaby's Picture Library: pp. 49 (BM), 58 (B), 61 (T, BL), 79, 88 (L, M); J. Allan Cash: p. 9 (M); © Stuart Chorley: pp. 1 (BR), 84; Coca-Cola Great Britain and Ireland: p. 41; Comstock: pp. 1 (TR), 48; Colorsport: p. 58 (B); Mary Evans Picture Library: p. 111 (L); Ford Motor Company Ltd: p. 25; © Fotex: p. 13 (TM); Fotomas: p. 19; Ronald Grant Archive: pp. 18 (BL, BR), 60, 64, 80 (R), 81/82, 108; Sally and Richard Greenhill: pp. 24 (B), 73/74, 79 (T); Robert Harding Picture Library: pp. 1/2, 5/6, 8, 9 (B), 24 (T), 49 (TR), 61/62 (M), 61 (BR), 62 (B), 73 (L), 88 (R), 99 (B), 101/102, 109/110, 113/114; Hemel Hempstead Fire Department: p. 7; Michael Holford: p. 119; Joe's: p. 87; The Kobal Collection: pp. 23, 40, 89/90, 92 (T), 116 (L); McDonald's: p. 41; Mirror Syndication: p. 1 (BL), 33/34; Modus: p. 41; National Motor Museum, Beaulieu: pp. 25/26; Nike (UK) Ltd: p. 41; The Office of Population Censuses and Surveys: p. 74; Pizza Hut (UK) Ltd: p. 41; Planet Earth Pictures: p. 111 (T, B); Popperfoto: pp. 3, 29 (TM), 36 (T), 43, 45/46, 49 (BL), 73 (4, 5, 6), 93, 100 (TR, BL), 112, 116 (R); Quadrant Picture Library: pp. 29/30; Range/Bettmann: pp. 12 (R), 32 (L), 38, 41/42, 49/50: Redferns: pp. 13 (TR, BL, BR) 20, 71 (L); Reebok International Ltd: p. 41; Rex Features: pp. 5 (L), 7, 9, 12 (L), 13 (TL), 17 (B), 20 (R), 21/22, 27, 29 (BM, B), 35, 48 (T), 49 (BR), 58 (T1, 2), 58 (4, 5), 59, 62 (T), 68 (T), 71 (R), 76, 79 (L), 85/86, 96, 99 (TL, TR), 100, (BR), 104, 105, 120 (BR), 120 (T); Rolls-Royce Motor Cars: p. 25; Sipa Press: p. 34 (B); Sipa Sport: pp. 53/54; Frank Spooner Pictures: pp. 34 (T), 51, 100; Tony Stone Images: pp. 32 (R), 36 (B), 68 (B), 79 (TM, TR), 92 (B): Levi Strauss (UK) Ltd: p. 41; Telegraph Colour Library: pp. 5 (M), 16 (T), 72; *Today*: p. 104; Volvo car UK Ltd: p. 25; John Walmsley: p. 1 (TL).

First published in 1996 by
Phoenix ELT
A division of Prentice Hall International
Campus 400, Spring Way,
Maylands Avenue,
Hemel Hempstead,
Hertfordshire, HP2 7EZ

© International Book Distributors 1996

Designed by Oxprint Design

Illustrations by Ray & Corrine Burrows, Robert Duncan, John Lawrence, David Lock, Brian Roll, Alan Rowe, Oxford Illustrators, Oxprint Design.

Cassettes produced by Ken Wilson

Printed and bound by Vincenzo Bona-Torino

Library of Congress Cataloging-in-Publication Data

British Library Cataloguing-in-Publication Data
A catalogue record of this book is available from the British Library

ISBN 0-13-325937-4

5 4 3 2 1
1999 98 97

Contents

Map of the Book iv

UNIT 1   Think big! 1

UNIT 2   Too dangerous for me! 5

UNIT 3   East to West 9

UNIT 4   I'll be there 13

UNIT 5   *Review Section* 17

UNIT 6   Computers are Magic! 21

UNIT 7   Fast cars 25

UNIT 8   Taking off 29

UNIT 9   Do animals talk? 33

UNIT 10   *Review Section* 37

UNIT 11   International Goods 41

UNIT 12   I love TV! 45

UNIT 13   The stars are out 49

UNIT 14   The biggest game on earth? 53

UNIT 15   *Review Section* 57

UNIT 16   What makes you different? 61

UNIT 17   Fit for life 65

UNIT 18   Amazing dreams 69

UNIT 19   Before you, who? 73

UNIT 20   *Review Section* 77

UNIT 21   Listen, boys and girls! 81

UNIT 22   It's not allowed! 85

UNIT 23   Here is the news 89

UNIT 24   Tall Stories 93

UNIT 25   *Review Section* 97

UNIT 26   Natural Explosions 101

UNIT 27   Shooting Stars 105

UNIT 28   Danger Signals 109

UNIT 29   Future perfect? 113

UNIT 30   *Review Section* 117

Keys and Communication Task 121

Tapescript 122

Grammar Check 136

Word List 139

BLOCK ONE Ambitions and work

UNIT 1   Pages 1–4

Expressing preferences
and ambitions

MAIN STRUCTURE
would prefer/rather
would like/love

PRONUNCIATION
/ɪ/ as in think

VOCABULARY
Ambitions

UNIT 2   Pages 5–8

Expressing obligation and
giving advice

MAIN STRUCTURE
have/had to
must/mustn't
should/shouldn't

PRONUNCIATION
/iː/ as in me

VOCABULARY
Occupations

UNIT 3   Pages 9–12

Comparing

MAIN STRUCTURE
Comparatives
superlatives

PRONUNCIATION
/e/ as in west

VOCABULARY
Ways of describing
places and jobs

UNIT 4   Pages 13–16

Talking about possibilities
and likely results

MAIN STRUCTURE
First conditional

PRONUNCIATION
/eə/ as in there

VOCABULARY
Music and video

UNIT 5 *Review section*   Pages 17–20

A LANGUAGE REVIEW
1 *Must* and *have to*
2 Comparatives

B SKILLS REVIEW
1 Reading: Comprehension
2 Listening: Note-taking
3 Writing: Parallel writing
4 Speaking: Information gap

C ACROSS CULTURES
Guy Fawkes (1570–1606) and The Gunpowder Plot

D COMPARATIVE PRON
1 /ɪ/ as in *think* and /iː/ as in *me*
2 /e/ as in *west* and /eə/ as in *there*

E COUNTDOWN TO BLOCK TWO

BLOCK TWO Communication

UNIT 6
Describing events in
the present

PRONUNCIATION
/æ/ as in magic

Pages 21–24

VOCABULARY
Computers and
computer games

MAIN STRUCTURE
Present simple

UNIT 7
Describing events in the past

PRONUNCIATION
/a:/ as in fast cars

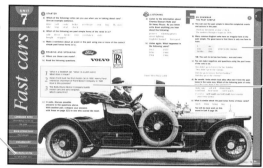

Pages 25–28

MAIN STRUCTURE
Past simple

VOCABULARY
Transport

UNIT 8
Comparing the past to
the present

PRONUNCIATION
/ɒ/ as in off

Pages 29–32

MAIN STRUCTURE
used to

VOCABULARY
Planes and air travel

UNIT 9
Imagining and speculating

PRONUNCIATION
/ɔ:/ as in talk

Pages 33–36

VOCABULARY
Animals and the
natural world

MAIN STRUCTURE
Second conditional

UNIT 10 *Review section*
Pages 37–40

A LANGUAGE REVIEW
1 The present simple
2 Present and past tense forms

B SKILLS REVIEW
1 Reading and Writing: Film reviews
2 Listening: Making a note of differences
3 Speaking: What I find difficult

C ACROSS CULTURES
Transport systems

D COMPARATIVE PRON
1 /æ/ as in *magic* and /a:/ as in *fast cars*
2 /ɒ/ as in *off* and /ɔ:/ as in *talk*

E COUNTDOWN TO BLOCK THREE

BLOCK THREE Hobbies and free time

UNIT 11

Defining things

PRONUNCIATION
/ʊ/ as in good

Pages 41–44

VOCABULARY
Fashion

MAIN STRUCTURE
Defining relative clauses

UNIT 12

Talking about time and place

PRONUNCIATION
/ʌ/ as in love

Pages 45–48

VOCABULARY
Television

MAIN STRUCTURE
Future tense with will and
prepositions of time

UNIT 13

Expressing achievements

PRONUNCIATION
/ə/ as in the

Pages 49–52

VOCABULARY
Films

MAIN STRUCTURE
Present perfect

UNIT 14

Describing events in the past

PRONUNCIATION
/ɜ:/ as in earth

Pages 53–56

VOCABULARY
Countries, football and
other sports

MAIN STRUCTURE
already, yet and still

UNIT 15 *Review section*

Pages 57–60

A   LANGUAGE REVIEW
1 The future tense with *will*
2 Questions with *ever* and *yet*

B   SKILLS REVIEW
1 Reading: Famous people
2 Writing: For and against
3 Listening: Radio advertisements
4 Speaking: 'Why I deserve to be President.'

C   ACROSS CULTURES
Stars in your country

D   COMPARATIVE PRON
1 /ʊ/ as in *good* and /ʌ/ as in *love*
2 /ə/ as in *the* and /ɜ:/ as in *earth*

E   COUNTDOWN TO BLOCK FOUR

BLOCK FOUR   You and your life

UNIT 16

Pages 61–64

Describing people

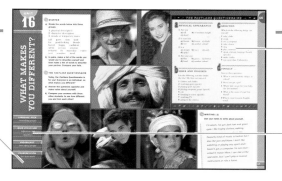

VOCABULARY
Describing people

PRONUNCIATION
/eɪ/ as in make

MAIN STRUCTURE
Adjectives and modifiers

UNIT 17

Pages 65–68

Idiomatic English

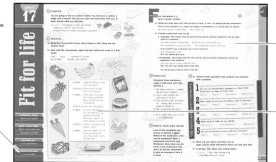

MAIN STRUCTURE
Multi-word verbs and
frequency adverbs

PRONUNCIATION
/aɪ/ as in life

VOCABULARY
Food and fitness

UNIT 18

Pages 69–72

Expressing possibilities

VOCABULARY
Dreams and nightmares

PRONUNCIATION
/əʊ/ as in most

MAIN STRUCTURE
might be, could be and may be

UNIT 19

Pages 73–76

Talking about the past

VOCABULARY
Families and
famous people

PRONUNCIATION
/uː/ as in who

MAIN STRUCTURE
Review of the past

UNIT 20   *Review section*

Pages 77–80

A   **LANGUAGE REVIEW**
  1 Multi-word verbs
  2 Adjectives and nouns

B   **SKILLS REVIEW**
  1 Writing: Improving on existing text
  2 Reading: Autobiography
  3 Listening: What teenagers think
  4 Speaking: What you think

C   **ACROSS CULTURES**
  Biographies and autobiographies

D   **COMPARATIVE PRON**
  1 /eɪ/ as in *make* and /aɪ/ as in *life*
  2 /əʊ/ as in *most* and /uː/ as in *who*

E   **COUNTDOWN TO BLOCK FIVE**

BLOCK FIVE — Good and bad news

UNIT 21

Pages 81–84

Telling stories
narrative

PRONUNCIATION
/ɔɪ/ as in boy

VOCABULARY
Shopping and comedy

MAIN STRUCTURE
Present simple and past
simple for telling a story

UNIT 22

Pages 85–88

Describing events in the past

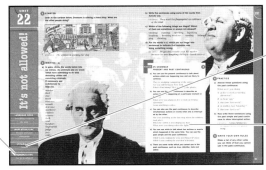

VOCABULARY
Crimes

PRONUNCIATION
/aʊ/ as in allowed

MAIN STRUCTURE
Present and past
continuous

UNIT 23

Pages 89–92

New stories

MAIN STRUCTURE
Past simple passive and
present perfect passive

PRONUNCIATION
/ɪə/ as in here

VOCABULARY
Newspapers, magazines,
TV and radio news

UNIT 24

Pages 93–96

Expressing doubt, surprise
and astonishment

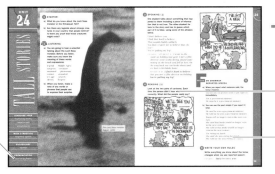

VOCABULARY
Various

PRONUNCIATION
/aʊə/ as in flower

MAIN STRUCTURE
Reported speech

UNIT 25   *Review section*

Pages 97–100

A   **LANGUAGE REVIEW**
  1 Describing two actions in the past
  2 Passive form or adjective?

B   **SKILLS REVIEW**
  1 Writing: Describing a famous crime
  2 Reading: Putting a narrative in order
  3 Listening: News item
  4 Speaking: Telling a story

C   **ACROSS CULTURES**
Folk tales and famous stories

D   **COMPARATIVE PRON**
  1 /aʊ/ as in *allowed* and /ɔɪ/ as in *boy*
  2 /aʊə/ as in *flower* and /ɪə/ as in *here*

E   **COUNTDOWN TO BLOCK SIX**

BLOCK SIX · Planet Earth

UNIT 26

Describing the natural world

PRONUNCIATION
/ʒ/ as in explosions

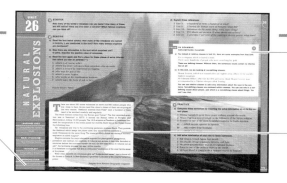

Pages 101–104

MAIN STRUCTURE
Non-defining clauses

VOCABULARY
Geographical features

UNIT 27

Explaining unusual events

PRONUNCIATION
/ʃ/ as in shooting

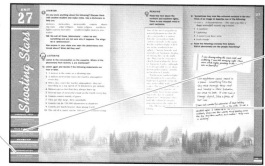

Pages 105–108

MAIN STRUCTURE
so/such
so/... that

VOCABULARY
Astronomy and
astrology

UNIT 28

Talking about the past

PRONUNCIATION
/dʒ/ as in danger

Pages 109–112

MAIN STRUCTURE
Time expressions

VOCABULARY
Animal and marine life

UNIT 29

Talking about the future

PRONUNCIATION
/tʃ/ as in future

Pages 113–116

MAIN STRUCTURE
will/won't be able to
will/won't have to

VOCABULARY
Technology

UNIT 30 *Review section*

Pages 117–120

A LANGUAGE REVIEW
1 Non-defining clauses
2 Non-defining clauses + *so ... that*

B SKILLS REVIEW
1 Reading: The English language
2 Writing: Choosing a subject
3 Listening: Train timetable
4 Speaking: A two-minute talk

C ACROSS CULTURES
The Norman Conquest

D COMPARATIVE PRON
1 /ʒ/ as in *shooting* and /ʃ/ as in *future*
2 /dʒ/ as in *explosions* and /tʃ/ as in *danger*

COUNTDOWN TO THE END OF THE BOOK

LANGUAGE AREA

Expressing preferences
and ambitions

MAIN STRUCTURE

would prefer/rather

would like/love

VOCABULARY

Ambitions

PRONUNCIATION

/ɪ/ as in *think*

1 **STARTER**

Look at the pictures and find a response in the list 1–4 below.

a) Would you like to
be an English
teacher?

c) Would you like to
work in an office?

b) Which ones
would you like?
The red ones
or the pink
ones?

d) Would you like a lift?

1 Actually, I'd prefer some white ones.
2 I'd rather teach Russian.
3 Thanks, but I'd rather walk.
4 No, I'd prefer to work in the open air.

2 **SPEAKING (1)**

a) **In pairs, ask and answer the
questions below using *I'd
prefer* or *I'd rather*. Give
reasons for your answers.**

EXAMPLE: *Would you like to
work in an office?
No, **I'd prefer** to work in
the open air.
Why?
I don't like staying inside
all day.*

1 Would you like to work in
another country?

2 Would you like to visit
New Zealand?

3 Would you like to meet
the President of the USA?

4 Would you like to study
Chinese?

b) **Now ask and answer your own
questions using *Would you
like ...?* and *I'd prefer* or *I'd
rather*.**

THE FASTLANE QUESTIONNAIRE → 💬

NAME: *Maggie Risley*

OCCUPATION: *British Airways pilot*

1 **When did you first decide that you
wanted to be a pilot?**

*My family tell me that when I was five I said that I
wanted to be an airline pilot. However, I think I expressed
a serious interest at 15 or 16. I didn't actually believe I
could achieve my ambition. I didn't have enough money to
pay for my own training and airlines were not sponsoring
students at that time.*

FOCUS ON GRAMMAR (1) ③ EXPRESSING PREFERENCES AND TALKING ABOUT AMBITIONS

a) You can express preferences in the following ways:

Would you like to go by car?
I *would prefer* to go by train.
I *would rather* go by train.

Would you like red roses?
I'*d prefer* white roses.
I'*d rather* have white roses.

NB: In spoken English, we usually say I'*d prefer* and I'*d rather*.

b) You can express what you want, or talk about your ambitions (things you really want to do) like this:

I'*d like* a cup of tea, please.

We'*d like* to come to your house at the weekend.

I'*d like* a Rolex watch for my birthday.

I'*d love* to visit Japan and China.

④ PRACTICE

Complete these sentences using *prefer* or *rather*.

a) I'd ... to work in a bank.

b) We'd ... stay at home.

c) Would you ... do this exercise at home?

d) I'd ... a red car.

⑤ SPEAKING (2)

In pairs, think about some of your ambitions. Tell your partner about them. Are any of your ambitions the same?

EXAMPLE: *I'd like to be a doctor.*
I'd love to work in Canada.
I'd like a big house in the country.

⑥ READING

a) **Maggie Risley is a British Airways pilot. You are going to read her answers to a questionnaire. *Before* you read, do a quick class survey of career ambitions.**

1 What is the most popular or common ambition in the class?

2 Does anyone in the class want to be a pilot?

b) **Now read Maggie's answers opposite and find out the following:**

1 Did she always want to be a pilot?

2 Did her schoolfriends have the same idea?

3 Did her parents feel the same way about her ambition?

2 Did you have friends with the same ambition?

Not while I was still at school, but later at university, I met quite a few who wanted to become RAF (Royal Air Force) pilots or airline pilots.

3 What was the first thing you did to achieve your ambition?

I went for an interview with BUAS (Bristol University Air Squadron) so I could have free flying training with the RAF. I was lucky enough to pass the interview and win one of two places for women that year (the squadron had about 70 members). You could only go for an interview if you were at a local university or college. The subject you were studying was not important, but I was doing an Aeronautical Engineering degree. I think that showed I was enthusiastic.

4 What did your family think of your ambition?

My sisters were excited and my dad was proud (although he'd never tell me that!), especially as I got closer to achieving my goal. My mother worried and I think she still does.

7 WRITING (1)

a) Decide which are the best definitions for the following words and phrases:

1 achieved   a) succeeded
   - b) told people
   - c) stopped

2 training   a) learning from books
   - b) the process of learning a skill
   - c) travelling on trains

3 quite a few   a) not many
   - b) less than
   - c) several

4 excited   a) went out of the room
   - b) exploded
   - c) felt happy and enthusiastic

b) Write down any other words and phrases you don't know. Discuss them with a partner and check them in a dictionary.

8 LISTENING

a) Here are some other questions that Maggie answered.

1 What kind of training did you have and how long did it last?

2 How long did it take you to get a job after your training finished?

3 Is the job everything that you expected it to be?

4 What's your working ambition for the future?

b) In pairs, role-play the rest of the interview using the questions above. Try to think of some extra questions to ask and answer.

STUDENT A: play the part of Maggie.
STUDENT B: play the part of the interviewer.

c) Take it in turns to act out your interview to another pair in the class.

d) Listen to Maggie's answers and take notes.

9 PRON SPOT: /ɪ/ AS IN THINK

a) *i* and *y* are the most common spellings of the /ɪ/ sound.

city   million   British   sister   fifty   system

Make a note of these exceptions:

busy   women   minute

b) **How many /ɪ/ sounds are there in these sentences?**

Maggie Risley is a British Airways pilot.

Fifty million Brazilian Indians live near the Amazon River.

I think I saw sixty busy women drinking quickly in Liverpool.

c) **Listen to the cassette and practise the sentences.**

STAR NAME

BILL AND HILLARY CLINTON
/bɪl/and/hɪlərɪ klɪntən/
President and First Lady of the USA

Read more about them on page 18.

FOCUS ON GRAMMAR (2) (10)
EXPRESSING PREFERENCES

You can express a preference for one thing more than another like this:

I'd *rather* go by train *than* (go) by car.

I'd *prefer* to go by skateboard *than* (go) by plane.

Would you *prefer* white roses *or* red ones?

Would you *rather* get a job *or* go to college?

(11) PRACTICE

Complete these sentences using one word only in each gap.

a) She'd ... stay here ... go out.

b) He'd ... to eat meat ... (eat) fish.

c) Would you ... to watch TV ... go out?

d) They'd ... to learn Russian ... (learn) Chinese.

e) Would you ... write ... phone her?

(12) WRITE YOUR OWN RULES

Look at the sentences in Focus on Grammar (2) again. I'*d prefer* and I'*d rather* mean the same thing. What are the differences in the way we use them?

(13) WRITING (2)

Your national airline has a weekend training course for teenagers. You want to apply but you have to prove your enthusiasm and interest. Write answers to the following questions:

a) Have you ever flown in a plane? When? Where?

b) If you haven't flown, would you like to?

c) Do you like machines? What kind of machines? Are you good at fixing them?

d) Do you know how to use a computer? What can you do with it?

e) Are you afraid of anything? Heights? Loud noises? Turbulence?

f) Are you a patient or impatient person? What makes you impatient?

(14) SPEAKING (3)

a) In groups, discuss the good and bad points about being an airline pilot. Read the list below and decide.

the chance to travel; being away from home; jet lag; turbulence; air traffic; meeting interesting people; delays; working with sophisticated machinery and technology

Think of some things to add to the list.

b) Who in the class would be a good airline pilot? Who would be a good steward or stewardess? Who would be a good check-in clerk? And who would be the passenger most likely to complain about something?

FOCUS ON YOUR COUNTRY (15)

It is often difficult to follow your career ambitions. How do you find out about different jobs in your country? Is there a positive attitude towards employment training for young people?

LANGUAGE AREA

Expressing obligation
and giving advice

MAIN STRUCTURE

have/had to, must/mustn't
should/shouldn't

VOCABULARY

Occupations

PRONUNCIATION

/i:/ as in *me*

1 STARTER

a) Which of the following people can you see on this page?

musician	greengrocer	soccer player
firefighter	gardener	street cleaner
priest	teacher	diplomat
police officer	hotel receptionist	newsreader

b) Which of the jobs listed in a) are dangerous? Discuss with other students.

EXAMPLE: *I think soccer players have a dangerous job because …*
Being a diplomat is dangerous because …

2 SPEAKING

In pairs, choose four people from the list above. What do they *have to* do in their working life? Think of things that are difficult or perhaps they don't like doing. Tell your partner.

EXAMPLE: *Hotel receptionists **have to** listen to complaints from guests.*

3 READING (1)

a) Read the text opposite about the London Fire Brigade and find the answers to the following questions:

1 How many firefighters are there in London?

2 What does LFCDA mean?

3 What codes are used to distinguish different teams of firefighters?

4 How many emergency calls are received by the London Fire Brigade every year?

b) Read the text again and find words or expressions that mean the following:

workers   almost
more than
answer/take action
knowledge

c) Underline verbs in the text that express obligation.

THE LONDON FIRE AND CIVIL DEFENCE AUTHORITY (LFCDA) employs 8,000 staff. Nearly six and a half thousand of them are firefighters. They have to deal with an area of 1,587 square kilometres covering Greater
5 London.

There are 114 fire stations in London and in 1991, they had to respond to 200,000 emergencies. In an average year, the Fire Brigade receives in excess of a quarter of a million telephone calls.

10 Each fire station operates a four-shift system. Each shift is known as a Watch, and each Watch has a colour code: Red, White, Blue or Green.

The Fire Safety Division of the LFCDA has to deal with fire prevention and public awareness of the dangers of fire.
15 Every year, fire safety officers visit 105,000 premises. They also organise advertising campaigns. (See page 7)

FOCUS ON GRAMMAR (1)
HAVE TO, MUST AND HAD TO
4

a) **You can express obligation in the present in two ways.**

Hotel managers *must* listen to complaints.

The Fire Safety Division *has to* deal with fire prevention.

He *must* wear a tie to the office.

You *mustn't* walk on the grass.

b) **You can use *had to* to talk about obligation in the past.**

In 1991, they *had to* respond to 200,000 emergencies.

She *had to* listen to complaints.

5 PRACTICE

Complete these sentences using *has to*, *have to*, *had to* and *must*.

a) Last year, they ... look for somewhere to live.
b) My brother and sister ... do the examination again soon.
c) My mother ... brake quickly when a dog ran in front of her car.
d) Policemen ... be at least 1 m 80 cms tall in my country.
e) Tom ... work tonight.

6 LISTENING

a) **Monica Stevens wants to be a firefighter. She is being interviewed for a place on a training scheme. Look at the list of things she wants to ask about.**

training   leisure facilities
age limit   location of workplace
sex discrimination driving fire engines

b) **Listen to the interview and make notes. What items from the list above does she ask about and in which order? Which ones does she forget to ask about?**

PRON SPOT: /iː/ AS IN *ME*

a) These are the most common spellings of the /iː/ sound.

we   deal   green   scene   chief
receive   meal   wheel

b) Make a note of these unusual spellings:

people   grand prix   machine   pizza
mosquito   Tina

c) Six of the occupations in Activity 1 contain the /iː/ sound. Which ones?

d) Find five other words in this Unit with the /iː/ sound.

e) Listen to the cassette and practise the /iː/ rap.

Tina is a cleaner from Parsons Green
She dreams of being in a grand prix team
She wants to make the scene with her green machine
She wants to be a racing queen!

STAR PRON SPOT NAME

STEVE McQUEEN
/stiːv məkwiːn/
American actor

Listen to more information about him in Unit 5.

8 READING (2)

November 5th is one of the Fire Brigade's busiest nights of the year. All over Britain, people light bonfires and organise firework displays to celebrate Guy Fawkes' night. In the advertisement, there are various things you should and shouldn't do with bonfires and fireworks.

a) Look at the pictures in the fire safety advertisement below. Match them with the words and expressions in the list below. Use your dictionary if you need to.

closed box   naked flame   torchlight
arm's length   fuse   wick   fences
dampen down   sheds   hose-pipe

b) Now read the advertisement to check your answers to a).

TEACH YOUR FAMILY THE FIREWORK CODE

1 Keep fireworks in a closed box. Take them out one at a time and put the top back on at once!

2 Follow the instructions on each firework carefully. Read them by torchlight, never by a naked flame!

3 Light end of firework fuse at arm's length, preferably with a safety firework lighter or fuse wick.

SAFETY ADVICE WITH BONFIRES

1 Don't leave it unattended. Someone should supervise it until it burns down. If it has to be left, dampen it down.

2 Build it well clear of buildings, garden sheds, firework display areas and fences.

3 Keep a bucket of water or a hose-pipe handy, just in case.

F FOCUS ON GRAMMAR (2)
SHOULD AND *SHOULDN'T*

9

You can ask for, give advice and say what you think is right, using *should* and *shouldn't*.

You *should* keep fireworks in a box.
You *shouldn't* tell lies.
Should we do this exercise?

Should and shouldn't are the same for all forms.

She *should* work harder.
You *should* visit your mother more often.

10 PRACTICE

a) **Complete these sentences using *should* or *shouldn't*.**

1 You ... stay up too late, you've got an exam tomorrow.
2 He ... take the handbag he's found to the police station.
3 ... we wait or ... we go?
4 I can't stay any longer, I ... be here at all.
5 You ... eat so much cake.

b) **Rewrite the information from the fire safety advertisement using *should* and *shouldn't*.**

EXAMPLE: *You **should** keep fireworks in a closed box. You **shouldn't** throw fireworks.*

NB: **For emphasis, you can say:**
You *should always* ... or
You *should never* ...

11 WRITING

In groups, make a list of the main domestic fire risks and devise an advertisement like the one opposite to warn people about them. Think about safety in the kitchen and electrical appliances.

→ 💬 ☞ ✗ ✉ ❝ ✎ → 💬 ☞

THE FASTLANE INTERVIEW

12 Barbara Vincent is a London police officer who trains other police officers in the use of safety equipment, such as riot shields.

● Listen to the interview.

● Don't worry if you don't understand everything.

● Make a note of three things that Barbara says about her work.

● Listen again. You can read the text of the interview on page 122.

13 WRITE YOUR OWN RULES

Make a note of everything you know about *have to*, *must* and *should*. What can you say about what they mean and how to use them? Make notes in your Workbook, and compare your notes with another student.

F FOCUS ON YOUR COUNTRY

14

Are there any dangerous jobs in your country which have not been mentioned in this Unit? What makes them dangerous?

EXAMPLE: *Digging the Channel Tunnel was dangerous because they used explosives and heavy equipment.*

Do you know anyone with a dangerous job? Describe what they do.

East to West

LANGUAGE AREA

Comparing

MAIN STRUCTURE

Comparatives/superlatives

VOCABULARY

Ways of describing places
and jobs

PRONUNCIATION

/e/ as in *west*

1 STARTER

a) **Listen to the English names of these European capital cities.**

Dublin   Madrid   Athens
Berlin   Ankara   Moscow

b) **In pairs, try to identify the famous buildings on the left.**

   Listen to the cassette and check.

c) **In pairs, decide which of the cities in a) is the biggest and which is the smallest.**

EXAMPLE: *We think Moscow is probably the biggest, and Berlin is the smallest ...*

Bay of Biscay

R. Tagus ○ **Madrid**

2 READING (1)

Read the information in the chart and answer the questions.

	Population	Area km^2	Average midday temperature °C (January)	Average midday temperature °C (July)	Distance from London (km)
DUBLIN	950,000	922	5	18	602
MADRID	3.2 million	1,629	9	36	2,000
ATHENS	2.4 million	1,934	11	37	2,400
MOSCOW	7.5 million	2,369	−2	16	2,942
BERLIN	5.1 million	1,824	3	21	1,266
ANKARA	2.3 million	1,132	13	40	2,560

Which city ...

a) covers the widest area? And the smallest?
b) has the hottest climate? And the coldest?
c) is the nearest to London? And the furthest away?

F

FOCUS ON GRAMMAR (1)
COMPARATIVES AND SUPERLATIVES

You can form comparative and superlative adjectives using
-*er* and -*est*, or *more* and *most*.

cold	colder	coldest
wide	wider	widest
hot	hotter	hottest
happy	happier	happiest

○ **Moscow**

attractive	*more* attractive	(*the*) *most* attractive
expensive	*more* expensive	(*the*) *most* expensive
dramatic	*more* dramatic	(*the*) *most* dramatic

EXAMPLE: *London is cold, Berlin is colder, but Moscow is the coldest.*
Berlin is colder than London.

Some of the most commonly used adjectives are irregular.

good	better	best
bad	worse	worst
far	further	furthest
much/many	more	most
little	less	least

○ **Berlin**

R. Seine

ire

R. Danube

R. Tiber

Adriatic

Black Sea

○ **Ankara**

Athens
○

Ionian Sea

Aegean Sea

Mediterranean

4 PRACTICE

Are these sentences correct?

a) Winter is colder than summer.
b) The River Thames is widest than the River Seine.
c) It's hot in Madrid than it is in London.
d) Oxford is nearer to London than Edinburgh (is).
e) Ferraris are the better cars in the world.

5 WRITE YOUR OWN RULES

a) *Cold, colder, coldest. Expensive, more expensive, most expensive.* When do you use *-er* and *-est* and when do you use *more* and *most*? Can you think of three more examples for each type?

b) *Hot, hotter, hottest.* Can you think of another adjective that changes like this?

c) Find an adjective like *cold* and another one like *wide.*

d) *Happy, happier, happiest.* Can you think of another adjective like this?

6 SPEAKING

In pairs, ask and answer questions about people in your family. Use superlatives in your questions (*oldest, youngest, tallest, shortest, biggest, most intelligent*).

EXAMPLE: *Who's **the oldest** person in your family?*

7 READING (2)

a) Angela Fox and Garry Marshall are college friends. They want to work and travel for a year before they decide what to do for a career. Read the two job advertisements below which they are considering.

b) Which word below best describes each job? Which words are unsuitable for any of the jobs? Add some adjectives of your own to the list.

unpleasant   well-paid   comfortable   exciting   dull   difficult

c) What do you think of the two jobs? Would you like to do either of them?

EARN $1,000 A WEEK IN A SHIPBOARD CASINO!

See the world and earn lots of money! Cruise from Europe to the West Indies and work on the most fantastic ocean liner in the world – the *Ocean Princess.* You will be working from ten at night until sunrise. Each cruise lasts a fun-filled three months. Experience is useful but not essential. We will train you to work in a casino.

MALAWI

WORK IN A FIELD HOSPITAL

We are looking for volunteers to help with non-medical duties. There is very little money and the work is hard. You don't need to have any experience of hospital work. Although Malawi is one of the world's poorest countries, this is a golden opportunity to see what is undoubtedly the most dramatic scenery in Africa.

FOCUS ON GRAMMAR (2) — 8
SUPERLATIVE EXPRESSIONS

Here are some common ways of using superlatives:

... undoubtedly *the most dramatic* scenery in Africa ...

... *the most fantastic* ocean liner in the world ...

... one of the world's *poorest* countries ...

9 PRACTICE

Complete these sentences using superlative expressions.

a) The Taj Mahal is ... buildings ... world.
b) Diego Maradona was ... soccer players.
c) Queen Elizabeth owns some ... art treasures.
d) Steven Spielberg is undoubtedly ... film director in Hollywood.
e) Hitchhiking is the ... way to see the world.

10 LISTENING

a) **Listen to Angela and Garry discussing the advertisements. Which jobs are they interested in?**

b) **Read these statements. Are they an accurate account of what Garry and Angela said?**

I don't want to work in Africa. It's too dangerous.

I think I'll apply for the job on the cruise because it pays the most.

Working in a casino sounds like fun, and especially on a boat.

I'm going to apply for the job in Malawi because I want to do something useful.

11 WRITING

a) **Read this letter to Garry from Angela in Malawi.**

Dear Garry,
Well, I'm in Malawi. What an incredible place. And what an incredible journey. The plane took 18 hours to get to Lilongwe, the capital, and then I spent two days on a bus to get here. But the scenery is absolutely fantastic, the best I've ever seen. And it's the hottest place I've ever been to, as well. I miss you very much and I wish you were here. Please write to me as soon as you can.

b) **Write a reply from Garry, who is working in a casino on a cruise ship in the Caribbean. Here are some words and phrases you can use, try to use some comparative and superlative adjectives.**

flight   cruise   job   interesting
boring   people   rich   pleasant
unpleasant   food   wonderful
disgusting   homesick   seasick
happy   depressed

12 PRON SPOT: /e/ AS IN *WEST*

a) *e* is the most common spelling of the /e/ sound.

spell   tense   well   best   ever

b) **Make a note of these exceptions.**

said   read (past tense)   lead (metal)
dead   unpleasant

c) **Find five more words in this Unit with the /e/ sound.**

STAR NAMES

ELVIS PRESLEY
/elvɪs prezli:/
American singer

NELSON MANDELA
nelsən mændelə
President of South Africa
(Mandela can also be pronounced /mændeilə/)

Read more about them on pages 18 and 19.

FOCUS ON YOUR COUNTRY 13

Is it common for students in your country to spend a year abroad? Where do they go? Where can they find information about the possibilities? Can they get help from the Government or other places to pay for their travelling?

I'll be there

LANGUAGE AREA

Talking about possibilities
and likely results

MAIN STRUCTURE

First conditional

VOCABULARY

Music and video

PRONUNCIATION

/eə/ as in *there*

1 STARTER

a) How many of these singers do you know? Where do they come from? Can you name any of their songs?

b) Three of their names contain the /ɪ/ sound (see Unit 1). Which ones?

You will find out more about all the singers in Review Unit 5 page 19.

2 READING (1)

a) Read the text below and think of a title for it.

Every week in the UK, more than a hundred new recordings are released. About thirty per cent of them are usually by unknown artists. Half of these unknown artists record on independent or 'first-time' labels. Videos are made of about forty per cent of the new releases. If the artists are famous, the video will appear on TV all over the world. If the artists are new or unknown, they probably won't get the chance to make a video.

There are more music programmes on radio, and radio disc jockeys are more interested in new material than TV disc jockeys. So, if the new artists are lucky, their song will be played on radio. If they're incredibly lucky, it will reach the bottom half of the Top 100 Hit Parade. If the first-time record isn't a hit, the artists will probably never make another one. They will probably have to change their name if they want a second chance. In a normal week, only one of the hundred new releases will be a hit.

b) Write a sentence using each of the following words:

release (noun and verb)
artist   label
disc jockey   hit (noun)

c) Now make questions using 'How many' to get the following answers:

EXAMPLE: *100: How many new albums and singles are released every week?*

1 Fifteen   2 Thirty   3 Forty   4 One

3 LISTENING

You're going to hear a song called *I'll be there*, sung by Jenny Page. The song was recorded on an independent label.

a) While you listen, write down as many examples as you can of *if* clauses.

EXAMPLE: *If you **want** to see me, I'll be there.*

b) After you listen, answer these questions.

1 When is Jenny leaving and by what means of transport?
2 When is she coming back?
3 Where does she want to meet her friend?
4 What should the friend do if he/she wants to see Jenny?
5 Will Jenny be angry if the friend doesn't want to see her?

F FOCUS ON GRAMMAR   4
THE FIRST CONDITIONAL

You can use the first conditional to talk about a possible situation and the likely result.

If you*'re* free, I*'ll come* and see you.
If you*'re* not there, I*'ll call* you tomorrow.
If you *come* to London, *call* me.
Don't worry *if* you *can't* come.

5 PRACTICE

a) Compare your examples of *if* clauses from the song with the sentences in Focus on Grammar. Which are similar?

b) Complete these sentences.

1 If you can come, I ... buy a ticket.
2 If you ... some free time, we ... meet at the Café Madrid.
3 Will you give me a call if you ... to London?
4 If you ... come, let me know and I ... meet you another day.
5 Don't worry, I ... be angry if I don't see you.

6 WRITE YOUR OWN RULES

a) What tenses are used to make the *if* sentences above?

b) What's wrong with these sentences?

1 If you'll see Tom, tell him to call me.
2 Don't worry if you won't see him.
3 If you can go to the party tomorrow, I go with you.

7 READING (2)

a) What is MTV? In pairs, talk about what you know.

b) Read the following text and make a note of any words that you don't know.

MUSIC TELIVISION

MTV stands for Music Television. It's a television channel dedicated to pop music. It was born on 1st August 1981 in the United States. Because of MTV's instant success in the US,
5 the company expanded into other areas. MTV Europe began operating on 1st August 1987. MTV Europe broadcasts 24 hours a day from its London studios. It can be seen in 33 countries and reaches an estimated audience
10 of 110 million viewers.

People of 19 different nationalities work at MTV's London headquarters, and they try to offer a mixture of music from all over Europe. The channel broadcasts in English but Ger-
15 many provides the biggest number of viewers. Currently, one fifth of the music is by German artists.

Most of MTV's output is video and concerts, but there is also a programme called
20 *Unplugged*, where major artists play live and acoustic in front of a small studio audience.

In addition to music, the channel's programmes deal with news, movie information and comedy. MTV has also broadcast special
25 reports on racism, immigration and unemployed teenagers.

c) Find words or phrases in the text that mean the same as the following:

immediate   started   approximate
at the moment   not recorded
not electric   report on   important
out of work

d) Discuss any words that you don't know with other students.

8 WRITING

Read this poem which was sent to an MTV disc jockey.

I write this poem
every day
To tell you the song
I want you to play.
But you still haven't
played it!
Why? Why? Why?
If you don't play it
soon, I think
I'll cry.

Write a poem or a letter to an MTV disc jockey asking him/her to play your favourite song. Say why you want to hear it.

9 PRON SPOT: /eə/ AS IN *THERE*

a) These are the most common spellings of the /eə/ sound.

bear   square   hair   there   their

b) Make a note of two exceptions:

mayor   Mary

c) Look at this list of words. Find words which are spelt differently but pronounced the same.

bear	square	hair	there	pear
care	pair	where	tear*	bare
air	their	wear	stare	chair
heir	rare	stair	fare	fair

* *tear* has two pronunciations: /teə/ **and** /tɪə/ **(rhymes with** *here*)
Use your dictionary to find what the two words mean.

d) Listen to the cassette to check the pronunciation.

THE FASTLANE INTERVIEW ✉ " ✎

10 Michael Klein is a record producer. In this interview, he talks about the process of making records.

- Listen to the interview.

- Don't worry if you don't understand everything.

- Write down three things that Michael thinks are essential for a successful pop song.

- Listen again. You can read the text of the interview on page 123.

11 SPEAKING

In groups, write down your Top 10 English-speaking singers and bands. Compare your views with other groups and agree a class Top 10. Make a bar chart to show the results.

EXAMPLE:

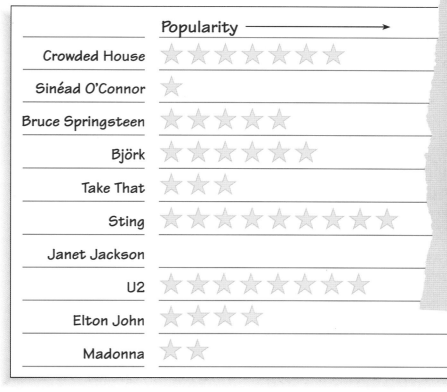

	Popularity ──────────➤
Crowded House	★ ★ ★ ★ ★ ★
Sinéad O'Connor	★
Bruce Springsteen	★ ★ ★ ★
Björk	★ ★ ★ ★ ★
Take That	★ ★
Sting	★ ★ ★ ★ ★ ★ ★
Janet Jackson	
U2	★ ★ ★ ★ ★ ★
Elton John	★ ★ ★
Madonna	★ ★

STAR ⭐ NAME

MARY PIERCE
/ meəri: pɪəs /
Franco-American tennis star

FOCUS ON YOUR COUNTRY   **12**

How many English language songs are there in your music charts? What do you think about this? How many students in the class think that English pop songs are good? How many people don't like them?

A LANGUAGE REVIEW

1 GRAMMAR EXTRA (1)
VERBS OF OBLIGATION

a) *Must* and *have to* can be used in the same way to indicate obligation.

He *must* do this exercise before he goes home.
You *have to* do this exercise before you go home.

b) *Mustn't* and *don't/doesn't have to* are completely different. *Mustn't* = it's illegal, immoral or dangerous.

You *mustn't* import illegal substances.
You *mustn't* tell lies.
You *mustn't* play with that electric cable.

c) *Don't/doesn't have to* = it isn't necessary, you are not obliged to do it.

You *don't have to* attend the meeting (if you don't want to).
You *don't have to* pay to get in (it's free).

2 PRACTICE

Complete these sentences using *mustn't* or *don't/doesn't have to.*

a) You ... light a match if you can smell gas.

b) She ... do this exercise if she doesn't want to.

c) It's Sunday. We ... go to school.

d) The minister ... tell anyone about the Government's secret plans.

e) It's very bad to steal sweets from the shop. You ... do it again.

3 GRAMMAR EXTRA (2)
COMPARATIVES

... *colder than* ... means the same as ... *not as hot as* ...
... *more expensive than* ... means the same as ... *not as cheap as* ...

4 PRACTICE

a) **Match the adjectives in the box on the left with their opposites in the box on the right.**

slow	old
dull	fast
poor	rich
young	intelligent
stupid	exciting

b) Write pairs of sentences using the words above.

EXAMPLE: *My English teacher is **younger than** my grandfather.*
*My English teacher is **not as old as** my grandfather.*

B SKILLS REVIEW

1 READING

a) Read the text about Bill and Hillary Clinton.

BILL CLINTON became President of the United States of America in 1993. He was the first Democrat to achieve this for 12 years. He isn't the youngest US President of
5 all time, but he's the first person since John F. Kennedy in 1961 to become President before the age of 50. As soon as he was elected, he appointed his wife Hillary to an important position in the government. She
10 became responsible for reforming the American health care system. Before moving to the White House, Bill was governor of the State of Arkansas, and Hillary was a Washington lawyer.

b) Now answer these questions.

1 What political party does Bill Clinton belong to?

2 Line 3: *to achieve this*: to achieve what?

3 How long did Bill wait before he gave his wife a job?

4 Does Hillary have to deal with doctors or lawyers?

5 What kind of work did they do before Bill became President?

2 LISTENING

a) You are going to hear some information about Stephen Spielberg and Steve McQueen. Look at the list of films below. Which starred McQueen? Which were directed or produced by Spielberg?

Jaws   Bullitt   ET
Close Encounters of the Third Kind
The Magnificent Seven
Jurassic Park
Schindler's List
Raiders of the Lost Ark
The Great Escape

b) Listen to the cassette and check your answers. When were they made?

3 WRITING

a) Read the text about Winston Churchill.

WINSTON CHURCHILL was born in 1874. He was the son of Lord Randolph Churchill and a descendant of the Duke of Marlborough. At the beginning of the century, he became an MP and was a Government minister at the age of 37, but he lost this position quite quickly and didn't get back into government until the beginning of the Second World War in 1939. He became Prime Minister in 1940 and was in power until the end of the war. He died at the age of 90.

b) Now write a paragraph about Nelson Mandela using this information.

NELSON MANDELA

1918: Born in Transkei, South Africa. The son of a chief of the Tembu tribe.

1930s: One of the first black South Africans to qualify as a lawyer.

1950s: Worked as a lawyer in Johannesburg. Became National Organiser for the African National Congress.

1964: Sentenced to life imprisonment for treason.

1990: Released from prison.

1994: Became President of the Republic of South Africa.

c) Add any more information you know about Nelson Mandela.

d) Find out about your head of state and write a similar paragraph.

4 SPEAKING

Some of this information about the singers pictured on page 13 is true, some of it is false.

a) **In pairs,**

STUDENT A: read the information to your partner one line at a time.

STUDENT B: close your book and listen. Say whether you think the information is true or not.

★ Sinéad O'Connor is a Scottish singer.
She makes dance records.

★ Elvis Presley was born in 1935 in Nashville, Tennessee.
He had lots of hit records but never made a film.

★ Crowded House are an American band.
Some of them used to be in a band called Split Enz.

★ Prince is one of the richest pop stars in the world.
He owns a massive recording studio called Paisley Park.

★ Sting was the singer in a band called The Fire Brigade.
He is an important campaigner for environmental issues.

★ Björk is the first ever pop star from her native country Greenland.
She was in a band called the Icecubes.

b) **Look at page 121 to find the correct information.**

c) **Ask and answer true and false questions about your favourite singers and bands.**

C ACROSS CULTURES Guy Fawkes (1570–1606) and The Gunpowder Plot.

Guy Fawkes was one of the conspirators who planned to assassinate King James I of England and his Government at the opening of Parliament on November 5th 1605. The conspiracy was called The Gunpowder Plot. Gunpowder was secretly stored in the cellars under the House of Lords, and Fawkes was responsible for igniting it at the appropriate time.

There was, of course, no explosion. A conspirator warned a relative not to attend Parliament that day. The relative was suspicious and informed the King. Police arrested Fawkes as he entered the cellar. The Gunpowder Plot is still remembered on November 5th every year.

Are there any famous traitors or conspirators in your country's history? What do you know about them? Find photos, drawings, articles and maps and start an ACROSS CULTURES scrapbook.

D COMPARATIVE PRON

STAR PRON SPOT NAMES

JIM REEVES
/ʤɪm riːvz/
Country singer

/ɪ/ as in **think** and
/iː/ as in **me.**

/ɪ/ is a short sound and
/iː/ is long.

FRED ASTAIRE
/fred əsteə/
Dancer and actor

/e/ as in **west** and
/eə/ as in **there.**

/e/ is a short sound and
/eə/ is long.

a) **Practise these expressions.**

eat and drink   listen and speak
meat and fish   cheese and biscuits

b) **Listen to them on the cassette.**

c) **Use one word from each of the pairs to complete these sentences.**

   1   Your problem is that you never ... when I'm talking to you.

   2   I eat chicken, but I don't eat red ...

   3   French Camembert is a very popular ... in England.

d) **Practise these words and expressions.**

Leicester Square   red hair   fresh air
Belfast airport   hairdresser

e) **Listen to them on the cassette.**

f) **Write a story using some of the expressions in a) and d).**

E COUNTDOWN TO BLOCK TWO

1   **In Block One, you have practised the following language:**

Expressing preferences.

I'*d prefer* to work in the open air.
I'*d rather* go by train.
I'*d prefer* to get a job than go to college.
I'*d rather* play football than watch TV.

Expressing obligation.

They *have to* deal with an area of 1,587 square kilometres.
They *had to* respond to 200,000 emergencies.
You *must* do this exercise before you eat.
You *mustn't* import illegal substances.
You *don't have to* pay to get in.

Talking about ambitions.

I'*d like* to be an airline pilot.

Giving advice.

You *should* keep fireworks in a box.
You *shouldn't* throw fireworks.
Should we do this exercise?

Comparatives and superlatives.

My teacher isn't *as old as* my father.
My teacher is *younger than* my father.
French films are *more exciting than* American ones.
... *the best* possible way to see the world.
... *the most* fantastic ocean liner in the world.

Talking about possibilities using the first conditional.

If you *come* to London, *call* me.
Don't worry *if* you *can't* come.
If you're free, I'*ll come* and see you.
If you're not there, I'*ll call* you tomorrow.

2   **Have you written all the new words you have learnt in the Words section of your Workbook? Check your list now.**

3   **Have you started your ACROSS CULTURES scrapbook?**

CONGRATULATIONS!
You are ready to start BLOCK TWO!

1 STARTER

In pairs, take it in turns to draw a character from a popular computer game. Can the rest of the class guess the game?

2 LISTENING

You're going to hear a conversation about computers and computer games.

a) Which of the following words do you think you will hear?

favourite   bicycle
problem   screen
graphics   obstacle
dinner   addictive

b) Listen to the cassette and answer the questions.

1 How many people are speaking?

2 How many of them own a computer?

3 What do the speakers use their computers for?

3 READING

a) Before you read, write down what you know about Sonic the Hedgehog.

LANGUAGE AREA

Describing events in the present

MAIN STRUCTURE

Present simple

VOCABULARY

Computers and computer games

PRONUNCIATION

/æ/ as in *magic*

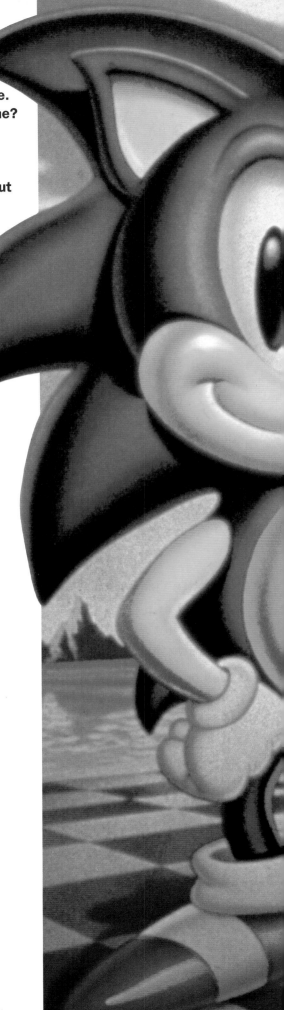

Sonic the Hedgehog is one of the world's best-selling computer games and appeared for the first time in August 1991. There are now many different Sonic games and also a CD version with techno music. What happens in a Sonic the Hedgehog game?

In Sonic 1, we meet a mad scientist called Doctor Robotnik. He decides to capture all the animals in the forest and turn them into robots. Fortunately, Sonic escapes and goes to save his friends. His journey involves fighting his way through six dangerous levels (see illustration).

In Sonic 2, Doctor Robotnik has more evil plans. He wants to capture Sonic's forest friends and convert them into robo-monsters. He needs them to help him build the Death Egg machine, which will help him to take over the world. With his friend, Miles 'Tails' Prower (a young fox with two tails), Sonic stops Robotnik and saves the world.

Sonic CD continues the story, this time with the addition of high-energy techno music. Doctor Robotnik invades the Little Planet, a place which has a strange effect on time and space. He tries to use this effect to take over the world in the past, present and future! Sonic catches Robotnik and saves the world again. He travels through time and defeats the Badniks.

b) Read the text and decide if these statements are true or false.

1 Doctor Robotnik plans to capture the animals in the forest in both Sonic 1 and Sonic 2.
2 The Death Egg machine will help Sonic take over the world.
3 Miles Prower is just an ordinary fox.
4 All Sonic games have a techno music soundtrack.
5 In Sonic CD, Sonic goes back in time to fight Doctor Robotnik and his army.

c) Find words or phrases that mean the following:

take as a prisoner   change
enter by force   control

F FOCUS ON GRAMMAR
THE PRESENT SIMPLE

 4

a) The present simple describes habitual action and routines.

I *ride* my bicycle to school every day.

How do you get to school? I *ride* my bicycle.

My mother *doesn't cook* very well.

I *don't write* to my grandparents very often.

b) You can also use it to describe the story of a film, a play, or a Sonic the Hedgehog game!

In *Back to the Future 1,* Marty *travels* back to 1955.

Romeo *falls* in love with Juliet but they both *die* at the end of the play.

Sonic *catches* Robotnik and *saves* the world again.

c) Make a note of these spellings.

catch catch**es**   try tri**es**   go go**es**

5 PRACTICE

a) Find the mistake in each sentence.

1 He never watchs television.

2 Her grandparents often writes to her.

3 Concorde flys from Paris to Rio de Janeiro.

4 Garry and Angela never washes their car.

5 She doesn't goes to college.

b) What's the third person singular form of these verbs?

do   write   fly   hurry   run
wash   fix   decide

6 WRITE YOUR OWN RULES

Write three rules about present simple spelling.

EXAMPLE: *If a verb ends in -ch or -sh you add -es for the third person singular.*

7 SPEAKING

a) In groups, devise a computer game.

1 Discuss the following: who are the heroes and villains? What is the situation? What problems do the heroes face?

2 Draw the characters.

3 Organise the scoring.

Remember – you can do <u>anything</u> with graphics!

b) Explain your game to other groups.

STAR SPOT NAME

BATMAN
/bætmæn/
American comic-strip character

 PRON SPOT: /æ/ **AS IN** *MAGIC*

a) All the following words contain the /æ/ sound. Put the words in four different categories (three words each).

cat   van   parrot   taxi
Sam   catch   Stan   hamster
carry   hang   Pat   ambulance

b) Make sentences using one word from each category.

23

THE FASTLANE QUESTIONNAIRE → 💬 ☞

9 **Name:** Steve Wallace
Occupation: Computer expert

Read Steve's answers to the questions. Unfortunately, there is an extra word in every sentence. Make a note of the extra words.

EXAMPLE: *The extra word in the first sentence is **my**.*

a WHAT IS A COMPUTER?

A machine which can my process data in digital form. It can favourite store data, display data and receive data. It's a machine that can hobby perform a series of tasks working from instructions. It's a machine that is can do anything, or nothing!

b HOW DOES IT WORK?

Not a fair playing question! It with works at many levels. A my game player sees a game, a programmer sees a program, an engineer sees a set of chips. I don't think anyone can computer see the whole picture, except my boss!

c WHAT'S THE BEST AGE TO START LEARNING COMPUTER SKILLS?

Start as soon I as you can! My son play George (21 months) uses my PC, he likes the colour and movement! More and more, you'll with find yourself using computers without realising it, in telephones, cars, even when you're making toast!

d WHAT IS YOUR FAVOURITE COMPUTER GAME?

My favourite it games are *Goodbye Galaxy* (Apogee Software) and *Monkey Island* (Lucas Arts). I like the every publicity for a game called *Another World*. It says: 'God created the day world in seven days, *Another World* took two years!'

10 WRITING

a) Your list of extra words from the Fastlane Questionnaire makes two sentences. What are they?

b) Write two similar sentences about yourself. Compare your sentences with your neighbour's.

FOCUS ON YOUR COUNTRY **11**

Are Sega and Nintendo games popular in your country? Are they very expensive?

1 **STARTER**

a) **Which of the following verbs can you use when you're talking about cars? Give an example sentence.**

drive   sell   cook   brake   accelerate   rent   buy   fly
overtake   stop   steal   check

b) **Which of the following are past simple forms of the verbs in a)?**

sold   drove   broke   rent   overtaken   stale
bought   stopped

c) **Make a sentence about an event in the past using one or more of the correct simple past tense forms in b).**

2 **READING AND SPEAKING**

a) **Where are these cars made?**

b) **Read the following questions.**

1 Volvo is a Swedish car. 'Volvo' is a Latin word.
What does it mean?

2 Henry Ford built his first motor car in 1892. Henry Ford retired as chairman of Ford Motor Company in 1980.
How is this possible?

3 The Rolls-Royce Motor Company builds motor cars and aero-engines.
Which came first?

c) **In pairs, discuss possible answers to the questions above. With another pair, compare your answers with those on page 121 to see who scored the most.**

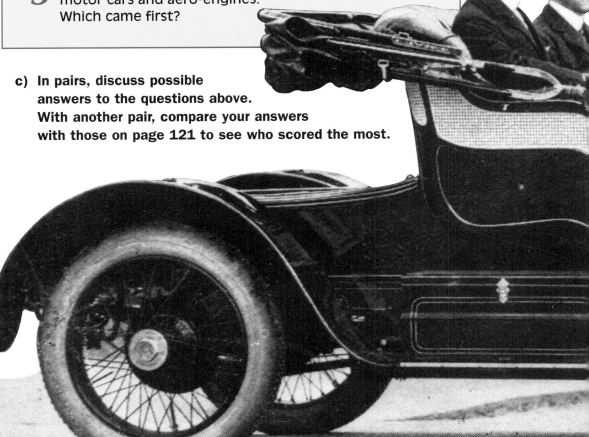

with those on page 121 to see who scored the most.

LANGUAGE AREA

Describing events in
the past

MAIN STRUCTURE

Past simple

VOCABULARY

Transport

PRONUNCIATION

/a:/ as in *fast cars*

3 LISTENING

a) Listen to the information about Charles Stewart Rolls and Sir Henry Royce. As you listen write down anything you hear about the following:

pioneer   winning prizes
street lighting
English Channel   Liverpool

b) Listen again. What happened in the following years?

1863	1877
1896	1900
1904	1906

Classic Rolls Royce 1906

FOCUS ON GRAMMAR
THE PAST SIMPLE

4

a) You can use the past simple to describe completed events and actions in the past.

> I *had* my breakfast at nine o'clock.
> The modern Olympics *began* in 1896.

b) Many common English verbs have an irregular form in the past simple. The good news is that there is only one form to learn.

I	we	
you	you	*went* to the cinema.
he/she	they	

NB: The verb *to be* has two forms – *was* and *were*.

c) You can make negatives and questions using the past tense of the verb *to do*.

> She *didn't go* to Greece for her holiday.
> They *didn't go* to the cinema.

> *Did* she *go* to Greece for her holiday?
> *Did* they *go* to the cinema?

d) Be careful. Verbs which look alike often don't form the past tense in the same way. Which of the following pairs of verbs have the same form in the past tense?

make take   sell tell   drink think
send lend   hear wear   catch watch

EXAMPLE: *sell (sold) and tell (told) have similar past tense forms.*

e) What is similar about the past tense forms of these verbs?

catch   think   bring   buy

You will do more work on this sound in Unit 9 page 36.

5 PRACTICE

a) Complete these sentences, choosing the correct verb and putting it in the past tense.

1 His sister (read/write) to him when she was on holiday.

2 Betty's grandfather (buy/sell) her a car for her 21st birthday.

3 The teacher (say/tell) me to stop worrying.

4 The cats (eat/drink) almost all the milk in the jug.

5 Harry (find/lose) his hat under the bed.

b) Now rewrite the sentences above as past simple questions.

EXAMPLE: *Did his sister **write** to him when she was on holiday?*

6 READING (2)

a) Read this text about Donald Campbell quickly. Which of the following does it refer to?

1 A man's relationship with his father.

2 The life of a car manufacturer.

3 Trying to be the best at something.

b) Which of the suggested meanings below makes sense in the context of the Donald Campbell story?

1 grew up in his shadow
   a) was much shorter than his father
   b) had a very successful father

2 longed to do well
   a) really wanted to do well
   b) wanted to be taller

3 came into his own
   a) drove his own car
   b) succeeded by his own efforts

4 embarked on a career
   a) started work
   b) worked on a boat

5 ended in tragedy
   a) finished his career as an actor
   b) was a disaster

DONALD CAMPBELL (1921-1967)
British land and water speed record holder

Donald Campbell was the son of Sir Malcolm Campbell, who in 1935 was the first man to drive a racing car faster than 300 mph (500 kph). For years, Sir Malcolm was very famous and the boy grew up in his shadow. He longed to do as well, better if possible, but was not encouraged while his father remained alive. Then, after 1949, Donald Campbell came
5 into his own.

With a fine team of engineers and backed by individuals and companies willing to finance him, he embarked on a splendid record-breaking career on land and water. He first broke the water speed record in 1955 and by 1964 had reached 276 mph (450 kph). Then, in 1967, on Lake Coniston, his last attempt to edge the speed higher still, ended in
10 tragedy when his speed craft blew up, killing him instantly.

Donald Campbell still holds the land speed record for a wheel-driven car. Bluebird reached 432 mph (690.9 kph) on 17th July 1964. In 1970, a rocket-engined car driven by Gary Gabelich reached 637 mph (1001.47 kph) and in 1983, Richard Noble drove a jet-engined car at 648.4 mph (1019.4) kph.

PRON SPOT: (1) PAST TENSE OF REGULAR VERBS

a) **There are three different sounds when you form the past simple tense of regular verbs using -ed:**

He fill**ed** /d/ my cup with very hot coffee.

She kiss**ed** /t/ her mother and left the room.

I wait**ed** /ɪd/ two hours for a bus.

b) **Find a verb in the text about Donald Campbell which matches each type.**

c) **Which pronunciation type are the verbs in this list?**

wanted	climbed	needed	stopped
cleaned	missed	started	dreamed

PRON SPOT: (2) /aː/ AS IN *FAST CARS*

a) **Here are some common spellings of words containing the /aː/ sound:**

bath   castle   darling   heart   laugh

It's not common to hear the /aː/ sound after *w* or *y*.

NB: The /aː/ sound is sometimes pronounced /æ/ by some native speakers; it depends where they come from.

b) **Say and explain this proverb:**

He who laughs last laughs longest.

STAR ★ NAME

ARSENAL FOOTBALL CLUB
/ɑːsənl/
Winners of the European Cup-Winners Cup (1994)

9 WRITING

a) **Imagine you are interviewing Donald Campbell on 18th July 1964. Write some questions that you would like to ask.**

EXAMPLE: *How did you feel yesterday when you broke the world record?*

b) **In pairs, ask and answer the questions.**

c) **Now write the interview as a short newspaper or magazine article. You may find the following vocabulary useful:**

excited   afraid   delighted
terrified   relieved

THE FASTLANE INTERVIEW

10 **Wendy Parkin owns a classic car, a 1963 Triumph Herald.**

- **Listen to the interview.**
- **Don't worry if you don't understand everything.**
- **Find out the following: where did she buy it? How much did she pay for it? What are the main problems with driving a classic car?**
- **Listen again. You can read the text of the interview on page 124.**

FOCUS **ON YOUR COUNTRY**   11

Which are the most common cars on the streets of your country? Are they built in your country? Are there traffic problems in your country? What is your Government's transport policy? Write to a minister and find out.

UNIT 8

Taking off

LANGUAGE AREA

Comparing the past
to the present

MAIN STRUCTURE

used to

VOCABULARY

Planes and air travel

PRONUNCIATION

/ɒ/ as in *off*

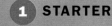

1   STARTER

**Look at these photographs. Do you recognise the people?
What do they do? What did they use to do?**

Sebastian Coe → Olympic athlete → Conservative politician
Glenda Jackson → Oscar-winning actress → Labour politician

EXAMPLE: *He's a ... He used to be a ...*

2   READING

a) Read the text opposite about British Airways.

b) Explain these references.

1 line 2: *the company:*   which company?
2 line 5: *from there:*   from where?
3 line 5: *when they arrived:*   arrived where?
4 line 7: *the journey:*   which journey?
5 line 9: *they used to carry:*   who? the pilots or
   the passengers?

BRITISH AIRWAYS, the biggest airline in the world, used to be called Imperial Airways. The company began a commercial London–Paris service in 1925. Douglas DC3 aircraft used to leave from Croydon Aerodrome in South London. Passengers met at a hotel in Central London and
5 travelled from there to the aerodrome in luxury limousines. When they arrived, they were given special warm clothing to wear during the flight.

The journey, which takes about 45 minutes nowadays, used to take much longer, maybe four or five hours. Pilots often landed four or five times between the two cities, often in farmers' fields, for repairs, refuelling and mechanical checks. They used to carry a five
10 pound note in case they had to buy extra fuel or arrange for their passengers to spend the night in a hotel. Planes landed at Le Bourget airport near Paris, and passengers were taken to the city centre in another limousine.

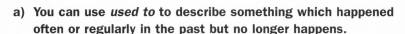

FOCUS ON GRAMMAR ③
USED TO

a) **You can use *used to* to describe something which happened often or regularly in the past but no longer happens.**

I *used to* smoke (but I don't now).

b) **You can also use *used to* to describe a situation or state in the past that no longer exists.**

We *used to* live in London (now we live in Paris).
There *used to* be a church here (now there is a school).

NB 1: ***Used to* is the same for all affirmative forms.**

She *used to* work here.
You *used to* be more interested in English.

c) **You can make negatives and questions using the past tense of the verb *to do*.**

Did you *use to* work for the Government?
She *didn't use to* wear make-up.

NB 2: ***Used to*** /juːstuː/ ***use to*** /juːstə/
The pronunciation is the same.

④ **PRACTICE**

Complete these sentences using the correct form of *used to*.

1 They (live) in Bristol but now they live in Glasgow.

2 She (smoke) 20 cigarettes a day but now she's stopped.

3 I (not like) flying, but now I really enjoy it.

4 You (smoke) ?

5 READING AND SPEAKING

a) Look at the old and new timetables for flights from London to Budapest.

b) Work out the answers to these questions:

1 If 7 means Sunday, on which days did flights use to go at 20:30?

2 On which days do flights go at 20:30 from January 1996?

3 What does FL.NO. mean? Not flying? Flight Number? Number of passengers?

c) In pairs, ask and answer questions about the old and new timetable.

LONDON TO BUDAPEST (until Dec 1995)					
DAYS	DEP.	ARR.	FL.NO.	PLANE	STOPS
——7	0930	1545	BA700	757	1
DAILY	1000	1330	BA868	757	0
——67	1800	2130	BA870	737	0
1-3-5-	2030	2350	BA872	737	0

LONDON TO BUDAPEST (from Jan 1996)					
DAYS	DEP.	ARR.	FL.NO.	PLANE	STOPS
——67	1030	1645	BA700	757	1
DAILY	1005	1335	BA871	767	0
——67	1700	2130	BA870	737	1
12345-	2030	2350	BA873	757	0

EXAMPLE: *When **did** flight BA870 **use to** arrive in Budapest? At 21:30. What time does flight BA871 leave London? At 10:05.*

FOCUS ON GRAMMAR
USED TO AND THE PAST SIMPLE   **6**

a) You can use the past simple or *used to* when describing habitual actions in the past. In this case the past simple is generally used with a specified time reference. This isn't necessary with *used to*.

British Airways, the biggest airline in the world, *used to* be called Imperial Airways.
In the 1930s British Airways *was* called Imperial Airways.

b) *Get used to* means to accustom yourself to something.

I'm *getting used to* driving on the left in England.
I can't *get used to* English food.
It was difficult but I quickly *got used to* it.

In these examples *used to* is pronounced /juːstə/.

c) Used /juːzd/ is also the past tense of the verb use /juːz/.

I *used* a mobile phone for the first time yesterday.

7 PRACTICE

Complete these sentences using the past simple or *used to*.

a) In 1992 I (go) to Canada on holiday.

b) I (catch) the train to work, but now I go by car.

c) I (work) for IBM until 1991.

d) I (work) for IBM.

e) I (not like) olives.

8 LISTENING

Look back at the timetable in Activity 5. Listen to a passenger asking for information about flights. There are three wrong pieces of information. Make a note of them.

PRON SPOT 9: /ɒ/ AS IN *OFF*

a) *o* is the most common spelling of the /ɒ/ sound. Practise these words. The letter *o* is followed by a different consonant in each case.

rob   doctor   body   off   fog   doll
Tom   long   stop   boss   pot

NB: Two alternative spellings can be found in *what* and *watch*.

b) The /ɒ/ sound is not made when the letter *o* is followed by *r*, *v*, *w* or *h*.

Listen and compare these sounds.

oh (dear)   or   love   power   work
move   lower

c) When the letter *o* is followed by a consonant and a vowel, the /ɒ/ sound is not produced. Listen to these words on the cassette and compare.

hop/hope   rob/robe   rod/rode

d) Make a note of these exceptions.

post /əʊ/   comb /əʊ/   only /əʊ/
old /əʊ/   gone /ɒ/   Roger /ɒ/
one /ʌ/

STAR PRON SPOT NAME

DOC HOLLIDAY
/dɒk hɒlɪdeɪ/
A friend of Wyatt Earp's.

See page 38 for more information about Wyatt Earp and Doc Holliday.

10 WRITING

Write a short story, using as many words from the lists in Activity 9 as you can. Read your story to the rest of the class.

EXAMPLE: *Tom found a body in the fog …*

11 SPEAKING (2)

Compare life in your present school to life in your last school.

Think about some of these things:

Homework
Sport
Friends
Teachers
The time you start and finish

EXAMPLE: *The time you start and finish. We **used to** start at … Now we start at …*

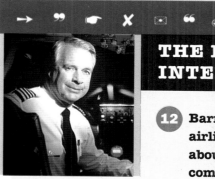

THE FASTLANE INTERVIEW

12 Barry Anderson, an airline pilot, talks about the history of commercial aviation.

- Listen to the interview.
- Don't worry if you don't understand everything.
- Make a note of any examples of *used to* that you hear.
- You can read the text of the interview on page 125.

FOCUS ON YOUR COUNTRY 13

What's the name of the main international airport in your country? What is the reason for this name? E.g. Is it named after a famous person? Has the airport always been in the same place, or did the main airport use to be somewhere else? When did the first international flight depart from there?

Do animals talk?

LANGUAGE AREA

Imagining and
speculating

MAIN STRUCTURE

Second conditional

VOCABULARY

Animals and the
natural world

PRONUNCIATION

/ɔ:/ as in *talk*

1   STARTER

If you were an animal, what kind of animal would you like to be?

2   READING (1)

a) Which creatures are the following texts about? Choose from the photos.

b) Check the words in *italics* in your dictionary. Choose a similar word
    from this list.

goes quickly   found   tell   make   a lot of   form   shown

The ... is a very intelligent animal
and leads a complicated life when
compared to other animals. However, it does not have a very large
number of sounds with which to
form a language. ..., like many
other mammals, can *inform* each
other of their feelings by using
facial expressions.

Animal Encyclopaedia.

When a ... arrives back, it performs a
special dance on the landing platform in
front of the entrance to the colony. First it
scurries around in a circle, then it bisects
the circle. Its track points directly to the
source of the food. Other ... immediately
fly off in the direction indicated. Then the
dancer goes into the hive to dance again.
The farther it goes from the entrance
before it dances, the farther away is the
flower that it has *discovered*.

Life on Earth.

... *produce* a great variety of
noises including ultrasounds,
and there has been *considerable*
speculation as to whether these
sounds *constitute* a language.
Some people say that if only we
were clever enough, we would
be able to understand what they
say and even exchange complex
messages with them. So far, we
have identified 20 complex
sounds that ... make. Some of
them probably keep a school
together when they are
travelling at speed. Some appear
to be warning cries. Some seem
to be call-signs so that they can
be recognised by others at a
distance. But no one has yet
demonstrated that ... put these
sounds together to form the
equivalent of the two-word
sentence that is the beginning of
true language.

Life on Earth.

3   LISTENING

Listen to the conversation about animal
communication. Which of the following
opinions are expressed?

a) If animals could speak, we
    wouldn't like what we heard.

b) It would be very useful if we
    learnt more about animal
    language.

c) Animals would have very little to
    tell us if they could speak.

d) If I was an animal, I would be
    very frightened of going near a
    human.

e) There is no point in talking about
    what animals would do if they
    could speak.

FOCUS ON GRAMMAR
THE SECOND CONDITIONAL (4)

a) You can use the second conditional to describe imaginary situations which are unlikely to come true.

If animals *could* speak, we *wouldn't* like what we heard.

b) You can also use it to give advice.

If I *were* you, I *wouldn't* do that.

c) You can use it to express a desire or longing.

If only we *were* clever enough, we *would* be able to understand them.
I *wish* I *could* swim with dolphins.

d) You can use *was* or *were* in the first and third person. *Were* is more formal.

If I *were* an animal, I *would* be a lion.
If I *was* an animal, I *would* be a lion.
What *would* he be if he *were* an animal?

(5) **PRACTICE**

Which of the following sentences indicate that it is raining, and which indicate that it isn't raining?

a) I wish it wasn't raining.

b) If it was raining, we could stay in and watch TV.

c) We could play tennis if it weren't raining.

d) It would be more comfortable if the sun stopped shining for a while.

e) I'd be happy if we saw a bit of rain.

6 WRITE YOUR OWN RULES

a) Look at this example and then write the grammatical explanation for the following three sentences.

EXAMPLE: *If I **had** a million dollars, I **would travel** round the world.*
= ***If** + ...*

If he *didn't go out* so often, he *would* have more money.
If he *didn't drink* so much, he *wouldn't* always have a headache.
If I *had* more money, I *wouldn't* have to work.

NB: In spoken English we usually contract *would* in the affirmative and *not* in the negative.

If I *had* a million dollars, I*'d* travel round the world.
If he *had* a million dollars, he *wouldn't* work.

b) Remember that *could* is also frequently used in the second conditional.

If it *wasn't raining*, we *could* go out and play football.

Complete the following sentences using *could*.

If I was 21, ...   If I had a car, ...
If we knew her name, ...

7 READING (2)

Read these three texts quickly. Which of them are in favour of zoos, and which are against zoos? Make a list of the different opinions.

a)   "It's all very well saying that we should close all the zoos in the world. What would happen? In most zoos, there are generations of animals which were born there. They would have no chance of surviving if they were sent back into the wild."

b)   "Zoos are nice places to visit, but it would be better if the animals were given a chance to live in their natural habitat. They are magnificent creatures who should be back where they belong, in the jungle, in the desert, in the forests, in the mountains or in the sea. In other words, in their natural habitat."

c)   "Personally, I don't like visiting zoos, but I feel very strongly that it would be a very dangerous thing to close them down. Firstly, many creatures would simply not exist if they didn't live in zoos. Secondly, the research which is done in the best zoos gives many species a better chance of survival than they would otherwise have."

8 SPEAKING

What is your opinion about zoos?

a) Divide into two groups, humans and animals.

HUMANS: add your own opinions to the list you made in Activity 7.

ANIMALS: in pairs, choose an animal and decide whether you want to live in a zoo or return to the wild.

b) Now try to convince the other group.

9 WRITING

a) Write a diary of a typical day at the zoo from the point of view of an animal. Don't write the name of the animal.

EXAMPLE: *At six o'clock the zoo keeper comes to my cage and gives me my breakfast, a big piece of meat ...*

In pairs, read your diary to each other. Can your partner guess which animal you are?

b) Write down the things that you would change if you ran the zoo.

EXAMPLE: *If I ran the zoo, I would give all the animals big cages.*

PRON SPOT: /ɔ:/ AS IN *TALK*

a) Here are some common spellings of words containing the /ɔ:/ sound.

caught   bought   horse   war   saw
water   fall   autumn

b) Here are some other words with similar spellings. Three of them do *not* contain the /ɔ:/ sound. Which are they?

taught   thought   worse   far   law
later   tall   Paul

c) Say these sentences quickly.

I caught a ball that Paul thought he saw in the hall.

What sort of storms fall in autumn? They're awful!

I bought a horse and taught it to haul water.

George Orwell was the author of *1984*.

Listen to the sentences on the cassette and practise them.

STAR NAME

GEORGE ORWELL
/dʒɔ:dʒ ɔ:wel/
Writer

Read more about him in Unit 10, page 39.

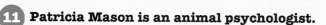

THE FASTLANE INTERVIEW

11 Patricia Mason is an animal psychologist.

● Listen to the interview.

● Don't worry if you don't understand everything.

● Make notes about the animals she refers to.

● What does she say about the following: animals in zoos, pets and fear of animals?

● You can read the text of the interview on page 125.

FOCUS ON YOUR COUNTRY

12

Do some research if necessary, and then talk or write about the following subjects: which animals are closely associated with your country? What animals do people in your country keep as pets? Where is the biggest zoo in your country? What kind of reputation has it got? Are any animals traditionally not liked or valued in your country? Why? How do you feel about this? Do a class survey on how many students have pets: what are the most common pets?

A LANGUAGE REVIEW

1 **GRAMMAR EXTRA (1)**
THE PRESENT SIMPLE

a) **The present simple can be used to describe routines, habits, things that *usually* happen.**

I *watch* TV for five hours a day.
I *get* annoyed when I *see* people shouting at their children.
The morning papers *arrive* at about six o'clock.

b) **Some verbs, when used in the present, are almost always used in the present simple rather than the present continuous, even if they refer to things which are happening now. Here are some of them:**

want	like	need	know	remember
mean	prefer	understand		realise
think (have an opinion)		seem	suppose	hate

Not you again! What do you *want* now?
I don't *understand* what you're talking about.
Do you *realise* what you're doing?

2 **PRACTICE**

a) **Look at the three examples in Grammar Extra 1b). Who said them? Who did they say them to? What was the situation? Write a short dialogue to put them in context.**

b) **Complete these sentences choosing a suitable verb from the list in Grammar Extra 1b).**

1 I don't ... the meaning of this word.
2 Do you ... me? We met last year.
3 She ... to see the manager immediately.
4 My brother ... some help with his maths homework.
5 They don't ... walking in the rain. They ... walking when the sun is shining.

3 **GRAMMAR EXTRA (2)**
PRESENT AND PAST TENSE FORMS

A lot of verbs ending in -*t* have the same form in the present and past (except for the third person singular *s* in the present). So, it is difficult to know whether the verb is in the past or the present.

They *hit* their dog.
I *hurt* my knee.
Those cars *cost* a lot of money.

4 PRACTICE

Complete these sentences.

1 Garry and Angela shut the door
2 I hit a tree
3 They put some money in the bank
4 I let the cat out
5 My feet hurt

a) when it miaows.
b) when I go climbing.
c) when they left the house.
d) when they get paid.
e) when I parked the car.

B SKILLS REVIEW

1 READING AND WRITING

a) You are going to read a review of a film about Wyatt Earp. In pairs, discuss what you know about the Wild West and the gunfight at the OK Corral.

b) Now read the text below quickly and write down three interesting facts about Wyatt Earp.

Wyatt Earp

 directed by LAWRENCE KASDAN • starring KEVIN COSTNER as Wyatt Earp and DENNIS QUAID as Doc Holliday.

Wyatt Earp (1848-1929) was an American law officer and gunfighter who worked as an armed guard for the Wells Fargo Company. In October 1881 he was involved in the gunfight at the OK Corral with his brothers Virgil and Morgan and their friend Doc Holliday.

The film begins in October 1881 as Earp (Kevin Costner) sits in a Tombstone saloon before going out with his brothers to fight the Clancy gang at the OK Corral. Kasdan takes us back to 1863 and we see the 15-year-old Wyatt on his father's farm in Iowa. He is envious of his older brothers who are fighting in the Civil War. His strict Protestant father (Gene Hackman) won't let him fight in the war so he decides to be a lawyer. Then when his pregnant wife dies of typhoid, he turns to drink and starts stealing horses. His father saves him from being hanged. He goes West again to start a new life.

Halfway through the film Earp begins his strange friendship with Doc Holliday, a Southern aristocrat, a part convincingly acted by Dennis Quaid. The film creates a believable portrait of Earp. Costner is both ordinary and charismatic at the same time, and leaves us wondering about the character.

At the end of the film, Earp goes to Alaska, still looking for his El Dorado.

38

c) **Now check the meaning of the following words from the text:**

saloon   envious   strict
pregnant   typhoid   convincingly
believable ordinary   charismatic
wondering

d) **Write a review of a film you have seen. Read these suggestions first:**

First paragraph: say the name of the film, where and when you saw it. Was it an English-speaking film? Was it subtitled or dubbed?

Second paragraph: write a summary of the story of the film. Notice in the review on page 38, past events are described in the present simple tense.

Third paragraph: give your opinion of the film, the actors, the story, the filming, the locations. Say if you would recommend the film to your friends.

2 ▶ LISTENING

Read the text about George Orwell and listen to the cassette. Make a note of any words that are different.

GEORGE ORWELL was born in 1913 in England. His family moved in India in 1917. In 1931, he joined the Imperial Police in Birmingham. His first novel *Burmese Days* shows how much he liked colonial rule. For seventeen years, he lived with the poor of two capital cities, London and Prague. He then worked as a beach guard, but had to stop because of ill health. In the late 1940s, Orwell went to Spain and fought in the Civil War, where he was wounded and wrote *Homage to Catalonia*. His two most famous novels are *Animal Farm*, which he read in 1945, and *1984*, which was a pessimistic view of the past. He chose the title *1984* by reversing the numbers of the year that he wrote the book, 1949.

3 SPEAKING

Look again at the list of verbs in Grammar Extra 1b). Some of them are very useful for saying what you find difficult in English.

EXAMPLES: *I don't **understand** the difference between 'like' and 'prefer'.*
*I don't **know** how to make a question with 'must.'*
*I don't **remember** the English word for …*
*I **need** to know the past tense form of the verb …*

Make a list of points that you have problems with in English. Make sentences like the examples above.

In groups, discuss the points together.

C ACROSS CULTURES

Do a project on transport in your country. Collect as much information as you can and add it to your ACROSS CULTURES scrapbook.

Find out how travelling around your country has changed in the last fifty years. When were the first motorways built? Are the original railway lines still working? Is there a tradition of sea travel in your country? How many airports are there in the country? When did they open?
You can find this information by writing to the airlines, railway companies and the Ministry of Transport.

D COMPARATIVE PRON

1 /æ/ **as in** *magic* **and** /a:/ **as in** *car.*

STAR PRON SPOT **NAME**

JACK CHARLTON
/dʒæk tʃa:ltn/
Manager of the Irish World Cup soccer team, 1994.

/æ/ **is a short sound and** /a:/ **is long.**

a) **Practise these expressions.**

jam jar   last lap   fat chance!
bad marks

**NB: Fat /æ/ chance /ɑː/ and last /ɑː/
lap /æ/ could be pronounced fat /æ/
chance /æ/ and last /æ/ lap /æ/ by
some native speakers.**

b) **Now listen to the cassette and check your
pronunciation.**

c) **Match the expressions with the correct
definitions.**

1 Towards the end of a race on a circular
   track.
2 A poor result in an examination.
3 A pessimistic exclamation.
4 A food container.

2 **/ɒ/ as in *off* and /ɔː/ as in *talk*.**

STAR ★ NAME
PRON SPOT

ROGER MOORE
/rɒdʒə mɔː/
(James Bond in the film *Octopussy*)

a) **Three of the following expressions contain
both sounds. Which ones?**

hot water
top drawer
daughter-in-law
lost cause
second thoughts

**Listen to them on the cassette and check
your pronunciation.**

b) **Make a list of 10 words containing the /æ/,
/ɑː/, /ɒ/ and /ɔː/ sounds. Swap lists with
a partner. Write a short story using all of the
words.**

E COUNTDOWN TO BLOCK THREE

1 **In Block Two, you have practised the
   following language:**

   Describing events in the present.

   I *ride* my bicycle to school every day.
   School *starts* at 8.30.

   Using the present tense to tell a story.

   Doctor Robotnik *invades* the Little Planet.
   At the end of the film, Earp *goes* to Alaska.

   Talking about the past.

   Henry Ford *built* his first motor car in
       1892.
   He *broke* the water speed record in 1955.

   Comparing the past to the present.

   British Airways *used to* be called Imperial
       Airways.
   I *used to* smoke but I don't now.
   We *live* in Paris. We *used to* live in
       London.

   **Talking about imaginary or unlikely
   situations, giving advice and expressing
   desires.**

   If only we *were* clever enough, we *would*
       be able to understand what they say.
   If I *were* you, I *wouldn't* do that.
   I *wish* it *wasn't* raining.

2 **Have you written all the new words you have
   learnt in the Words section of your
   Workbook? Check your list now.**

3 **Have you added new information to your
   ACROSS CULTURES scrapbook?**

   CONGRATULATIONS!
   You are ready to start BLOCK THREE!

UNIT 11

International GOODS

LANGUAGE AREA

Defining things

MAIN STRUCTURE

Defining relative clauses

VOCABULARY

Fashion

PRONUNCIATION

/ʊ/ as in *good*

1 STARTER

a) How many of the following places and product names do you recognise? Which of them can you find in your town?

b) Which of the following statements are true?

1 Nike is a company which manufactures clothes.

2 DR MARTENS is a famous brand of footwear which is made in England.

3 Coca-Cola is a drink which is commonly known as Coke.

4 Benetton is a clothes company which is based in Italy.

5 Pizza Hut is a famous fast food restaurant which sells burgers.

2 LISTENING

Listen to the conversation about famous products. Which of the products in Activity 1 are mentioned?

3 READING

a) You are going to read a text about jeans. Before you read, write down anything you know about the history of jeans.

b) In the text there is a word missing from the first *or* the last sentence of each paragraph. These are the missing words.

coast   means   explain   continued   wear

Read the text opposite and decide where the missing words go.

Klondike miners washing out gold 1897

The man who made the first pair of jeans was Levi Strauss, a German who went to live in the United States at the time of the Gold Rush. Before he went to live in the USA, he lived in France. Here, in the southern French city of Nîmes, he discovered the material which we now call *denim*. Denim is really a short form of *de Nîmes*, which from Nîmes.

But this still doesn't why jeans are called jeans, does it? Well, Strauss decided to take the material that he found to America. He knew that there were hundreds of people who were searching for gold in California and further North in cold Alaska and that they needed clothing and protection.

He packed a large quantity of denim and went to Genoa, a small port which is on the Italian near the French border. In Genoa, he found people who were able to weave the denim into cloth.

The French name for Genoa is *Gênes* (the *s* is not pronounced). In America, denim was called Genes material and eventually *jean* material. Even when he was rich and famous, Strauss to use the Italian port to import denim.

Originally, Strauss wanted to use denim to make tents. The problem was it wasn't waterproof! So he started making work clothing with it. And that's why we jeans, and don't go camping in them!

LEVI'S

c) **Listen to the cassette and check your answers.**

FOCUS **ON GRAMMAR** **4**
DEFINING THINGS AND PEOPLE

a) **You can define things and places using *that* or *which*. The information given in a defining relative clause is essential to the meaning of the sentence.**

... a company *which* is based in Italy ...
... the material *that* he found ...
... a small port *which* is on the Italian coast ...

You can use either *that* or *which* in these sentences.

b) **You can express the same idea without using the relative pronoun (*that* or *which*) when it is the object of the verb.**

A company (*which* is) based in Taiwan.
A port (*that* is) on the south coast of France.

c) **You can usually use *who* to define people.**

Levi Strauss was a German *who* went to live in the USA.
There were hundreds of people *who* were searching for gold.

5 PRACTICE

Rewrite these sentences, using *who*, *which* or *that*.

EXAMPLE: *Denim is a material from France.*
*Denim is a material **which** comes from France.*

a) Levi Strauss was a man from Germany.

b) Genoa is a port situated in Italy.

c) Doc Martens are shoes designed in England.

d) Pizza is a food from Italy.

6 PRON SPOT: /ʊ/ AS IN *GOOD*

a) **Here are some common spellings of words containing the /ʊ/ sound:**

g**oo**d w**oo**d c**ou**ld w**ou**ld sh**ou**ld

b) **The /ʊ/ sound is also in some words containing the letter *u*.**

put /ʊ/   pull /ʊ/   push /ʊ/
bush /ʊ/ (see Star Name)   bully /ʊ/

The letter *u* can also be pronounced /ʌ/.

but /ʌ/   dull /ʌ/   rush /ʌ/

c) **Listen to the cassette and practise this chant.**

Don't push, don't push, pushing isn't good
You want me to move and I would if I could
You're putting me out with your pushing and pulling
You shouldn't be such a great big bully!

STAR ⭐ NAME

GEORGE BUSH
/dʒɔːdʒ bʊʃ/
Former US President

7 WRITING

a) **Write two sentences about things you like and don't like under the headings: places, things and people.**

EXAMPLE: *People: I like people **who** have a good sense of humour. I don't like people **who** are cruel to animals.*

b) **Swap your piece of paper with another person in the class. Tell the rest of the class about that person.**

EXAMPLE: *George likes people with a good sense of humour and he doesn't like people **who** are cruel to animals.*

8 WRITING AND SPEAKING

a) **In groups, look at the illustration. What do you think the products are?**

EXAMPLE: *Gleam is a powder **that** cleans your teeth.*
*Gleam is a powder **that** you use to clean your teeth.*

b) **Devise a television commercial to advertise one of the products.**

Think about the following:

1 **Who are you trying to persuade to buy the product?**

2 **What's special and different about the product?**

3 **In your television commercial, what kinds of people will appear? Will the commercial be serious or funny?**

c) **Act out your commercial to the rest of the class.**

9 WRITE YOUR OWN RULES

a) Make a note of everything you know about the use of *who*, *which* and *that*.

b) Write examples from your own experience in your Workbook for reference.

THE FASTLANE INTERVIEW

10 Helen Rowan studied Fashion at Epsom College of Art, near London. She answered this questionnaire. The answers are with the wrong questions. Connect the questions with their answers.

a What's your favourite style of clothes?

A friend made me a T-shirt with a heart on it and that's my favourite at the moment.

b Where in the world are the most stylish young people?

A good quality classic coat, a tailored trouser suit and an expensive pair of shoes, preferably made in Italy.

c Do you have to spend a lot of money to be stylish?

I like clothes that are individual, not necessarily fashionable.

d What's your favourite T-shirt?

No. Style comes from individuality. You can dress in second-hand clothes and be more stylish than those who spend a lot of money.

e If you had a thousand pounds to spend on clothes today, what would you buy?

Most people think France or Italy, but a lot of style comes from personality. I was in Mexico recently and I think Mexican young people are very stylish.

How would you answer these questions?

FOCUS ON YOUR COUNTRY 11

What clothing styles are fashionable in your country at the moment? Do you like them? What fashion item is your country famous for? Do you like it?

1 **STARTER**

a) What are your favourite TV programmes? Why do you like them?

b) Write down your five favourite TV programmes. Share your ideas with the rest of the class and agree a class Top 10.

2 **READING (1)**

a) Look at the TV listings opposite. Find an example of each of the programmes below.

documentary
news programme
sports programme
soap opera
game show
comedy programme
film
cartoon

BBC 1

6.00 **The News**

6.20 **Adventures of Mickey Mouse**

6.30 **Down Our Street**
Scandal and fun in TV's oldest soap.

7.00 **Have a shot!**
More madness from the strangest game show on TV at the moment. This week, contestants try to shoot apples off a tree.

7.30 **Boys in Blue**
More dull comedy from the boys (and girls) at Dover Street Police Station.

8.00 **Vista**
The award-winning documentary team examine the scandal of half-empty hospitals.

9.00 **Evening news**

9.40 **Rosemary**
The top American comedy series of the year. Does anyone know why?

10.10 **Score!**
All tonight's sports news.

LANGUAGE AREA

Talking about time and place

MAIN STRUCTURE

Future tense with *will* and prepositions of time

VOCABULARY

Television

PRONUNCIATION

/ʌ/ as in *love*

BBC 2

6.00 Wildlife on 2
The lions of the Serengetti.

6.30 Crisis
This week's documentary looks at the problems of sudden amnesia.

7.00 Film: Road to Ruin (1959)
Comedy about two bank managers who try to rob their own bank.

9.20 History Now
A look at 1926, the year of the General Strike and a wonderful Cup Final.

9.50 Say what you mean
The quiz programme for intellectuals.

10.15 News and views
Lively round-up of the day's news with Karen Rogers interviewing the newsmakers.

b) Now match these comments with the relevant programme.

1 It seems that ... will be with us forever, but I'm sure I'm not the only one who hopes that the BBC will get rid of this boring police show sooner rather than later. The characters are not interesting and the comedy never works.

2 This classic comedy from the 1950s will make you laugh and cry at the same time. It's a real classic. Don't miss it!

3 Another chance to see this visually stunning piece, filmed on location on the African plain. The programme covers a year in the life of these powerful and effective hunters.

3 SPEAKING (1)

In pairs, ask and answer questions about the TV programmes.

STUDENT A: close your book and ask about the programmes.

STUDENT B: tell your partner which programmes are on.

EXAMPLE: *A: What's on **at** seven o'clock on BBC1?*
B: A programme called ...
A: What kind of programme is it?

Now swap places.

ON GRAMMAR (1) 4
PREPOSITIONS OF TIME

a) You can use the prepositions *on*, *at* and *in* to talk about time.

The documentary starts *at* eight o'clock.
Boys in Blue is *on* Thursdays.
In the second week of August, I always go to the seaside.
My birthday is *in* March.
I never watch TV *in* winter.
I was born *in* 1984.

b) You can use *from* and *to* or *until* (*till*) to indicate the start and finish of a period of time.

Crisis is on *from* 6.30 *to* 7.00.
The News goes *from* 9.00 *till* 9.40.

5 WRITE YOUR OWN RULES

Look at the sentences in Focus on Grammar 4a) and make a note about the use of *on*, *at* and *in* to talk about time. Think about the following: specific times, days, weeks, months, seasons and years.

6 WRITING

In pairs, think about programmes you really like or dislike. Write a short review and read it to your partner.

7 READING (2)

a) Quickly read paragraphs 1–4 below. (There is a sentence missing from each paragraph.) Decide on an appropriate heading for the text.

1   It is estimated that by the year 2005, there will be at least 2,000 TV channels world-wide. This is not really surprising. People who live in Europe will be able to see programmes which were made in China. Advertisers from Argentina will be able to advertise their products on televisions from Brussels to Beijing.

2   With 2,000 channels to choose from, how will we be able to decide what to watch? There will be two different ways that we can find out what's on TV.

3

METHOD 1

Your personal computer will be attached to an international database of TV information. You will be able to ask your computer to find details of what is on at specific times. For example, if you decide that you want to stay home next Wednesday evening and watch a comedy programme, you can ask your computer. The computer will print out all the comedy programmes that will be broadcast in your language on that evening.

4   **METHOD 2**

The lazy viewer's method. Experts predict that in most countries, there will be a five-hour information programme every Sunday afternoon. With a maximum of 30 seconds about each programme, there will be information about six hundred programmes.

b) Read the paragraphs again. Put the sentences below into the correct place in each paragraph. (They are in the correct order.)

1   What *is* surprising is this: we will all be able to see *all* the channels, wherever we live!

2   Don't worry, the television people have found the answer!

3   This will give you instant information about the available programmes.

4   This will give information about a selection of programmes that will be broadcast in the next seven days.

c) Without looking at the page, describe the two methods from the text in your own words.

FOCUS ON GRAMMAR (2) — THE FUTURE TENSE WITH *WILL* — 8

You can use *will* and *won't* when making a prediction about future events.

There *will* be a five-hour information programme.

There'*ll* be information about six hundred programmes.

You *won't* need a special TV.

The future of *can* is *will be able to*.

You *will be able to* ask your computer.

9 PRACTICE

Complete these sentences using *will* or *won't*.

a) When I'm old and grey, ... you still love me?

b) When we go on holiday next month to the USA, we ... need our passports.

c) In 1997, Hong Kong ... belong to Britain any longer.

d) San Marino probably ... win the next World Cup.

PRON SPOT: /ʌ/ AS IN *LOVE*

a) *u* or *a* are the most common spellings of the /ʌ/ sound. Practise these words and then listen to them on the cassette.

bus   butter   club   fun   gum   rugby
run   Sunday   come   company   compass
done   honey   London

b) Make a note of these unusual spellings and listen to the pronunciation.

enough   rough   tough   young

c) Practise this advertising rap.

Hey there, son, come to the rugby club
Sunday lunch time up in London
If you're young and you can run
You can have fun, rain or sun
It's rough, it's tough, it's rugby
It's rough, it's tough — that's enough!

STAR NAME

JEREMY GUSCOTT
/dʒerəmi: gʌsgət/
England rugby international player

11 SPEAKING (2)

The situation described in Activity 7 is a real possibility. What do you think about having 2000 channels?

THE FASTLANE INTERVIEW

12 Sue Sullivan is an autocue operator (she makes sure that TV presenters can see their scripts when they are in front of the cameras).

● Listen to the interview.

● Don't worry if you don't understand everything.

● Is she in favour of having more TV channels or not?

● You can read the text of the interview on page 126.

FOCUS ON YOUR COUNTRY

13

How many TV channels can you watch in your country? Do many people have satellite TV? Are the programmes better? Do people watch more TV now than five years ago? If so, how is this affecting life in your country?

UNIT
13

The stars are out

LANGUAGE AREA

Expressing achievements

MAIN STRUCTURE

Present perfect

VOCABULARY

Films

PRONUNCIATION

/ə/ as in *the*

1 **STARTER**

a) **Look at the list of films and film stars. Can you match the right name to the right film? Listen to the cassette and check your answers.**

Four Weddings and a Funeral   Beverley Hills Cop   Casablanca
The General   Mad Max 3   Batman   Wolf   Green Card   Cousins

Hugh Grant   Eddie Murphy   Gérard Depardieu
Buster Keaton   Ingrid Bergman   Isabella Rossellini
Tina Turner   Michelle Pfeiffer   Jack Nicholson

b) **Match the statements below with the people in the photographs.**

1 She's made fourteen films.
2 She never made a film.
3 She made nineteen films.
4 She's never made a film.

FOCUS **ON GRAMMAR** **2**
THE PRESENT PERFECT

a) **You can use the present perfect to talk about actions or events that began in the past and have some importance in the present, or to talk about unfinished actions.**

I*'ve lost* my passport. (It is still lost.)
I*'ve spilt* the milk. (It is still on the floor.)

b) **You can use the present perfect to talk about life experiences without saying when things happened.**

She*'s made* fourteen films. (She is still alive and possibly making films.)
I*'ve read* all Shakespeare's plays.
He*'s seen* Jurassic Park fifteen times.
I*'ve been* to Egypt.
I*'ve met* the President of Iceland.

c) **Compare these sentences with the ones above.**

She made fourteen films before she was 35.
I read all of Shakespeare's plays while I was at university.
I saw *Jurassic Park* fifteen times in one year!
I visited the Pyramids when I was in Egypt.
I met the President of Iceland during her visit to Europe.

3 PRACTICE

a) Write about yourself using the present perfect (remember not to use a time expression).

EXAMPLE: *I've been to the USA.*
I've seen Queen Elizabeth.

b) Now show your answers to another student. Ask and answer questions using the past simple.

EXAMPLE: *When **did you go** to the USA?*
*Where **did you go**?*
*When /Where **did you see** the Queen?*

4 SPEAKING (1)

Famous people and you! What do you know about the people in Activity 1?

EXAMPLE: *I've read a book about Marilyn Monroe.*
I've never heard of Buster Keaton.
I've never seen a film starring Isabella Rossellini.

5 WRITE YOUR OWN RULES

How do you form the present perfect? Write some rules in your Workbook. How is it different to the past simple?

6 READING

a) Read the text below quickly. How many different film styles are mentioned?

WHY HOLLYWOOD?

I went to the cinema for the first time when I was three. I don't remember anything about it, of course, although my sister said that I screamed at the monsters on the screen. It was a Mickey Mouse cartoon! By the time I was 12, I was a movie addict. I went to the
5 cinema as often as I could and I rented videos on the days that I couldn't.

When I was 14, they built a huge multi-screen cinema in my town, there were 18 films playing at the same time! I started going three or four times a week. I think I've been there more than a thousand
10 times. I've seen them all: action films, horror films, comedy films, thrillers, historical films, romantic films and cartoons!

One day, something occurred to me. Why are all these films in American English? Don't they make films in Britain? And when I was taking a French exam, I thought, aren't there any films in French?
15 The answer to the first question is: yes, they do, but only a few. Only a handful of British films are made each year. The most successful British film ever is *Four Weddings and a Funeral*. And the answer to the second question is: yes, of course! Hundreds! But they have never shown a French (or Italian, Spanish, Polish, Greek,
20 Russian or Chinese) film on any of the 18 screens at my local cinema.

b) Explain these references:

1 Line 5: *I rented videos on the days that I couldn't.* Couldn't what?

2 Line 9: *I've been there more than a thousand times.* Been where?

3 Line 15: *the first question:* what was it?

4 Line 18: *the second question:* what was it?

7 SPEAKING (2)

a) In groups, talk about what kind of films you like. Then share your ideas with the rest of the class.

b) Do you like American films? Are they successful in your country? Try to find reasons for this. Here are some ideas to get you started.

1 They spend a lot of money on them.
2 The stars and their lifestyles are glamorous.
3 There's a lot of action in them.
4 The stories are easy to follow.
5 The music is good.

8 PRON SPOT: /ə/ AS IN *THE*

a) /ə/ is the most common unstressed sound in British English. Look at the different spellings of this sound in the following words.

horror   action   thriller   Tina Turner
theatre   funeral   syllable   American
Iceland   Nicholson   Pfeiffer

b) If you say these common words by themselves, they don't contain the /ə/ sound.

at /æ/   to /uː/   of /ɒ/   was /ɒ/
can /æ/   have /æ/   for /ɔː/   were /ɜː/

But when they are spoken in a sentence, they usually become unstressed and contain the /ə/ sound.

I've been **at** the cinema.

I want **to** tell you something.

London is the capital **of** the United Kingdom.

He **was** here yesterday.

She **can** swim well, can't she?

Where **have** you been?

I'm waiting **for** a friend.

Were you here yesterday?

Listen to them and practise the sentences and individual words on the cassette.

STAR NAME

SARAH FERGUSON
/seərə fɜːrgəsən/
The Duchess of York

9 LISTENING

a) Read the following extract aloud and circle the words which contain the /ə/ sound.

> I closed the door and turned round. He was standing there, next to the picture of his father, the movie actor. 'Where have you been?' he asked. 'At the cinema,' I answered. He wasn't listening. He was thinking about something else. 'Was it raining at the cinema?' he asked suddenly. 'What do you mean?' I replied. 'Your coat is rather wet.' 'I walked back,' I said. 'I couldn't get a taxi.' The smile disappeared from his face. 'You haven't been anywhere near a cinema,' he said. 'Perhaps you'd better leave now.'

b) Now listen to the extract on the cassette. How many /ə/ sounds can you hear? Did you find them all when you read the text aloud?

c) Listen again. Who do you think the characters are? What has happened and what will happen next?

10 WRITING

a) Read the following dialogue. It's a continuation of the story in Activity 9.

WOMAN:	Look! We have to talk!
MAN:	Don't shout at me!
WOMAN:	Then listen! I'm in terrible trouble!
MAN:	I couldn't care less.
WOMAN:	I've been to see Melrose.
MAN:	And ...?
WOMAN:	He didn't want to talk.
MAN:	So what did you do?
WOMAN:	I got angry. I hit him. I ... I think I've killed him.

b) Were your ideas about the story in Activity 9c) correct? Discuss the characters and the situation again, now that you have more information.

1 Where is this scene taking place? In which town and in what kind of building?

2 What is the relationship between the characters?

3 Why is the woman so anxious?

4 Why is the man so suspicious?

5 Who is Melrose? Why has she been to see him?

c) Write the continuation of the story.

d) In pairs, act out the story for the rest of the class.

THE FASTLANE INTERVIEW

11 Stuart Nurse is an English stage actor who wants to work in films.

● Listen to the first part of the interview.

● Make notes about his career so far.

● Don't worry if you don't understand everything.

● Listen to the second part.

● Make notes about the kind of films he would like to appear in.

● You can read the text of the interview on page 127.

FOCUS ON YOUR COUNTRY 12

Who are the most famous actors, actresses and directors (film and stage) in your country? What films have they starred in or directed? Is there a strong film industry in your country or are most films American?

1 STARTER

a) Only six countries have ever won the soccer World Cup. In pairs, look at the flags of those countries. Which countries are they?

b) Can you write down one year when each of them won the World Cup? If you don't know, have a guess. Remember that the World Cup only happens every four years!

2 LISTENING AND SPEAKING

a) Listen and check your answers to Activity 1b).

b) In pairs, listen again and fill in *half* of the chart below each (each person listen for information in two of the columns only). Don't show your partner your information.

c) Now ask and answer questions to complete the chart together. Don't look at your partner's chart!

EXAMPLE: *What was the score in 1966 when England won?*
It was four two.

Who did Sweden lose to in 1958?
Who did Argentina beat in 1978?
Who were the losing finalists in 1994?

YEAR	WINNERS	LOSING FINALISTS	SCORE
	Uruguay		
		Czechoslovakia	
		Hungary	
1950			
	West Germany		
		Sweden	
			3-1
1966			
		Italy	
		Netherlands	
	Argentina		
1982			
	Argentina		
1990			(penalties)
	Brazil		

LANGUAGE AREA

Describing events in the past

MAIN STRUCTURE

already, yet and *still*

VOCABULARY

Countries, football and other sports

PRONUNCIATION

/ɜː/ as in *earth*

3 READING (1)

Read this text. Decide which statements are true and which are false.

SOUTH AMERICAN countries have dominated the World Cup. Brazil have already won it four times and Bolivia twice. European teams have won five times. The most successful European team is Italy who have already won four times, with Germany not far behind. The Netherlands have played in three finals but have still not won the trophy. England haven't won yet either. Three countries which no longer exist have appeared in World Cup finals.

WHEN ARE ENGLAND GOING TO WIN THE WORLD CUP?

WE'VE WON IT ONCE ALREADY.

BRAZIL

ENGLAND

FOCUS ON GRAMMAR
ALREADY AND *YET*

4

a) You can use *already* to emphasise that something has happened in the past earlier than expected.

I've *already* cleaned my room.
Has she *already* arrived?/ Is she *already* here?
He's finished his homework *already*.

b) You can often use *already*, as emphasis, in response to a question or statement made by someone else.

Why don't you clean your room? I've *already* cleaned it.
When is she going to arrive? She's *already* arrived.
Is she *already* here? Yes, she is.
Why isn't he doing his homework? He's finished it *already*.

c) You can use *yet* in questions, when you expect someone to do something, or you expect that someone has done something.

Have you cleaned your room *yet*?
Have you seen the new Disney cartoon *yet*?

d) You can use *yet* in negative sentences, when you haven't done something, but are planning to do it or expecting it to happen.

My country hasn't won the World Cup *yet*.
I haven't seen the new Disney film *yet*.

e) You can use *still* to talk about an event or action that began in the past which you expect to stop soon.

The Netherlands *still* haven't won the World Cup.
I *still* haven't finished my homework.
Is he *still* the world champion?

PRACTICE

Answer these questions using *already*, *yet* or *still*.

a) When are you going to make some coffee?

b) Where's your ticket?

c) Are you going to see the new Disney film?

d) I hear that you lost your car keys. Any news?

e) Did the shop write to you about your complaint?

6 **WRITE YOUR OWN RULES**

a) **Make a note of everything you know about *already*, *yet* and *still*.**

EXAMPLE: *You can't use **yet** with positive statements.*

b) **Make a note of the way you use *already*, *yet* and *still* in your own language. Is it similar or completely different?**

7 **READING (2)**

You are going to read a text about football. The first part is about Liverpool football club. The second is about footballer Gary Mabbutt.

a) **Read the text and find a place for the following words:**

seen won had played said asked refused

b) **Find words in the text that mean *the opposite* of these words:**

ended
unknown
failure
funny
whispered

c) **Find words or phrases in the text that mean *the same* as these:**

if not
spoke loudly (two examples)
said he was sorry
give permission to
things that have happened

Football—A matter of life and death?

Liverpool have the European Cup four times. Their success began in the 1960's when their manager was Bill Shankly, a man famous for saying memorable things about the game. His most famous remark was:

'People have to me that football in Liverpool is a matter of life and death. They're quite wrong - it's much more serious than that!'

Over the years, many Liverpool fans have if they can have their ashes spread over the Liverpool ground after they die. The club have always these requests. 'If we allow one supporter to do this, we will have to allow them all. We would have the ashes of dead Liverpool fans all over the ground!'

Gary Mabbutt is still the only diabetic soccer player who has for England. He plays for Tottenham Hotspur (Spurs). He has already many interesting experiences in his career. Once, he played for Bristol City, a much smaller club than Spurs. At the end of every away match, the players drank tea and ate biscuits on their way home on the team bus.

One day, the manager was so angry with their performance that he refused to let them have their tea. 'I have never such a terrible display' he shouted. Mabbutt raised his hand. 'Can I have a biscuit?' he asked quietly. 'Why?' yelled the manager. 'Give me one good reason!'

'I have to eat something,' said Mabbutt. 'Otherwise, I may go into a coma and die.'

The manager apologised and the team had their tea and biscuits.

PRON SPOT: /ɜː/ AS IN *EARTH*

a) This is a commonly mispronounced sound. Listen to the sound on the cassette.

b) Here are some common spellings. Listen to them on the cassette.

ir words	er words	ear words	or words*	ur words
bird	person	heard	word	burn
third	serve	earth	worm	hurt
first	alert	learn	world	turn

*only words beginning with *w*. But: wore /ɔː/, worn /ɔː/ and worry /ʌ/.

c) Make a note of these words which *don't* contain the /ɜː/ sound.

pear	wear	bear	tear	/eə/
near	fear	hear	dear	/ɪə/

d) What do you think these expressions mean?

First come, first served.
The early bird catches the worm.

Listen to them on the cassette. Do you have any expressions in your language which mean the same thing?

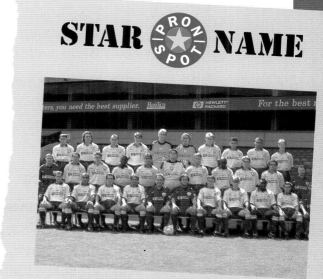

STAR NAME

SPURS FOOTBALL CLUB
/spɜːz/
(Tottenham Hotspur)

9 WRITING

What is your opinion of football? Write a paragraph describing your feelings about 'the biggest game on earth'. Use these words and expressions to help you.

brings people together / exciting spectator sport
the World Cup makes people proud of their country

too much soccer on TV / players are overpaid
it's impossible to get tickets for big games / some players
set a bad example to young people

10 SPEAKING (2)

In 1994, Diego Maradona, the Argentine footballer, was sent home from the USA World Cup for taking drugs. Why do sports people sometimes take drugs? Should they be banned from playing sport for life?

FOCUS ON YOUR COUNTRY 11

What is the most successful thing your national football team has done? What about the best football club? Does it matter to you if your national team plays badly?

A LANGUAGE REVIEW

**1 GRAMMAR EXTRA (1)
THE FUTURE TENSE WITH *WILL***

a) *Will* **can be used to make predictions about the future.**

By the year 2005, there *will* be at least 2,000 TV channels.

b) **The *will* future can be used when you are not sure about the future.**

I don't know what I'*ll* do this weekend.
Maybe he'*ll* be here in a few minutes.
We've no idea what kind of jobs we'*ll* get.

c) **The *will* future can also be used when you make an instant decision.**

I think I'*ll* make some coffee.
Don't worry, we'*ll* take the dog for a walk.

2 PRACTICE

Complete these sentences using *will* or *won't*.

a) I ... be here tomorrow, see you then!
b) She says she ... climb that wall. She's too scared.
c) Sorry, but we ... be able to come to your party.
d) Don't worry, my brother ... clean the kitchen!
e) Can we talk about it now? I ... be here this afternoon.

**3 GRAMMAR EXTRA (2)
QUESTIONS WITH *EVER* AND *YET***

Have you ever ...? Ever = in your life.

Have you ever been to England?
Have you ever been to that café?
NOT: *Have you ever* seen Peter this morning?

***Been* is the past participle of the verb *to be* and can also be the past participle of the verb *to go*. It indicates that the speaker has visited somewhere and returned.**

EXAMPLE: *I've **been** to New York. (i.e. I am back home now.)*

***Gone* is also the past participle of the verb *to go*. It is used in the same way as *been* but has a different meaning. It indicates that the speaker is visiting somewhere (and is still there).**

EXAMPLE: *She's **gone** to New York. (i.e. she has not returned yet.)*

Make questions with the following verbs using the present perfect with *ever* or *yet*.

go   visit   eat   meet   see

If you want more information about something, the question will probably be in the past simple.

Have you ever been to England?
Yes, I have.
Oh, really? When (*did you go* to England)?
(I *went* to England) two years ago.

In pairs, practise short conversations with the questions you created using *ever* and *yet*.

Have you … yet? **indicates that you expect someone has done something or is going to do it.**

Have you cleaned your room *yet*? (You have to clean it or you said you were going to clean it.)

4 PRACTICE

Look at Sam's timetable below for Saturday.

SATURDAY

9am:	*Clean my room*
10am:	*Go to music shop*
11am:	*Have coffee with Anita and Fred*
12 noon:	*Buy some new trainers*
1pm:	*Have lunch with Mum at her shop*
2pm:	*Visit Uncle Herbert in hospital*
3pm:	*Watch the rugby match on TV*
5pm:	*Make dinner for Mum and Alan*
6pm:	*Iron shirt and get ready to go out*
7pm:	*Meet Dan at Roxy Cinema*

In pairs, take it in turns to ask and answer the questions.

EXAMPLES: *A: It's two o'clock. What time did he iron his shirt?*
*B: He hasn't ironed it **yet**.*
A: It's six o'clock. What time is he going to have lunch with Mum?
*B: He's **already** had lunch with her.*

a) It's nine o'clock. What time did he have coffee with Anita and Fred?

b) It's two o'clock. What time is he going to buy some new trainers?

c) It's three o'clock. What time is he going to visit Uncle Herbert in hospital?

d) It's one o'clock. What time did he watch the rugby match on TV?

e) It's seven o'clock. What time is he going to meet Dan at the Roxy Cinema?

B SKILLS REVIEW

1 READING

a) In pairs, discuss what the following people have got in common, then read and find out.

Marilyn Monroe was born Norma Jean Baker. John Wayne, star of many Hollywood cowboy films was originally Marion Michael Morrison. Elton John's real name is Reg Dwight, and Sting was christened Gordon Sumner. Bob Dylan's real name is Robert Zimmerman and Woody Allen was born Allen Stewart Konigsberg. Bebeto, star of the Brazilian soccer team, is really called José de Oliveira.

There are several different reasons why pop stars, film stars and football players change their names. Almost all Brazilian football players are known by a nickname. Pelé, one of the greatest players in the history of the game is the best known example. His real name, by the way, is Edson Arantes do Nascimento.

Monroe and Wayne had to change their names! The studios insisted on more glamorous names. Almost all the big stars of the 40s and 50s changed their names. Some actors in the 50s like Marlon Brando and James Dean refused to change their names. Woody Allen changed his name because it was thought that a Jewish-sounding name would not help his career. Barbra Streisand and Elliot Gould are Jewish actors who refused to change their names.

Elton John thought his real name sounded like a soccer player's. In fact, his cousin Roy Dwight *was* a professional soccer player. Sting changed his name during the punk music era when he was in a band called *The Police*. All around him were musicians with names like Johnny Rotten and Sid Vicious. Bob Dylan changed his name because he liked the work of the Welsh poet Dylan Thomas.

b) Give three reasons why these famous people changed their names.

c) Can you think of five other movie stars or pop stars who changed their names. Do stars in your country do the same?

2 WRITING

a) Look at these arguments for and against an increase in the number of TV channels. Add one more argument to each box.

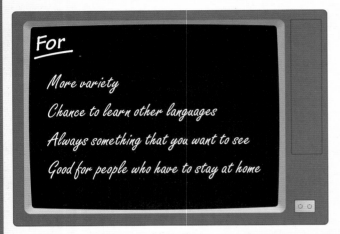

For

More variety

Chance to learn other languages

Always something that you want to see

Good for people who have to stay at home

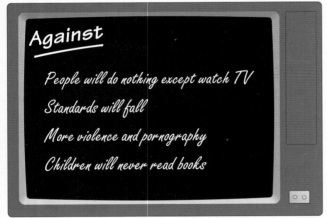

Against

People will do nothing except watch TV

Standards will fall

More violence and pornography

Children will never read books

b) Now write a paragraph including arguments for and against. Make sentences using one argument from each box.

EXAMPLES: *There will be ... but ...*
This will happen. However, ...

3 LISTENING

a) What products do you think these adjectives could describe?

spacious   new   terrifying   clean
fresh   quiet   fun   exciting
reliable   fast   nervous   bright

b) Now listen to the cassette and find which advertisements the words are used in.

4 SPEAKING

'Why I deserve to be President.'

a) In groups, choose one person to stand for President of your country. Think of reasons why he/she should be President.

b) Help your candidate to write a short speech about his/her views and suitability.

c) Listen to all the candidates' speeches.

d) Vote for the next President!

C ACROSS CULTURES

Who are the stars in your country? Make a list of people that the whole class agree are stars. When you have agreed on a list of stars, find pictures and articles about them and put them in your ACROSS CULTURES scrapbook.
Put them in the following categories:

Film
Music
Politics
Sport
Television
Literature

D COMPARATIVE PRON

1 /ʊ/ as in *good* and /ʌ/ as in *love*.

STAR **PRONI SPOT** NAME

NUTBUSH CITY LIMITS
/nʌtbʊʃ/
A song by Tina Turner

2 /ə/ as in *the* and /ɜː/ as in *earth*.

STAR PRONI SPOT NAME

UMA THURMAN
/uːmə θɜːrmæn/
American actress

a) Practise these words. Listen to the cassette to check your pronunciation.

good	wood	put	push	bush
bull	bully	up	butter	fun
rugby	London	money		

b) Here are some words and expressions using both sounds.

good fun   cut wood   wonderful
put up   running bulls

Put them in sentences.

EXAMPLE: *We had **good fun** when we went to the beach.*

c) Practise this tongue-twister and then listen to it on the cassette.

How much wood could a woodchuck chuck if a woodchuck could chuck wood?

NB: A *woodchuck* is a kind of bird. Chuck means throw.

d) Practise using *the* with words containing the /ɜː/ sound.

the first
the third
the birds
the words

Make sentences with the expressions that you have practised.

e) Complete this sentence. Discuss it with the rest of the class.

The first words I learnt in English were ...

E COUNTDOWN TO BLOCK FOUR

1 In Block Three, you have practised the following language:

Defining things, people and places.

... a company *which* is based in Italy ...
... a port (*which* is) on the Italian coast ...
... people *who* were searching for gold ...

Prepositions of time.

It starts *at* six o'clock.
Boys in Blue is *on* Thursdays.
Her birthday is *in* August.
I take my holidays *in* (the) spring.
My great-grandmother was born *in* 1899.

The future tense with *will/won't*.

There *will* be a five-hour programme.
It is estimated that a million people *will* read this book.
You *will* be able to go where you like.
I*'ll* make some coffee.
You *won't* need a special TV.

Talking about life experiences using the present perfect tense.

She*'s made* several films.
I*'ve read* all Chekhov's plays in Russian.
He*'s seen Jurassic Park* five times.
I*'ve been* to England, Wales and Scotland.
She*'s eaten* Malaysian food.

***Ever, never, yet, already* and *still*.**

Have you *ever* met a famous person?
I've *never* told a lie.
They've *already* done it.
Have you cleaned up that mess *yet*?
I *still* haven't finished my homework.

2 Have you written all the new words you have learnt in the Words section of your Workbook? Check your list now.

3 Have you added new information to your ACROSS CULTURES scrapbook yet?

CONGRATULATIONS!
You are ready to start BLOCK FOUR!

1 STARTER

a) Divide the words below into three groups:

1 physical description
2 character description
3 moods or temporary states

tall   quiet   slim   kind
fat   good-looking   blonde
bored   happy   confident
silent   serious   anxious
relaxed   fit   muscular
extrovert   sensitive   tired

b) In pairs, make a list of the words you would use to describe yourself and then make a list of words to describe your partner. Compare your lists.

2 THE *FASTLANE* QUESTIONNAIRE

Today, the *Fastlane* Questionnaire is for you! Everyone is an individual, so what makes *you* different?

a) Answer the questions opposite and make notes about yourself.

b) Compare your answers with three other students to see how different you are from each other!

LANGUAGE AREA

Describing people

MAIN STRUCTURE

Adjectives and modifiers

VOCABULARY

Describing people

PRONUNCIATION

/eɪ/ as in *make*

a PHYSICAL APPEARANCE

1 Are you
  a) tall   **b)** of medium height
  c) short?

2 Is your hair
  a) blonde **b)** brown **c)** black
  d) red   **e)** another colour?

3 Is it
  a) straight **b)** wavy **c)** curly
  d) spiky?

4 Are your eyes
  a) blue **b)** green **c)** brown
  d) hazel **e)** another colour?

b LIKES AND DISLIKES

List the following activities under:
like / don't like / hate / not interested

1 fashion and clothes
2 watching sport (specify)
3 playing sport (specify)
4 playing computer games (specify)
5 cars
6 listening to music (specify)
7 watching TV
8 going to the cinema

c ABILITIES

Which of the following things can you do?

1 ride a bike
2 swim
3 use a computer
4 ride a horse
5 sing
6 play a musical instrument (specify)
7 speak a foreign language fluently (specify)
8 make clothes
9 run more than 5 kilometres

d FINALLY …

Answer these questions:

1 What is your favourite subject at school?
2 Have you got a pet?
3 Where did you go for your holiday last summer?
4 What is the name of your best friend?
5 What is your favourite English word?

3 WRITING (1)

Use your notes to write about yourself.

I'm short, I've got dark hair and green eyes. I like buying clothes, walking, swimming and playing chess. My favourite kind of music is techno but I also like jazz and blues. I don't like watching or playing any sport and I haven't got a computer. I'm not interested in motor bikes. I can ride a bike and swim, but I can't play a musical instrument or ride a horse.

4 SPEAKING (1)

a) In pairs, describe the appearance of the people in the photographs on pages 61 and 62, using the following words:

beautiful attractive wrinkly
funny handsome gorgeous
pretty plain old

EXAMPLE: *What does she look like?*
She's beautiful.

b) Think of three people you know and write sentences describing their personality or abilities. You can use some of the following words.

talented terrible boring clever
impatient moody exciting
old-fashioned amazing awful

EXAMPLE: *What is your friend like?*
He's very funny.

c) Look at the arrow of modifying words below and use some of them to rewrite your sentences in a) and b).

extremely
really
very
rather/pretty
quite
fairly
not very

EXAMPLE: *I think she's extremely beautiful.*
I don't think he's very funny.

5 LISTENING (1)

a) Look at the picture. What do you think has happened?

b) Listen to the conversation. Were you right?

c) Listen again and find words that mean the following:

very wet very stupid very angry
very nice

d) Write the conversation between Angela and Mr Evans.

F FOCUS ON GRAMMAR   6
ADJECTIVES AND MODIFIERS

a) Adjectives come before nouns and do not change.

She's very *tall.*
She's a very *tall* girl.
They're very *tall.*
They're very *tall* girls.

Not: They're very talls girls.

b) Don't confuse *rather* and *I'd rather* (see Unit 1).

It's *rather* late, I have to go home.
I have to go home but *I'd rather* stay here. (I'd prefer to stay here.)

c) Some adjectives describe an extreme condition or state.

It's a *terrifying* film.
(i.e. it can't be more terrifying.)

Absolutely is only used with these sorts of adjectives and emphasises how extreme the condition is.

It's an *absolutely* terrifying film.

These are some of the adjectives you can use *absolutely* with.
wonderful extraordinary fantastic
incredible amazing terrifying
awful terrible ridiculous
stupid furious brilliant

You can't use *absolutely* with other adjectives.
good well-dressed intelligent
dull sad etc.

7 PRACTICE

Choose modifying words from Activities 4 and 5 to complete these sentences.

a) She didn't say anything, but I think the teacher was ... pleased.

b) The team was ... awful! They lost 13-0!

c) I'm sorry. I think romantic films are ... dull!

d) The view from the top of the mountain is ... amazing.

e) That dog is either ... bad or ... stupid.

8 WRITE YOUR OWN RULES

To help you remember the difference between all these modifiers, write a list of your own examples in your Workbook.

EXAMPLE: *My sister is **rather** untidy.*
*My new bike is **absolutely** brilliant.*
*My cousin Michael is **extremely** tall.*
*English is **quite** easy.*

9 SPEAKING (2)

In pairs, describe someone in a photograph.

a) STUDENT A: turn to page 121. Describe the person in the photograph.

STUDENT B: draw the person that Student A is describing. Don't let Student A see your drawing until you have finished.

b) When you have finished, compare your drawing with the picture. Tell your partner what you thought of his/her description.

10 PRON SPOT: /eɪ/ AS IN *MAKE*

a) *a* is the most common spelling of the /eɪ/ sound, especially when followed by a consonant and a vowel.

label	place	made	age	cake
male	same	lane	tape	late
wave	lazy			

Listen to the words on the cassette and make a list of more words like this.

b) Here are some other common spellings of this sound:

gain	mail	wait	sailor	available
day	lay	may	play	stay	way
eight	weigh	weight	straight	

Listen to the words on the cassette and practise them.

STAR NAME

Doris Day,
/dɒrɪs deɪ/
American actress

11 LISTENING (2)

Listen to the descriptions of the people in the photographs on pages 61 and 62. Make a note of who is being described.

12 WRITING (2)

Write a short description of someone in the class. Don't write the name, and don't say if it's a boy or a girl.

EXAMPLE: *I'm writing about someone with **long hair** ...*
*This person has **blue eyes** ...*
*The person I'm writing about is **very attractive** ...*

FOCUS ON YOUR COUNTRY 13

Who is on the front covers of the 10 most popular magazines in your town this month? Find out who the people are. Are they famous? Are they unknown models? Write a description of one of them.

Fit for life

LANGUAGE AREA

Idiomatic English

MAIN STRUCTURE

Multi-word verbs and
frequency adverbs

VOCABULARY

Food and fitness

PRONUNCIATION

/aɪ/ as in *life*

1 STARTER

You are going to live on a desert island. You will have a cooker, a fridge and a freezer! You can only take ten food items with you. In pairs, decide what you will take.

EXAMPLE: *I'm going to take sun-dried tomatoes, olives, mozzarella, strawberry ice cream, sausages, potatoes ...*

2 READING

a) Read the conversation below about Angela's diet. Does she eat healthy food?

b) Now read the conversation again and find multi-word verbs in it that mean:

stop   start   continue (2 verbs)
try to find   finally, you will be

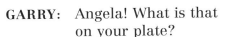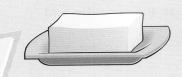

GARRY: Angela! What is that on your plate?

ANGELA: What does it look like? I'm hungry.

GARRY: Yeah, but if you go on eating stuff like that, you'll end up in hospital.

ANGELA: Don't be ridiculous.

GARRY: It's not ridiculous. You should give up greasy food and take up a sport, or start going to a gym.

ANGELA: There's no gym near where I live.

GARRY: I'm sure there is. I'll help you look for one. You can't carry on like this.

F FOCUS ON GRAMMAR (1)
MULTI-WORD VERBS

3

a) **Multi-word verbs have more than one part to them. A verb + an adverb particle/preposition.**

They can be transitive (i.e. require an object) or intransitive (i.e. cannot take an object).

He *broke up* the relationship.   They *broke up*.

b) **Transitive multi-word verbs can be:**

1 **Separable. This means that the verb and the adverb particle/preposition can be separated in a sentence.**

He *broke up* the relationship.   He *broke* the relationship *up*.

You should *give up* greasy food.   You should *give* greasy food *up*.

If you want to use a pronoun (e.g. *it*) you *must* say:

You should *give* it *up*.
Not: You should *give up* it.

2 **Inseparable. This means that the verb and the adverb particle/preposition cannot be separated in the sentence.**

You can't *go on* eating stuff like that.
Not: You can't *go* eating stuff *on* like that.

You will do more work on this in Unit 20.

---

4 PRACTICE

Complete these sentences using a multi-word verb from Activity 2.

1 My Mum tried to ... smoking but she couldn't.
2 Garry and Angela are ... somewhere to live.
3 The teacher says we have to ... doing this exercise until we finish it.
4 She wanted to do more exercise, so she ... judo.
5 If we drive this way, we'll ... in Edinburgh!

5 WRITE YOUR OWN RULES

Look at the completed sentences in Activity 4 again. Which of the multi-word verbs can be separated? Start a multi-word verb list in your Workbook. Every time you discover a new multi-word verb, add it to the list. Remember to give an example of how it is used.

---

6 a) **Answer these questions and compare your answers with a partner.**

THE FASTLANE QUESTIONNAIRE

1 ....
Do you eat hamburgers, sausages or other fried foods such as chips or fried rice?

Daily 3   Often 2   Sometimes 1   Hardly ever 0

2 ....
How often do you eat chocolate, cakes or biscuits?

Daily 3   Often 2   Sometimes 1   Hardly ever 0

3 ....
How often do you eat crisps or nuts?

Daily 3   Often 2   Sometimes 1   Hardly ever 0

4 ....
What kind of milk do you drink?

Full cream 2   Semi-skimmed 1   Skimmed 0

5 ....
Do you eat bread or toast with lots of butter?

Daily 3   Often 2   Sometimes 1   Hardly ever 0

b) **Work out your score and then turn to page 121 for more information about you and your diet.**

c) **In groups, talk about your eating habits.**

EXAMPLE: *I eat chips every day.*
I hardly ever eat crisps.

FOCUS ON GRAMMAR (2)
FREQUENCY ADVERBS

7

	MONDAY	TUESDAY	WEDNESDAY	THURSDAY	FRIDAY	SATURDAY	SUNDAY
Hamburger				A L W A Y S			
Chips			U S U A L L Y				
Eggs			O F T E N				
Pasta	S O M E T I M E S						
Salad	H A R D L Y E V E R						
Green veg.				N E V E R			

Adverbs of frequency usually come before a main verb but after *to be* or auxiliary verbs.

I *hardly ever* eat potatoes.
I'm *usually* too late for breakfast.
I can *sometimes* eat five sandwiches on the same day.
I've *often* tried to give up eating hamburgers.

8 PRACTICE

a) **Complete these sentences choosing a suitable frequency adverb.**

1 You should ... tell lies.
2 I've ... visited the Taj Mahal.
3 My uncle and aunt ... write to me.
4 We ... spend our holidays on the beach.
5 I ... get up later at the weekend.

b) **Put a frequency adverb in these sentences.**

1 I've seen my grandmother without her false teeth.
2 They drink wine at lunch time.
3 He was bad-tempered in the mornings.

9 WRITE YOUR OWN RULES (2)

Read the sentences below. Write a rule for each one describing the position of the adverb.

a) I always wash my hair in the mornings.
b) They are never on time.
c) She has often dreamed of being famous.

10 LISTENING

a) **What do you think are the main elements of a healthy diet? What things shouldn't you eat?**

b) **Listen to the interview with a nutritionist. Which of the following does she mention?**

salt   minerals   calories   sugar
carbohydrates   meat   fish
olive oil   sausages   fat

c) **Listen again and decide if these statements are a true or false account of what was said.**

1 You should never eat meat.
2 Vegetarians don't get enough protein.
3 We get Vitamin C from fruit.
4 You should try to eat less sugar, butter and salt.
5 Dairy products are an important source of calcium and iron.

11 PRON SPOT: /aɪ/ AS IN *LIFE*

a) ***i* followed by a single consonant and another vowel is the most common spelling of the /aɪ/ sound.**

dine   fine   line   mine   nine
pine   wine   lime   time   bike
like   life   wife

b) **The /aɪ/ sound is made by two vowels together.**

die   lie   tie

67

c) *y* is another spelling of the /aɪ/ sound.

apply	by	cry	fly	July
rhyme	sky	try		

d) The /aɪ/ sound is also in words with the letters *igh*.

delighted   high   light   might   night
sight   tight   tonight

e) Complete this poem with words from the lists above and on page 67.

Simon said to Michael and Michael told his wife
I have never been so excited in all my ...
I'm delighted to say that I'm going to dine
With the Prime Minister, tonight at ....
I think this means he's going to resign
I must go out and buy some ... .

Now listen to the cassette and check your answers.

STAR NAME

MICHAEL STIPE
/maɪkəl staɪp/
Singer with the band REM

12 SPEAKING

When you were a child, did your parents ever make you eat food you didn't like? Do you think children should be allowed to eat whatever they want?

THE FASTLANE INTERVIEW

13 Lauren Brewer is a holistic therapist. She tries to cure illnesses by treating the whole person: their job, what they eat and drink, how they live, etc. Lauren specialises in treating young people. She believes that young people should be allowed to eat what they want and should never be told to give up anything.

● Listen to the interview.
● Don't worry if you don't understand everything.
● Make notes about the boy she describes.
● You can read the text of the interview on page 128.

FOCUS ON YOUR COUNTRY   **14**

Is food an important part of your country's culture and tradition?
What are the national dishes? Are they healthy? Are they popular in other parts of the world?

UNIT
18

Amazing dreams

LANGUAGE AREA
Expressing possibilities

MAIN STRUCTURE
might be, could be
may be

VOCABULARY
Dreams and nightmares

PRONUNCIATION
/əʊ/ as in *most*

1 STARTER

This child's painting represents a dream he had. What could the different things represent?

EXAMPLE: *The two people on the left could be ...*

2 LISTENING

a) Look at these five illustrations which all represent dreams. What do you think the dreams were about. Were they pleasant dreams or nightmares?

b) Listen to people talking about their dreams and nightmares. Match the descriptions to the illustrations.

3 READING

a) Read the text opposite about five different kinds of dreams. There are five misspelt words, one in each section. Which are they?

b) Find words or expressions in the text that mean:

worried
more or less
to be told something you already know
happen
well known

c) What kind of dreams did you hear about in Activity 2? Match them to the descriptions in the text.

Dreams and NIGHTMARES

mean different things to different people. Dreaming about your family or your school could be nice for some people and depressing for others. But there are some common themes.

1 Anxiety dreams

Everybody suffers to a greater or lesser extent from anxiety. In our daily lives, we may not show it, but it's there and the brain sometimes decides to remind us about it. We might be anxious about school, examinations, family or frends ... the dream will tell us.

2 Guilt dreams

We all feel guilty about something - forgetting a birthday, not keeping in contact with other members of the family - and we need to be reminded of it. The *interesting* thing about guilt dreams is that you only feel gilty when you wake up!

3 Warnings

We are sometimes surprised by bad dreams and nightmares. They often occur when everything seems to be going well in our lives. We may be happy at school or at work and *suddenly* we dream about death and destruction. In these dreams, everything we have is destroyed or damaged. We wake up thinking, *why me?*

4 Emptiness

Sometimes dreams remind us that nothing much is happening in our lives. These dreams might be very nice; you might be at a party with interesting and famous people. You could be in a film, *or* you might be playing for your national sports teem. It's wonderful, until you wake up. Then you feel depressed.

5 Narrative dreams

Some dreams are complex and colourful stories, with hundreds of characters and locations. You might be in another country with people you don't know. You might do something together *which takes you to* another interesting location. People you know may pass by. You often wake up before the story has ended, disapointed that you didn't see more.

F

MIGHT BE, COULD BE AND *MAY BE*

4

a) You can use these expressions to indicate possibility in the present and future.

You *might be* anxious about school.
Dreaming about your family *could be* nice for some people.
I *may* go swimming at lunchtime.
I *could* meet you next week.

Remember *might*, *could* and *may* are the same in all forms.

b) In the negative you use *might not* and *may not* (but not *could not* when expressing possibility).

I *might not* go away this summer.
In our daily lives we *may not* show our anxiety.

5 **PRACTICE**

Answer these questions using one of the expressions from Focus on Grammar.

EXAMPLE: *Where will you be this time tomorrow?*
*I don't know. I **might be** at home.*

a) Where's your brother?
b) What time is it?
c) Who's that woman with the teacher?
d) What do you think is in this parcel?
e) What's the population of India?

6 **LISTENING AND WRITING**

Listen to the cassette. You will hear a series of sounds. Use the images you see to write the story of a nightmare. Write it in the present tense.

Here's a possible start to the story. You can start it a different way, if you prefer.

It's three o'clock in the morning. It's raining. I can hear the sound of thunder. Suddenly there's another sound. It could be ...

7 **PRON SPOT:** /əʊ/ **AS IN** *MOST*

a) *o* followed by a consonant and another vowel is the most common spelling of this sound.

grocer	rode	joke	home
alone	hope	note	

b) Which of these words is pronounced differently?

love	move	stove	wove	whose
close	lose	nose	pose	

NB: The pronounciation of the *ol* combination in *gold*, *sold*, and *hole* etc. varies according to the accent of the native speaker. Listen to these variations. Both are correct.

c) Words spelt *ore* are always pronounced differently /ɔː/ (see Unit 9).

wore	store	more	bore	core

d) Here are some other common words with the /əʊ/ sound.

only	no	go	so
don't	most	folk	toast

Listen to the words on the cassette.

e) Say these sentences quickly.

Joe's the only one who saw *Home Alone*.
Grocers don't close until everything's sold.
Don't you like folk music? No! Only rock and roll!

STAR NAMES

THE ROLLING STONES
/ðə rəʊlɪŋ stəʊnz/
British rock band

HOME ALONE
/həʊm ələʊn/
American film starring Macauley Culkin

8 SPEAKING (1)

In pairs, ask and answer questions about dreams.

STUDENT A: you are a hypnotist helping someone to remember a childhood dream.

STUDENT B: close your eyes and think of a dream. Describe it to your partner.

You can use some of the words below. Remember that this is not serious hypnosis!

sleepy   monster   imagine   frightened   excited   huge
dark   chase   lost   forest   falling

EXAMPLE: ***Hypnotist:*** *You're feeling **sleepy**, very very **sleepy**, I want you to imagine that you're five years old. What can you see?*

*Client: I can see something. I don't know what it is. It **might be** a **monster**.*

9 SPEAKING (2)

Talk about a nightmare you have had. Has anyone else had a similar nightmare?

THE FASTLANE INTERVIEW

10 **Edward Wayne is a psychologist who specialises in dreams. Here he talks about the powerful effect that dreams have on children and teenagers.**

● **Listen to the conversation.**
● **Don't worry if you don't understand every word.**
● **Make a note of three types of dream that he talks about.**
● **Listen again. You can read the text of the interview on page 129.**

FOCUS ON YOUR COUNTRY   11

Children's stories are often based on common nightmares. For example, Roald Dahl's *The BFG* begins with a giant taking a young girl from her house and running away with her. Are there any children's stories in your language that are frightening in this way? Do they usually have a happy ending?

Queen Victoria

Princess Diana

Winston Churchill

Jenny Jerome

Barbara Cartland

Prince Charles

Before you, who?

1 STARTER

a) **Look at the photographs above and try and work out who is related to who and what their relationship might be. It doesn't matter if you don't know the right answers!**

EXAMPLE: *I think Jenny Jerome may be Winston Churchill's mother.*

b) **Now listen to the cassette and check your answers.**

2 LISTENING

a) **What's it like to have the same name as a famous person? Listen to five people talking about their experiences and answer the questions below.**

1 How does Diana Spencer prove who she is?

2 Why is it strange that people think Paul McCartney is the famous one?

3 Does Julie Roberts enjoy being confused with Julia Roberts?

4 How did Alan Shakespeare avoid being arrested?

5 What's the difference between Michael Jackson and the singer with the same name?

b) **Listen again and read these sentences. Are they exactly what you hear?**

1 You can imagine how difficult life is.

2 I'm about thirteen years younger than Paul McCartney.

3 What's it like having the same name as a film star?

4 As far as I know, I am not related at all to William Shakespeare.

5 For a start, I'm white and I'm nearly bored.

c) **Do you, or does anyone you know, share a name with a famous person?**

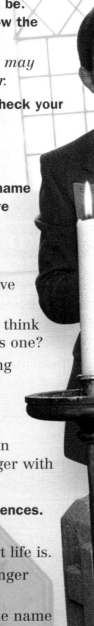

The OPCS at St Catherine's House

80

Population Trends

Trends in marriage and cohabitation; the decline in marriage and the changing patterns of living in partnerships

Suicide deaths in England and Wales, 1982–92; the contribution of occupation and geography

Males and females – some vital differences

Social class differences in mortality of men; recent evidence from the OPCS Longitudinal Study

Annual and quarterly statistics on:
Population
Population change
Vital statistics summary
Births
Deaths
Abortions
Migration
Marriages
Divorces

OPCS   A publication of the Government Statistical Service

The Office of Population Censuses and Surveys is responsible for finding out how many people live in Britain. But it is also open to any member of the public who wishes to trace his or her ancestry. The Public Search Room is always full of people who are trying to find out about their family history.

The Public Search Room has records relating to births, marriages and deaths in England and Wales since 1st July 1837. The records used to be kept in alphabetical order in yearly quarters. In 1984, they began to arrange the indexes in alphabetical order for the whole year.

You can compile a family tree at St Catherine's House. If you want to trace the record of your father's birth, you can first of all look for the record of your parents' marriage. A certificate of marriage should give your father's name and provide a starting point for tracing his date of birth.

What happens when you reach 1837? Before 1837, churches kept records of births, marriages and deaths. Unfortunately, not all churches were very careful about these records and many have none at all. In this case, you can employ a professional genealogist, who may be able to find out about your family from other sources.

3 READING

a) Before you read the text above about St Catherine's House, look at the brochure cover. Try to imagine why hundreds of people visit these offices every day.

b) Now read the text and find a place for the words and phrases below:

(OPCS)
(including births and deaths at sea)
(that is, one for every three months)
(but you don't know when he was born)
(and the name of his father)
(you will hear an interview with one later in this Unit)

c) Now listen to the cassette and check your answers.

4 SPEAKING (1)

In groups, talk about what you know of your family and ancestors. Make a note of the following information about yourself. Compare your notes with other students.

a) How long has your family lived in this town?

b) Who's the oldest relation that you know or have met?

c) Where did your ancestors live?

d) Where do other people in your family live?

5 WRITING

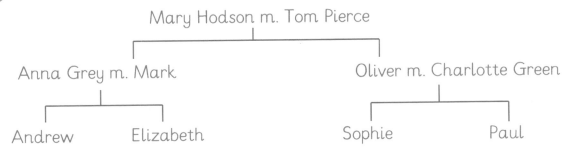

a) Look at the family tree above. Talk about the relationships using the words below.

grandmother/father   grandson/daughter
great-uncle/aunt   great-nephew/niece

b) Now read these relationships and decide if they are true or false:

The novelist, Barbara Cartland, is related to Princess Diana.
Isabella Rossellini is Ingrid Bergman's sister.
Warren Beatty is Shirley Maclaine's cousin.

c) Make a family tree for your own family.

d) Write a paragraph describing the family relationships.

EXAMPLE: *Albert is my **grandfather**. He married Clara and they had one **daughter** called Jean. She's my **mother**.*

FOCUS ON GRAMMAR
REVIEW OF THE PAST

6

a) You can use the past simple to describe actions and events which happened in the past and are finished.

Before 1837, churches *kept* records of births, marriages and deaths.
My family *came* to England with the Norman invasion.

b) You can use the present perfect in three ways.

1. To describe actions and events which started in the past and still continue.

My family *has lived* in this town for 300 years.

2. To describe actions and events that started in the past and have some importance in the present.

I*'ve finished* reading the book.

3. To describe actions and events which happened in the past but where the precise timing is not important.

Have you ever *been* to France?
I*'ve* never *eaten* Chinese food.

c) You can use *used to* to describe actions and events that happened regularly in the past and no longer occur.

The records *used to* be kept in alphabetical order.

7 PRACTICE

Read the following text and fill in the gaps using the past simple, present perfect or *used to*.

Garry and Angela _____ (live) in London for five years. Angela _____ (travel) to work on the train every day but then they _____ (decide) to move house. They _____ (move) from Oxford to London in 1991. Now she gets the tube to work.

Garry hates travelling by tube and so he _____ (buy) a bicycle. Now they both go cycling every weekend.

1

9 SPEAKING (2)

The ghost of a person from the last century visits you. What would you like to ask him or her? In groups, make a list of questions, using the past simple. Use these topics as starting points:

Music	Jobs
Sport	Homes
Holidays	Family
Transport and travel	Food
Having fun	Clothes

EXAMPLE: **Did you ever travel to another country?**
What music did you like?

8 PRON SPOT: /uː/ AS IN *WHO*

a) There are many spellings of the /uː/ sound. Here are the most common ones:

blue	clue	glue	true	blew
crew	flew	grew	Jewish	
moon	zoo	too	June	rule

NB: The pronunciation of the *ool* combination in *pool* and *fool*, etc. varies according to the accent of the native speaker. Listen to these variations. Both are correct.

b) Make a note of these unusual spellings:

do   two   who   you   usual   suit   route

Listen to the cassette and practise all the words.

THE FASTLANE INTERVIEW

10 **Frank Kincade is a genealogist. He traces people's ancestors.**

- **Listen to the interview.**
- **Don't worry if you don't understand everything.**
- **How does he start looking for information about people's ancestors?**
- **What's the most unusual thing he has discovered?**
- **Are people always pleased with what they find out?**
- **You can read the text of the interview on page 130.**

STAR ★ NAME

Lulu
/luːluː/
Scottish singer

F FOCUS ON YOUR COUNTRY 11

In groups, make a family tree for a famous family in your country. Collect photographs of as many members of the family as you can and stick them onto the tree. Write a paragraph of biographical information about each member of the family.

A LANGUAGE REVIEW

1 **GRAMMAR EXTRA (1)**
MULTI-WORD VERBS

A lot of multi-word verbs consist of three words, a verb (e.g. *catch*) and two other words (e.g. *up with*). Multi-word verbs with three words are always *inseparable*. Look at the examples below. Can you work out the meaning from these sentences?

In the 100 metres, Linford Christie started slowly but *caught up with* Carl Lewis and won the gold medal.

Most English people like Scottish people, but some can't *get on with* them at all.

I love Ireland and I always *look forward to* visiting my aunt there.

It was impossible to *put up with* the noise from the airport.

The thieves robbed the bank and *got away with* a million pounds.

2 **PRACTICE**

Some of these sentences mean the same as the examples in Grammar Extra (1)? Which ones?

a) English and Scottish people usually like each other.

b) I don't like visiting my aunt in Ireland.

c) It was impossible to stop the noise of the airport.

d) The thieves escaped with a million pounds.

e) Christie was behind Lewis but passed him and won the gold medal.

3 **GRAMMAR EXTRA (2)**
ADJECTIVES AND NOUNS

You can double your vocabulary by learning the nouns which can be formed from the adjectives that you know. All the adjectives in this Activity were in Unit 16.

All the adjectives below form abstract nouns in the same way. Use your dictionary to find out how, and make notes in your Workbook.

dark   fit   good   happy   kind
lonely   sad   serious   tired

What is similar about the way these groups of adjectives form nouns?

(1) anxious   sensitive   stupid   generous
(2) confident   intelligent   patient   silent

These adjectives don't have a noun form that is commonly used.

clever   nice   old   strange   tall

Find a noun that matches the meaning of any of the adjectives above.

4 PRACTICE

Complete these sentences using a noun from Grammar Extra (2).

a) I don't think you understand the ... of your crime.

b) My mother enjoys living alone. ... is not a problem for her.

c) Dolphins are very clever. You can see the ... in their eyes.

d) Bob Geldof thanked the crowd at the Live Aid concert for their ... .

e) I want to thank you for all the ... you have shown me while I was a guest in your house.

B SKILLS REVIEW

1 WRITING

a) **Here is the text from the Writing Activity in Unit 16. Look at the notes in the margins and read the new version.**

b) **Either: Find the text you wrote about yourself in Unit 16 and rewrite it being as positive as you can about yourself!**

Or: **In pairs, exchange the piece you wrote with another student.**

too negative - 'quite tall' →

beautiful dark hair

'I like all kinds of music, especially ...' →

you sound old-fashioned. Invent a computer! →

you sound dull! Invent a sport that you like!

too negative!

change to 'I'm learning to play ...'

I'm short, I've got dark hair and green eyes. I like buying clothes, walking, swimming and playing chess. My favourite kind of music is techno but I also like jazz and blues. I don't like watching or playing any sport and I haven't got a computer. I'm not interested in motor bikes. I can ride a bike and swim, but I can't play a musical instrument or ride a horse.

I'm quite tall, I've got beautiful dark hair and green eyes. I like buying clothes, walking, swimming and playing chess. I like all kinds of music, and my special favourites are techno, jazz and blues. I love all sports and I play as many as I can regularly. I have just bought a computer and I'm really enjoying learning how to use it. I'm very interested in motor bikes and model aircraft. I can ride a bike and swim, and I'm learning to play the piano and guitar and to ride a horse.

2 READING

a) This is an extract from *Is That It?*, Bob Geldof's autobiography. Before you read, tell other students what you know about Bob Geldof.

b) Before he became famous, Bob Geldof worked as an English teacher. Read the extract and find out the following:

1 Where did he go to teach English?
2 Did he go alone?
3 Was he a qualified English teacher?
4 What did he think of the school?
5 Which students did he like best?

We looked through the train window at the dusty plains of La Mancha. The railway meandered down to the valley floor and the little provincial capital of Murcia.

We checked into a cheap hotel near the bullring, which Finnegan quickly located, and then set off to find the language school's director. We climbed the stairs and knocked on the big oak door and went in. We were an odd couple, me tall with long hair and a beard and wearing an old jacket, and Finnegan, small, red-haired and in a suit ...

The sole qualification for teaching at the school was that you knew no Spanish, a qualification I was able to meet perfectly. My pupils varied from schoolboys trying to supplement their schoolwork, to secretaries from the local bank, a retired admiral, the governor of a bank and a history professor.

I worked hard at the theory of English grammar that I had neglected to learn at school. I wasn't a bad teacher. The young kids between seven and eleven were the best. Every Friday, we had a party with cakes and sweets. It was strange hearing small Spanish children speaking English with a Dublin accent.

Adapted from Is That It? by Bob Geldof.

3 LISTENING

a) You're going to hear Sandra, Ravi and Gina answering the following questions about themselves:

1 What makes you smile?
2 What makes you want to stay in bed in the morning?
3 What makes you very angry?

Which of the following words do you expect to hear?

hospital   football   cartoons
grandmother   raining   stupid
mathematics   litter   bicycle
sister   government

b) Now listen to the cassette and check your answers.

4 SPEAKING

a) In pairs, think about the questions in Activity 3. What would your answers be? Discuss them with your partner.

b) Go round the class and make a list of other people's answers. Does anyone have the same answers as you? Who has the funniest answers?

C ACROSS CULTURES

a) In groups, discuss which biographies and/or autobiographies have been popular in your country.

b) Put them into categories. Here are some suggestions:

Politicians and other leaders
Artists, musicians and film stars
Inventors
Military people
TV personalities
Ex-criminals

c) Make a list of 5 famous people (past and present) who you would be interested in reading a biography about.

D COMPARATIVE PRON

STAR  NAMES

David Icke
/ˈdeɪvɪd aɪk/
Athlete and sports commentator
/eɪ/ as in *make* and /aɪ/ as in *life.*

Peter O'Toole
/ˈpiːtə əˈtuːl/
Irish actor
/əʊ/ as in *most* and /uː/ as in *who.*

a) **Practise these words and expressions which contain the /eɪ/ sound and the /aɪ/ sound.**

eighty-nine	at the same time
seatbelts save lives	break time
five past eight	take your time

b) **Listen to them on the cassette.**

c) **Practise these words and expressions which contain the /əʊ/ sound and the /uː/ sound:**

So do I	No through road
Oh no! Not you!	Opening soon

d) **Listen to them on the cassette.**

e) **When would you *say* or *see* the two expressions in a)?**

f) **Which of these words contain the /əʊ/ sound?**

though   slow   cough   allow   robot

g) **Which of these words contain the /uː/ sound?**

through   enough   shoe   does   blue

E COUNTDOWN TO BLOCK FIVE

1   **In Block Four, you practised the following language:**

Describing people and things using adjectives and modifiers.

He's *extremely* attractive.
This book is *really* interesting.
My sister is *rather* untidy.
It's an *absolutely* terrifying film.

Multi-word verbs – separable.

You should *give up* greasy food.
You should *give* greasy food *up*.
You should *give* it *up*.

Multi-word verbs – inseparable.

I'll help you *look for* your purse.
I'll help you *look for* it.

Multi-word verbs with three parts.

Christie *caught up with* Lewis.
Christie *caught up with* him.

Expressing possibilities.

You *might be* anxious about school.
He *could be* her great-great-grandson.

Review of past tenses: past simple, present perfect and *used to*.

Before 1837, churches *kept* records.
They *have kept* records since 1837.
Churches *used to* keep records.

2   **Have you written all the new words you have learnt in the Words section of your Workbook? Check you list now.**

3   **Have you added any new information to your ACROSS CULTURES scrapbook?**

CONGRATULATIONS!
You are ready to start BLOCK FIVE!

1 STARTER

a) In pairs, talk about the comedians who make you laugh. Do you know any English-speaking comedians? Have you seen any of their films?

b) Has anything funny ever happened to you? It could be something which happened on holiday, on a journey, when you were out with friends or at school. Tell your partner about it.

EXAMPLE: *One day, when I was going up an escalator, a man roared at me, like a lion!*

2 🎧 LISTENING

a) Listen to this conversation which takes place in a railway station. There are extra words in the dialogue below. Make a note of these as you read. Write down the last thing that the rail employee says.

PASSENGER:	Excuse me, please.
RAIL EMPLOYEE:	Good morning, can I help you?
PASSENGER:	Yes. I want to buy a ticket.
RAIL EMPLOYEE:	You want a ticket.
PASSENGER:	Yes. I want a ticket for the train to Birmingham.
RAIL EMPLOYEE:	You want a ticket to Birmingham?
PASSENGER:	Yes, please.
RAIL EMPLOYEE:	Why?
PASSENGER:	What did you say?
RAIL EMPLOYEE:	Why do you want a ticket to Birmingham?
PASSENGER:	Because I live there.
RAIL EMPLOYEE:	Birmingham's a terrible place.
PASSENGER:	Actually, I live there.
RAIL EMPLOYEE:	Why don't you go to Oxford?
PASSENGER:	Listen, I live there!
RAIL EMPLOYEE:	What? In Oxford?
PASSENGER:	No, I live in Birmingham.
RAIL EMPLOYEE:	Oh.
PASSENGER:	I live in Birmingham, I work in Birmingham, I was born in Birmingham ...
RAIL EMPLOYEE:	And ...

b) Now listen to the next part of the sketch. Say what happens in you own words. Remember that you can use the present tense to tell stories.

EXAMPLE: *A man **walks** into a railway station ticket office and **asks** for ...*

LANGUAGE AREA

Telling stories

MAIN STRUCTURE

Present simple and past simple for story-telling

VOCABULARY

Shopping and comedy

PRONUNCIATION

/ɔɪ/ as in *boy*

c) In pairs, think of a reason why it is impossible to go to Birmingham.

STUDENT A: you are the passenger.

STUDENT B: you are the railway employee. Think of reasons why the passenger cannot travel to Birmingham.

d) Listen to the end of the sketch and answer these questions.

1 Why can't the passenger buy a ticket?
2 When is the train going to leave?
3 Why isn't it necessary to hurry?

3 READING (1)

a) Look at the cartoon below. What do you think the story below could be about?

b) Rearrange the sentences below to make a story. (Number 1 is the first sentence of the story. The last sentence is missing.)

1 An Englishman went to stay in Paris.

2 He replied by saying his own name, 'Sidebottom.' This happened every day for a week.

3 On the first morning, he went to have breakfast. There were no tables free, so he sat at the same table as a Frenchman.

4 'That isn't his name,' said Sidebottom's friend. 'That's what French people say before they eat something.'

5 When the Englishman's breakfast arrived, the Frenchman said, '*Bon appetit.*' The Englishman thought that it was his name.

6 At the end of the week, an English friend of Sidebottom's arrived at the hotel. 'I want you to meet my friend, Mr *Bon Appetit*,' said Sidebottom.

c) How do you think the story ends? Write the final sentence. Now listen to the end of the story on the cassette. Were you right?

4 SPEAKING (1)

a) Now read the dialogues and look at the cartoons below. Try to think of an ending.

1 CUSTOMER: Excuse me?
  WAITRESS: Yes?
  CUSTOMER: What's this fly doing in my soup?
  WAITRESS: ...

2 WOMAN: What's the matter?
  MAN: I've lost my dog.
  WOMAN: Why don't you put an advertisement in the newspaper?
  MAN: I can't do that. ...

b) Now listen to the cassette and compare your answers.

FOCUS ON GRAMMAR   **5**
PRESENT SIMPLE AND PAST SIMPLE FOR STORY-TELLING

NB: Focus on Present Simple   Unit 6
       Focus on Past Simple   Unit 7

You can use either the present simple or the past simple when you are telling a story.

A man *walks* into the ticket office of a railway station and *says* ...

An Englishman *went* to stay in a hotel in Paris ...

Once upon a time, three bears *lived* in a little house in a forest ...

6 PRACTICE

a) What is the past tense of these verbs?

> carry   play   arrive   die   stop
> hope   cut   rent   look   watch

b) Listen to the past tense forms on the cassette and practise them.

c) Complete these sentences using positive and negative past simple forms from the list above.

> EXAMPLE: *Manchester United **didn't play** well in the Cup Final.*

1 Sarah ... beautiful in her wedding dress.

2 Angela ... a flat in Paris last summer.

3 I ... the chair up seven flights of stairs.

4 The plane ... late because of traffic congestion.

5 I ... my finger when I opened that tin.

6 She ... biting her finger nails.

7 WRITE YOUR OWN RULES

Write everything you know about the spellings of the regular verbs in the list in Activity 6a).

> EXAMPLE: *If the verb ends in -y ...*
> *If the verb ends in -ay ...*

8 WRITING

a) Write down the funny experience which you told your partner about in Activity 1).

> *about two weeks ago. Something really*
> *funny happened when we went to the*
> *theatre. It was a really boring play.*
> *Suddenly, a very old woman stood*
> *up in the front row and said: 'Is*
> *there a doctor in the theatre?'*
> *Everything went quiet. The actors*
> *just stopped and looked at her. She*
> *said it again: 'Is there a doctor in the*
> *theatre?' A woman at the back stood,*
> *up and said: 'Yes, I'm a doctor. What's*
> *the matter?' 'What's the matter?'*
> *repeated the old woman. 'This play.*
> *It's rubbish!' And then she walked out.*

b) Tell your partner's funny story to the rest of the class in your own words.

9 READING (2)

a) Read this story about a Spanish man visiting a clothes shop and explain the ending.

Eso si que es!

A Spanish man goes into a clothes shop to buy some clothes. He can't speak English and he isn't very good at describing things with gestures. The woman in the clothes shop is very helpful. She shows him a pair of trousers. He shakes his head. She shows him a suit. He shakes his head. She shows him overcoats, scarves, shirts, pullovers, underwear, ties and suits, and he keeps shaking his head. Finally, she shows him a pair of shoes. He looks at them, and points inside the shoe. She nods and takes out a pair of socks.

'*Eso si que es!*' says the Spanish man, looking very pleased. ('*Eso si que es*' is a Spanish expression which means 'That's it!'). The woman looks puzzled. 'If you knew how to spell it, why didn't you tell me when you came in?'

b) Listen to the cassette for an explanation of the ending.

10 PRON SPOT: /ɔɪ/ AS IN *BOY*

a) *oy* and *oi* are the most common spellings of the /ɔɪ/ sound.

> boy   joy   Roy   toy   destroy
> loyal   oyster   royal   boil   coil
> foil   soil   toil   avoid

Listen to the words on the cassette and practise them.

b) Practise these sentences and then listen to them on the cassette to check your pronunciation.

> A boy called Roy destroyed my toys.
> I boiled the oysters in oil and covered them with foil.

NB: New Jersey is in the USA. In British English, Jersey is pronounced /dʒɜːzɪ/. People from New Jersey pronounce the /ɜː/ sound in Jersey as /ɔɪ/. Listen to the cassette and compare.

STAR NAME

PAUL GASCOIGNE
/pɔːl ɡæskɔɪn/
Footballer

11 SPEAKING (2)

a) Who or what do you think is funny? Discuss with other students the kind of comedy films and TV programmes that you like.

b) In your country, is there a tradition of making jokes about certain groups of people? What do you think about this? Is it unfair?

THE FASTLANE QUESTIONNAIRE

12 Richard Vranch is a member of the Comedy Store Players – a group who perform sketches (short funny scenes). They appear twice a week at a venue for comedians called the Comedy Store in London. Read his answers to the questionnaire and try to fill in the missing words.

a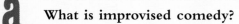

What is improvised comedy?

Comedy without a ... . We create the scenes and sketches as we ... them. At the Comedy Store, people in the audience suggest the characters and locations.

b

Do people from other countries visit the Comedy Store?

Yes. Many ... in central London go to theatres and clubs to see shows. Sometimes they're ... , sometimes they're confused!

c

Who's your favourite comedian?

I haven't got a single favourite comedian. My favourite British comedians are Spike Milligan and John Cleese (*see Unit 25 for more information about John Cleese*). My favourite ... comedians are Groucho Marx and Garry Shandling.

d

Have you ever tried to tell a joke in a foreign language?

Yes, I know a joke in ... The problem is that when I tell it to German ... , they think I can speak German really well and they start telling me other ... that I can't understand at all.

Now listen to the cassette and check your answers.

F FOCUS ON YOUR COUNTRY

13

Who are the most famous comedians in your country? What kind of jokes do they tell? Do a survey of the class to see if everyone likes the same kind of comedy.

84

1 STARTER

Look at the cartoon below. Someone is robbing a video shop. What are the other people doing?

EXAMPLE: *The woman is walking her dog.*

2 WRITING (1)

a) In pairs, divide the words below into (a) crimes, (b) criminals and (c) words which have something to do with detecting crimes and convicting criminals. If necessary, use a dictionary to help you.

murder
thief
clue
fraud
evidence
assault
detective
murderer
robbery
witness
theft
trial
burglary
fingerprint
judge
jury
robber

LANGUAGE AREA

Describing events in
the past

MAIN STRUCTURE

Present and past
continuous

VOCABULARY

Crimes

PRONUNCIATION

/aʊ/ as in *allowed*

b) Write five sentences using some of the words from Activity 2a).

EXAMPLE: *They used the **fingerprint** as evidence at the trial*.

c) Which of the following things are illegal? Which of them are sometimes or always not allowed?

smoking   running   speeding   hijacking
laughing   breaking windows   stealing
kidnapping   shouting

d) Put the words in c) which are *not* illegal into sentences to indicate that someone was doing something wrong.

EXAMPLE: *He got into trouble with his mother because he was **laughing** during a church service*.

FOCUS ON GRAMMAR   **3**
PRESENT AND PAST CONTINUOUS

a) You can use the present continuous to talk about actions which are happening now and are likely to continue.

They*'re studying* computing at the university.
Are you still *living* in New York.
What*'s* Paul *doing*? He*'s watering* the plants.

b) You can use the past continuous to describe an action that was happening at a particular moment in the past.

What *were* you *doing at five o'clock on Friday afternoon?*
I *was watching* a video.

c) You can also use the past continuous to describe simultaneous actions or events when one is interrupted by the other.

She *was standing* at the bus stop when the robbery *took place*.
When he *called*, I *was drying* my hair.
What *were* you *doing* when the lights *went out*?

d) You can use *while* to talk about two actions or events which happened at the same time. You can use the past simple and the past continuous.

While I *was cooking* he *was watching* television.
While I *was cooking* he *watched* television.

e) There are some verbs which you cannot use in the past continuous, such as *love, (dis)like, hate* and *adore*.

4   **PRACTICE**

a) Answer these questions using the past continuous.

What were you doing ...

1 at five o'clock yesterday afternoon?

2 an hour ago?

3 this time last week?

4 at midday last Saturday?

5 this time last year?

b) Now write three sentences using the past simple and past continuous to show interrupted action.

EXAMPLE: *I was eating my breakfast when the phone rang*.

5   **WRITE YOUR OWN RULES**

Make a list of any other verbs you can think of that you cannot use in the past continuous.

6 SPEAKING

a) After the video shop robbery the police interviewed Sid Smiley. Read the comic strip below. Do you think Sid is guilty?

POLICEMAN: 'Where were you at 5 o'clock on Friday afternoon?'
SID: 'I was at home.'

POLICEMAN: 'What were you doing?'
SID: 'I was watching a video.'

POLICEMAN: 'Were you anywhere near Bentall's video shop in Railway Street?'
SID: 'No, I wasn't.'

POLICEMAN: 'We saw you at Cross Street market on Saturday morning. You were selling a video machine'
SID: 'No, I wasn't.'

POLICEMAN: 'Well, what were you doing then?'
SID: 'I wasn't selling a video machine, I was buying one.'

POLICEMAN: 'So you were buying a video machine on Saturday ... and you were watching a video on Friday?'

b) In pairs, role-play the following situation.

STUDENT A: you are the police officer. Ask Sid's wife questions about Friday afternoon.

STUDENT B: you are Sid's wife. Answer questions about where Sid was on Friday afternoon.

7 READING

a) Read the confession below by someone who robbed a petrol station.

OFFICIAL STATEMENT

I was driving down Swan Road when I saw the garage. It was empty. The man who works there was in the kiosk, reading a newspaper. I pulled my balaclava over my face and asked him for money. He looked frightened but gave me about a hundred pounds from the till. I ran out, got into my car and drove away.

I drove for about a kilometre and stopped at some traffic lights. I saw there was a police road block stopping all the cars that were passing. I turned left at the lights, then left again and when I came to the main road, I turned right, so I was travelling in the opposite direction to the police road block.

I looked at the petrol gauge on the dashboard and saw that I was running out of petrol, so I pulled in a garage. Unfortunately, it was the same garage that I had robbed ten minutes before. When I arrived, the man was talking to a police officer, who arrested me.

b) Now tell the same story from the point of view of the man in the garage.

8 ▶ LISTENING

On the cassette, you will hear advertisements for a series of security features. Match the photos of the security features with the advertisements.

9 WRITING (2)

On your way to school you saw a man steal an old lady's handbag and run away down the street. The police need you as a witness. Write an account of what you saw. Include the following information about the crime: the date, time, where you were and a description of the man.

10 PRON SPOT: /aʊ/ AS IN *ALLOWED*

a) All these words contain the /aʊ/ sound. Practise them *before* you listen to the cassette.

allow   brown   cow   how   now
wow!   about   plough   house
loud   mouse   out

Now listen to the cassette and check your pronunciation.

b) The *ow* spelling can be pronounced two ways. Check the different meanings of these two words in your dictionary:

bow/aʊ/ and /əʊ/   row/aʊ/ and /əʊ/

c) The words below are pronounced like the *second* of the words above.

follow   know   low   mow   tow

THE FASTLANE INTERVIEW

11 Hazel Garvey had all her jewellery stolen from her flat while she was away for the weekend. In the interview, she talks about how she felt, and what she did.

● Listen to the interview.

● Don't worry if you don't understand everything.

● How much was the jewellery worth?

● What did the police do?

● Did she get any of the jewellery back?

● You can read the text of the interview on page 131.

F FOCUS ON YOUR COUNTRY 12

Is crime increasing in your country? Why? What are the most common crimes? What are the police and Government doing to fight crime? Why do people commit crimes?

Here is the news

LANGUAGE AREA

News stories

MAIN STRUCTURE

Past simple passive and
present perfect passive

VOCABULARY

Newspapers, magazines,
TV and radio news

PRONUNCIATION

/ɪə/ as in *here*

1 STARTER

a) Read this conversation between Garry and Angela.
What is Garry's reaction to the news about Vince Savage?

ANGELA: Guess what Garry! You won't believe this!
GARRY: What?
ANGELA: Vince Savage has been arrested!
GARRY: Who?
ANGELA: Vince Savage, the lead singer of that new band.
GARRY: No! You're joking. Has he really?
ANGELA: Yes!
GARRY: Why?

b) Now listen to the rest of the conversation.
Why did the police arrest Vince Savage?

2 READING

a) Match the headlines with the
stories below.

b) Now choose one of the stories
and write more details about it.

Girls see monster in Loch Ness

POP STAR MEETS BIGGEST FAN

Teenager wins top fashion prize

ENGLAND LOSE IN 8-GOAL FIASCO

ALIENS BUILD MILITARY BASE ON MOON

The Montana Prize, Britain's most important fashion prize, has been won by 19-year old Paul Kennedy, a student at Epping Forest Art College. Paul's revolutionary casual wear was considered to be the most inventive of the 1,200 items that were examined by the judges.

England manager Lee Sharpe was sacked after England were beaten 5-3 by Albania at Wembley last night. Sharpe said it was the most embarrassing night of his professional life and he was happy to leave.

Susan Morgan (18) and her friend Beryl Costello (19) claim that they saw the Loch Ness monster while they were walking around the Loch last Saturday. The monster, which hasn't been 'seen' for several years, looked very healthy, they said.

BOBBIE SHARON, twenty-something star of TV series The People Next Door was in London last night to promote her new record, *All the Poor People*. At a party, she was introduced to Sam Parrish, who is 6 feet 5 inches tall (1 metre 95).

Space experts in California say that buildings have been seen on the moon. They are convinced that the buildings, which may contain military weapons, have been built by creatures from another

Robin Williams as DJ and newsreader in the film Good Morning Vietnam

3 LISTENING

a) Listen to the first three news stories from Activity 2 and write down any extra details that you hear.

b) Read and listen to the radio reports of the last two news stories in Activity 2. Make a note of any differences between the written version and what you hear.

Last week soap star Bobbie Sharon was disappointed when she got the chance to meet Sam Parrish, who describes himself as her biggest enemy. You can see why he says that, Sam is an incredible 1 metre 35 tall. He was introduced to Bobbie at her record company's party to advertise Bobbie's latest book, *All the Poor People*. Bobbie was interviewed by Bill Bright for Rock Sound Radio.

'I'm just so pleased to be here. English people are so awful!'

You can hear the complete interview on David Wayne's What's New? programme tonight at 9.30.

And yet another story about the Loch Ness Monster! Nessie has been seen by two Swedish teenagers. They say they saw the monster during a walk round Loch Ness. 18-year old Susan Morgan talked to Rock Sound Radio.

'We just turned the corner and there she was! She looked very happy and healthy.'

Susan and her friend, Karen Costello, were interviewed by doctors when they returned to their hospital in Aberdeen.

23

90

FOCUS ON GRAMMAR
PAST SIMPLE PASSIVE AND PRESENT PERFECT PASSIVE

a) You can use the passive tense to make the object of an active sentence into the subject of a passive sentence.

The police have arrested Vince Savage.
Vince Savage *has been arrested*.

You could say:

Vince Savage *has been arrested by the police*.

but *we know* it was the police, so it isn't necessary to say this.

b) You can also use the passive if you don't know who performed the action or if it isn't important to know.

The England manager *was sacked* last night.
Buildings *have been seen* on the moon.

c) The object may be more important than the subject.

The Montana prize *has been won* by Paul Kennedy.

In this sentence we are more interested in the Montana Prize than in Paul Kennedy.

5 PRACTICE

Complete these sentences in the passive using the following prompts.

a) Mona Lisa/stolen/Louvre.

b) The Queen/take/hospital.

c) Aliens/see/London.

d) London/take over/aliens.

e) England/beat/World Cup final.

6 WRITING

a) The five newspaper headlines in Activity 2 all contain an *active* verb in the present tense, e.g. Pop star *meets* biggest fan. Here are five more headlines which contain a *passive* verb, but part of the verb is missing (this is normal in newspaper headlines in English). Rewrite each headline including the missing part of the verb.

Presley tapes found in library

Buckingham Palace sold to film producer

WHITE WHALE SEEN IN RIVER THAMES

LONDON PUB INVADED BY CATS

VAN GOGH PAINTING STOLEN FROM TAXI

b) Read this extra information about the first headline.

c) Now choose one of the headlines in Activity 6 and write a similar article. Think about the following:

1 What is the news story about?

2 When did it happen?

3 Where did it happen?

4 Do we know who was involved?

5 Is it a serious news story?

Tapes of several unknown Elvis Presley songs have been found in a library in Nashville. They were found by librarian Alice Spritzer while she was clearing out a cupboard full of old books. Presley experts are convinced that the tapes are genuine and were probably recorded by Presley when he was still a teenager.

91

PRON SPOT: /ɪə/ AS IN *HERE*

7

a) *ear* and *eer* are the most common spellings of the /ɪə/ sound.

ear	clear	dear	fear	gear
hear	near	tear	year	beer
career	cheers!	deer	steer	

Make a note of these words which contain the *ear* spelling but are pronounced differently.

bear   pear   tear   wear

Check the difference between these words.

tear /ɪə/ and tear /eə/

b) Here are some other common words containing the /ɪə/ sound.

here   mere   pier   tier
we're (we are)

c) These occupations and activities all end in the /ɪə/ sound.

auctioneer   engineer   mountaineer
pioneer

d) Some place names contain the /ɪə/ sound when they are said in English.

Andalusia   Korea   Kampuchea
Nicosia   Aramathea

Listen to the words on the cassette and practise the pronunciation.

e) Now practise this poem and check your pronunciation and stress on the cassette.

We're here, we're here
Can you hear? Can you hear?
Oh dear, no one here
Are they near? Are they near?
Never fear, have a beer, cheers!

STAR  NAME

RICHARD GERE /rɪtʃəd gɪə/
American actor

8 SPEAKING

In pairs, think of a famous person. Do not tell anyone else in the class who you have chosen.

STUDENT A: you are a journalist.

STUDENT B: you are a famous person.
Prepare an interview between the journalist and the famous person and act out the interview in front of the rest of the class. (Remember not to mention the famous person's name!) The rest of the class has to try and guess who the famous person is.

THE FASTLANE INTERVIEW

9 Gillian Dickinson is a freelance journalist. She sells stories to lots of different newspapers.

- Listen to the interview.
- Don't worry if you don't understand everything.
- What kind of stories does she write?
- How does she sell them?
- What's the most dangerous situation she's been in?
- You can read the text of the interview on page 132.

F FOCUS ON YOUR COUNTRY

10

Which are the most popular newspapers and magazines in your country? Does anyone in the class read them? Do a survey and find out. Do you think most newspapers report the news accurately? What type of news interests you the most – politics, international affairs, sports or the arts?

TALL STORIES

LANGUAGE AREA

Expressing doubt,
surprise and
astonishment

MAIN STRUCTURE

Reported speech

VOCABULARY

Various

PRONUNCIATION

/aʊə/ as in *flower*

1 STARTER

a) What do you know about the Loch Ness monster or the Himalayan Yeti?

b) Are there any legends about strange creatures in your country that people believe? Is there any proof that these creatures might exist?

2 LISTENING

a) You are going to hear a scientist talking about the Loch Ness monster. Before you listen, make sure you know the meaning of these words and expressions:

legend	Middle Ages
surgeon	creature
mammal	plesiosaur
extinct	stranded
ice age	search
theory	forgery

b) When you listen, make a note of any words or phrases that people use to express their surprise.

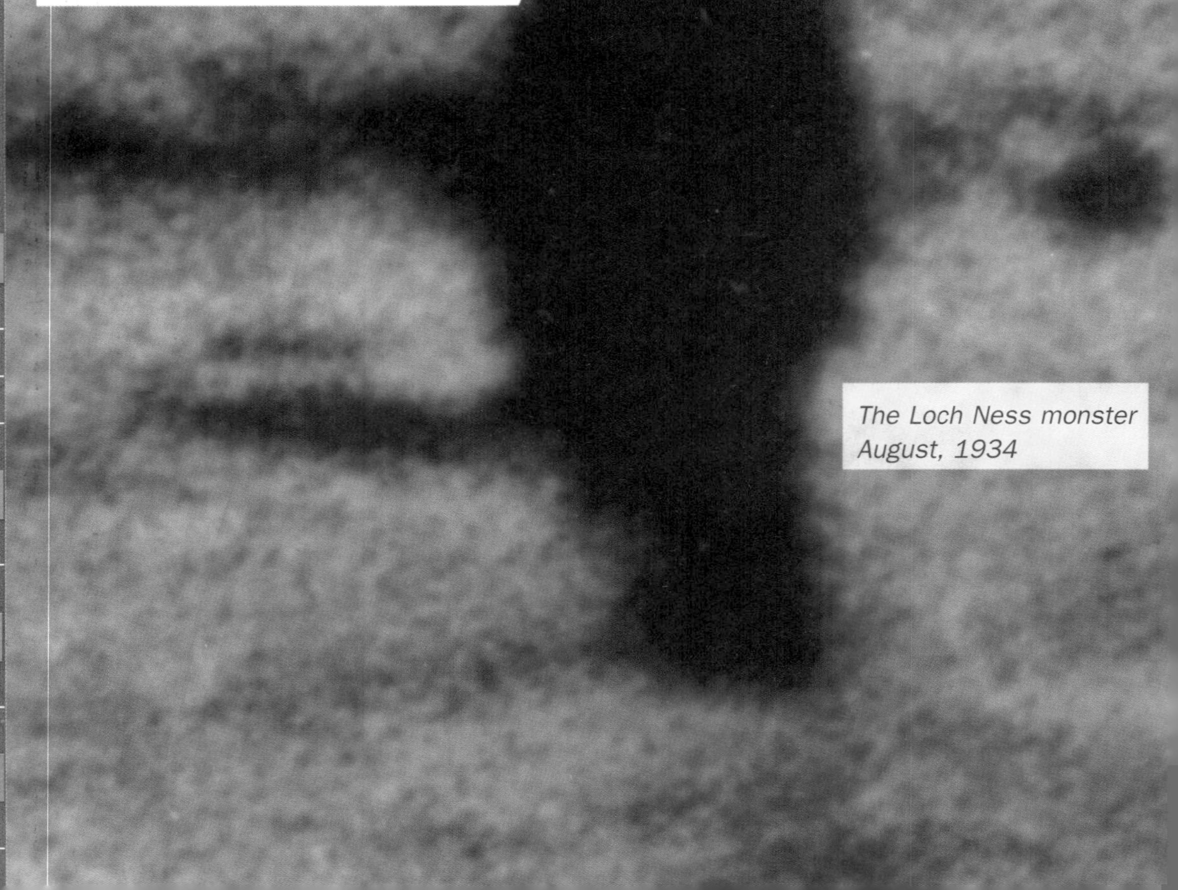

*The Loch Ness monster
August, 1934*

3 SPEAKING (1)

One student talks about something that happened to them including a piece of information that is not true. The other student listens to the story and has to guess which part of it is false, using some of the phrases below.

I don't believe you.
I find that hard to believe.
That sounds highly unlikely.
You don't expect me to believe that, do you?
You're pulling my leg!

EXAMPLE: *STUDENT A: I went to the coast on holiday last year. I met a film director, went scuba diving, found some money on the beach and fell in love. On the way back our car broke down and we had to hitchhike home.*

*STUDENT B: **I find it hard to believe that you met a film director on holiday. You're pulling my leg!***

4 READING (1)

Look at the two pairs of cartoons. Each time the person didn't hear what was said correctly. What did the people *really* say?

F FOCUS ON GRAMMAR 5
REPORTED SPEECH

a) **When you report what someone said, the tense changes.**
You can use the present tense if you report it immediately.

I'*m* a government minister.
He *says* he's a government minister.

b) **You can use the past simple if you report it later.**

He *said* he *was* a government minister.
He *told* me he *was* a government minister.

Books *will* no longer exist in the next century.
She *said* that books *would* no longer exist in the next century.
She *told* us that books *would* no longer exist in the next century.

I'*m eating* my lunch.
She *said* she *was eating* her lunch.
She *told* me she *was eating* her lunch.

6 WRITE YOUR OWN RULES

Write everything you know about the tense changes when you use reported speech.

EXAMPLE: *Am/is becomes was.*

7 PRACTICE

What did these people actually say?

a) He said he wanted to meet the Prime Minister.

b) She told the teacher that she couldn't do her homework.

c) The teacher said she knew who was responsible for the graffiti.

d) My Mum told me that I had to come home early.

e) Paul McCartney told reporters that he didn't want to tour any more.

8 SPEAKING (2)

Sit in a circle of at least five people. One person should whisper something to the next person, who should then whisper what he or she heard to the next person and so on. The last person in the group should tell the others, using reported speech, what the first person said.

EXAMPLE: *First person: I'm going to Rome at Easter.*

*Last person: He **said** he was going to Rome at Easter.*

9 READING (2)

a) **'Tall stories' are stories that you find hard to believe. Read these three stories and find words or phrases that mean the following:**

amazement   travel card   resembled   king   helpers   killed   temporary

b) **Match the stories below with a title from this list.**

The Punk in the Café   The Driving Dog
Teaching Henry to Drive   Sharing a Chocolate Bar
The King's Double   Tragedy at Monza

An old man went to his favourite café for a cup of tea and a chocolate bar. He noticed that there weren't any free tables. In fact, the only free seat was at a table with an angry-looking young woman with a ring in her nose and a strange spiky haircut. He sat at the table and began drinking his tea. To his astonishment, the girl opened his chocolate bar and began to eat it! He stared at her in disbelief, but she carried on eating. The old man stood up, angrily poured his tea on the girl's leather jacket and walked out. Still angry, he got on a bus and put his hand in his pocket to take out his bus pass. In his pocket, he found his chocolate bar ...

Umberto the Second of Italy went to the races in Monza. He was eating in a restaurant when he noticed that the restaurant owner looked exactly like him. He then discovered that the man was also called Umberto, had the same birthday and had a wife with the same name. Umberto the monarch invited Umberto the restaurateur to join him at the races the next day. The next day, one of the King's aides brought him some bad news. Umberto the restaurateur was dead, probably murdered. Moments later, King Umberto was assassinated.

When Wayne Devlon of Charlottetown, Illinois, lost his driving licence for speeding, he thought it would be a good idea to teach his dog to drive. He bought an old dual control automatic car from a driving school, and taught Henry, his St Bernard, to control the steering wheel while he controlled the pedals. He even applied for a provisional driving licence for the dog, in the name of Henry St Bernard. Eventually, the police stopped the car and arrested the dog for driving after dark with just a provisional licence.

10 WRITING

Choose one of the opening lines in box A, and one of the closing lines in box C and write a story. Try to use at least one word from box B. Use a dictionary to help you with any words or phrases you don't understand.

A In the Middle Ages, a knight was riding his horse through a terrible snowstorm.

In 1894, a fisherman was swept overboard in a storm in the South Atlantic.

Charles Coghlan, an actor, was interred in a mausoleum in Galveston, Texas.

B arrive   swallow   flood   midnight
whale   destroy   harpoon   town
exhausted   post

C They found the coffin 3,000 kilometres away on Prince Edward Island, Canada, the place where he was born.

They opened up the whale, and found their shipmate inside, still alive.

When he woke up, he was lying in the town square. His horse was tied to a lamppost in the main square.

11 PRON SPOT: /aʊəː/ AS IN *FLOWER*

a) **There are two common spellings of the /aʊə/ sound.**

bower   cower   flower   power
tower   flour   hour   sour

b) **Make a note of these exceptions.**

grower /əʊə/   lower   lawnmower
rower

NB: These are all associated with a verb or an adjective: grow, low, mow, row.

Listen to the cassette to check the pronunciation.

c) **Practise these sentences.**

Flowers grow bigger in lower fields.
A rower rowed with power past the tower.
Our flour will be ready in an hour.

STAR ⭐ NAME

TYRONE POWER
/taɪrəʊn paʊə(r)/
American actor

THE FASTLANE INTERVIEW

12 **John Chilwell is an actor/comedian from the North of England. He is famous for telling tall stories.**

● **Listen to the interview.**

● **Don't worry if you don't understand everything.**

● **Write down five words that you hear.**

● **Discuss the story with other students.**

● **You can read the text of the interview on page 133.**

FOCUS ON YOUR COUNTRY   13

Are there any famous tall stories which people tell in your country? In groups, make notes about them, and then talk about them with the rest of the class.

A LANGUAGE REVIEW

1 **GRAMMAR EXTRA (1)**
DESCRIBING TWO ACTIONS IN THE PAST

a) **The past continuous is used to describe a continuous action at a point in time.**

I *was cooking* when the phone *rang*.
When you *phoned*, I *was drying* my hair.
What *were you doing at eight o'clock*?
I *was writing* a letter to my grandmother.

b) **The past simple is used to describe one action followed by another in the past.**

I *stopped* when I *saw* him.
(1. I saw him   2. I stopped)

When the door *opened*, we *went* in.
(1. the door opened   2. we went in)

c) ***Before* or *after* can sometimes be used.**

I bought some flowers *before* I went to see my aunt.
After I locked the door, I heard the telephone ring.

d) **You don't use the past continuous to talk about regular events in the past, you use *used to*.**

When we lived in Birmingham, we *used to* support Aston Villa football team. (We don't live in Birmingham any more, so we don't support Aston Villa.)

NB: In sentences with *when*, *before* and *after*, when do you use a comma? Look at the sentences above.

2 **PRACTICE**

Make questions using the words in brackets.

a) Where (live) when you (meet) each other?

b) What (do) when the volcano (erupt)?

c) What (talk) about when I (be) upstairs?

d) Why (laugh) when I (come) in?

3 **GRAMMAR EXTRA (2)**

Look at these four sentences. Two have passive verbs, the other two have the verb *to be* + adjective. Which is which?

Vince Savage *was arrested* last night.
Bobby Sharon *was amazed* when she met Sam Parrish.
My Mum *was disappointed* when she saw my exam results.
My bicycle *was stolen* this morning.

Here are some common adjectives ending in **-ed**. All these adjectives describe people, *not* things.

amazed	annoyed	astonished
bored	delighted	disappointed
excited	impressed	interested
puzzled	shocked	surprised

Complete these sentences.

Bobby Sharon was amazed when ...
The whole town was shocked when ...
We were so bored when ...

With two exceptions, all of the adjectives above have an -ing form which describes things, situations or people.

Sam Parrish was *amazing*.
My exam results were *disappointing*.

Which are the two exceptions? What form do the two exceptions take?

Write three more sentences like the ones above using the -ing form.

NB: All these adjectives can be made into verbs.

Bobby Sharon was *amazed*.
Sam Parrish was *amazing*.
Sam Parrish *amazed* Bobby Sharon.
My Mum was *disappointed* when she saw my exam results.
My exam results were *disappointing*.
My exam results *disappointed* my Mum.

4 PRACTICE

Complete these sentences using an adjective from Grammar Extra (2).

a) She was expecting a lot of birthday cards so she was very ... when she only received three.

b) I was ... when he said he was my Uncle Sid. I haven't got an Uncle Sid.

c) That was the worst film I've ever seen. It was so ...!

d) We were all ... when we heard about the train crash.

B SKILLS REVIEW

1 WRITING

a) Read this account of one of the most famous robberies that took place in Britain.

The Great Train Robbery

On August 8th 1963, more than a million pounds was stolen from a mail train which was travelling from Edinburgh to London. At the time, it was the largest robbery ever committed in Britain.

The train stopped in a rural area north of London because of a red light. But the red light was put there by the thieves who knew that if the real green light was removed or broken, an alarm would ring and a warning light would flash in a nearby signal box. This problem was solved in a very clever way. A glove was placed over the green light. It was still on, but it could not be seen.

Fortunately for the police, the glove was not removed after the robbery, and became an important piece of evidence. Also, after the gang's last meal at a cottage near the scene of the crime, the plates and cups were not washed. More clues for the police.

The driver of the train was attacked during the robbery and never fully recovered from the shock of that night. All the train robbers were sent to prison. One of them, Ronald Biggs, escaped and went to live in Brazil.

b) In groups, think of a famous crime, or a crime that has happened recently in your country. Talk about it together.

c) On your own, write about the crime. Use the story of The Great Train Robbery as a guide. Think about the following when you write:

1 When and where did the crime take place?

2 What kind of crime was it?

3 What happened?

4 Were the criminals caught and sent to prison? Are the criminals still in prison?

5 What clues and other evidence did the police have when they were looking for the criminals?

NB: Remember to use the passive.

2 READING

The actor/comedian John Cleese is famous for many successful films and TV programmes such as *Monty Python's Flying Circus*, Fawlty Towers, *Clockwise* and *A Fish Called Wanda*. Tom Stoppard is a famous British playwright. Below are two true stories about incidents that happened to them. The two stories are in the right order but they have been mixed up. Can you work out what the two stories are?

John Cleese, the actor, comedian and film maker, an extremely tall man, was having breakfast at his London home when he heard a noise in the street.

Tom Stoppard writes plays. Something strange or absurd usually happens in them.

He lives in a big house in the country with a large garden, where he keeps a lot of Canadian geese.

He went to the window of his kitchen, which faces the street, and looked out.

A teenage boy and a woman of about 25 were struggling in the street. It was clear that the boy was trying to steal the woman's handbag.

He was shaving in his bathroom one morning. He was wearing pyjama bottoms and slippers. Suddenly, he heard the sound of a car screeching to a halt.

He was wearing his dressing gown and slippers, but he immediately ran to the front door of his house.

The woman was standing alone in the street and shouting. The teenager was running away.

He looked out of his window and he saw that one of the animals was walking across the road.

He ran out of the back door and into the garden. Some more geese were walking towards the gate.

He immediately began to chase the boy. When he caught up with him, he threw him to the ground and jumped on top of him.

He ran outside and closed the gate. Then he ran across the road and picked up the goose.

He held out his hand to stop a car so he could go back to his house. The driver of the car looked astonished.

Because of the actor's great height, this was quite painful for the boy. He screamed with pain and turned and shouted.

When he recognised who it was, he stopped shouting. 'I know who you are,' said the boy. 'What's going on? Are you making a film?'

He realised that it was like a scene from one of his plays. He was standing half-naked in the street, he had shaving foam over half of his face, he was holding a Canada goose and he was ordering cars to stop so that he could cross the road.

3 LISTENING

a) Match the news items you hear with the photos below.

b) Now invent some more information about one of the news items.

4 SPEAKING

Most of Block Five has been about stories ... news stories, funny stories, tall stories. In groups, or as a whole class, tell a story together. Use the 7 prompts below to divide your story into parts. Each student should only tell *one* sentence from the story but try as a group or class to make at least three or four sentences for each part so that the story has plenty of detail.

a) When did the story take place?

EXAMPLE: *It all happened **a hundred years ago**. It was **the 24th December**. It was **the middle of the afternoon**.*

b) Who are the main characters?

EXAMPLE: *A **group of people** were walking in a forest. They were a **brother** and his **two sisters**. They had their **dog, Toby**, with them.*

c) One of the main characters saw something. What was it? Something terrible happened – what was it?

d) What did the characters decide to do?

e) What did the characters do to put things right?

f) Something else went wrong. What was it?

g) What happened at the end? What was the outcome?

C ACROSS CULTURES

Who are some famous characters that appear in folk tales and other famous stories in your country? Try to find pictures of them and explain who they are in English in your ACROSS CULTURES scrapbook.

D COMPARATIVE PRON

STAR ★ PRON SPOT ★ NAMES

CHAIRMAN MAO
/maʊ/
(Chinese Communist Leader)
/aʊ/ as in *allowed*.

PRESIDENT MOI
/mɔɪ/
(President of Kenya)
/ɔɪ/ as in *boy*.

PRESIDENT EISENHOWER
/ɑɪz(ə)nhaʊə/
(President of the USA
1953–61)
/aʊə/ as in *flower*.

MIA FARROW
/mɪə færəʊ/
(American actress)
/ɪə/ as in *here*.

a) **Which of these words contain the /aʊ/ sound?**

tow   brown   thrown   mouse
town

b) **Which of these words contain the /ɔɪ/ sound?**

soul   soil   bowl   boil   destroy

c) **Which of these words contain the /ɪə/ sound?**

bear   dear   ear   here   hear
pear   there   wear   were   year

d) **Which of these words contain the /aʊə/ sound?**

shower   blower   tower   pour
hour   flour   grower

E COUNTDOWN TO BLOCK SIX

1 **In Block Five, you practised the following language:**

Present and past tenses for story-telling.

A woman *walks* into a restaurant and *says* …
An American *arrived* in Rome and *went* to a hotel.

The past continuous tense.

What *were you doing* this time last year?
I *was sitting* here listening to you.
She *was standing* at the bus stop when the robbery took place.
While *you were sleeping*, I was cleaning the house!

Past simple passive and present perfect passive.

Vince Savage *has been sent* to prison.
He *was arrested* in a hotel last night.

Reported speech, using present and past tenses.

She *says* she's a government minister.
He *said* people wouldn't read books in the next century.
She *said* she was eating her lunch.

2 **Have you written all the new words you have learnt in the Words section of your Workbook? Check your list now.**

3 **Have you added any new information to your ACROSS CULTURES scrapbook?**

CONGRATULATIONS! You are ready to start THE FINAL BLOCK OF *Fastlane*!

NATURAL EXPLOSIONS

LANGUAGE AREA

Describing the natural world

MAIN STRUCTURE

Non-defining clauses

VOCABULARY

Geographical features

PRONUNCIATION

/ʒ/ as in *explosions*

1 **STARTER**

How many of the world's volcanoes can you name? How many of these are still active? Have you ever seen a volcano? Which famous eruptions can you think of?

2 **READING**

a) Read the text below quickly. How many of the volcanoes you named in Activity 1 are mentioned in the text? How many famous eruptions are mentioned?

b) Was there any information in the text which surprised you? In pairs, describe the positive value of volcanoes.

c) Read the text again and find a place for these pieces of extra information where you see an asterisk (*).

1 ,which is of course softer

2 ,which has more volcanoes than anywhere else on earth,

3 ,which is heated by subterranean magma,

4 ,who was the god of fire

5 ,which is near Naples,

6 ,who works at the Smithsonian Institute,

7 ,which takes the form of ash or lava

Kilauea Volcano, Hawaii

There are about 550 active volcanoes on earth and 500 million people who live close to them. As you read this, about a dozen of them are erupting at this very minute. Research scientist Dick Fiske* says a hundred of them need to be watched carefully and regularly.

5 The word volcano comes from the Roman god, Vulcan*. The first recorded eruption was at Vesuvius* in AD79. It buried the Roman towns of Pompeii and Herculaneum, killing 16,000 people. The 1815 eruption at Tambora in Indonesia lowered the temperature of the entire planet for months. Snow fell in the United States the following June.

10 Yet volcanoes are vital to the continuing existence of planet Earth. They provide the lifeblood which keeps the planet alive. Our blood carries nutrients around our body. Volcanoes do the same thing. The material which shoots out during a volcanic explosion is called magma*.

Magma contains the major elements required for plant growth: phosphorus,
15 potassium and calcium, for example. If it shoots out as lava, it may take decades or centuries before the nutrients benefit the soil. On the other hand, if it shoots out as ash*, the fertilising process can start within months.

It is therefore no surprise that Java in Indonesia* is also one of the most fertile areas of the planet.

20 What other benefits do volcanoes give us? Underground water* heats almost all the houses in Iceland. In New Zealand, it provides 7 per cent of the country's electric power.

Adapted from National Geographic magazine.

d) Explain these references:

1 Line 3:   *a hundred of them*: a hundred of what?
2 Line 6:   *it buried the Roman town of Pompeii*: what did?
3 Line 12:   *Volcanoes do the same thing*: what same thing?
4 Line 15:   *If it shoots out as lava*: if what shoots out as lava?
5 Line 21:   *it provides 7 per cent of the country's electric power*: what does?

FOCUS **ON GRAMMAR**
NON-DEFINING CLAUSES ③

a) You looked at relative clauses in Unit 11. Here are some examples from that Unit:

It's a company *which* is based in Italy.
There were hundreds of people *who* were searching for gold.

These are *defining* clauses. Without them, the sentences would contain no information at all!

b) In this Unit, we are looking at *non-defining* clauses.

Mount Everest, *which* was named after an English army officer, is the world's highest mountain.
Sir Edmund Hillary, *who* was the first person to climb Mount Everest, was accompanied by a Tibetan sherpa called Tensing.

You can use relative clauses to add extra information about the noun in the sentence. Non-defining clauses are enclosed within commas. You can use *who* in a non-defining clause about people, and *which* in a non-defining clause about things. You can't use *that*.

④ PRACTICE

a) Complete these sentences by inserting the extra information a)–c) in the correct place.

1 Ffyona Campbell spent three years walking around the world.
2 Mount Fuji is a sacred temple to the followers of the Shinto religion.
3 Ecuador is one of the most beautiful countries in South America.

a) ... ,which means *equator* in Spanish,

b) ... ,who comes from Scotland,

c) ... ,which is in Japan,

b) Add extra information of your own to these sentences.

1 Bill Clinton visited Japan last month.
2 The Pacific Ocean separates America and Asia.
3 My great-grandmother was an exceptional woman.
4 Rome is one of the noisiest cities in the world.
5 My best friend is going to do a summer course in England.

5 WRITE YOUR OWN RULES

Write everything you know about the main differences between defining and non-defining clauses.

6 LISTENING

a) You are going to listen to someone talking about the San Andreas fault. Before you listen, read the following sentences and decide if you think they are true or false.

1 A fault is where two types of rock meet and pressure occurs.
2 Faults are caused by earthquakes.
3 The San Andreas Fault is in California.
4 It is the only fault in the area.
5 It is 12 kilometres long.
6 The San Francisco earthquake occurred in 1960.
7 The earthquake that occurred on 17th October 1989 was the worst one that will ever happen.

b) Now listen to the cassette and check your answers.

c) Listen again and make a note of any extra information that you hear.

7 SPEAKING

Imagine you are a television journalist reporting from the scene of a volcanic eruption or earthquake. Describe what you have seen and who you have spoken to.

8 WRITING (1)

a) Match the natural features on the left with a suitable adjective on the right.

forest	deep
valley	snow-covered
river	dense
lake	winding
mountain	fertile

b) Look at the words below that can be used to talk about mountains. Find words which relate to RIVERS, LAKES, FORESTS and VALLEYS.

EXAMPLE: *MOUNTAINS; slope, high, climb, steep, range, peak, rocks*

9 WRITING (2)

a) Read this letter about a visit to Italy.

I'm really pleased to hear that you're planning a visit to Italy, which is one of my favourite countries in the world. I understand that you're planning to fly to Pisa, is that right? I have a suggestion. Instead of going to Florence, which is packed with tourists at this time of the year, why don't you travel north along the coast? La Spezia, which is north of Pisa, is an ideal base for touring the area. And you must go to Portovenere, which is the most beautiful place I have ever visited.

b) Write a letter to a friend who is planning to visit your country for the first time. The friend wants to spend the entire visit in the capital city. Encourage him/her to visit a different part of the country, and describe the area using non-defining clauses. Try to use some of the vocabulary from Activity 8.

10 PRON SPOT: /ʒ/ AS IN *EXPLOSION*

a) Here are three common words containing the /ʒ/ sound:

pleasure   television   usually

Make a sentence using all three words.

b) Here are some other words ending in *-sure*.

leisure   measure   treasure
disclosure   enclosure   exposure

c) Here are some other words ending in *-sion*.

collision   decision   precision
revision   vision

Listen to the words on the cassette and practise the pronunciation.

STAR PRON SPOT NAME

Jean-Michel Jarre
/ʒɒ mɪʃel ʒɑː/
French musician and performer

11 Ffyona Campbell is the first woman to walk around the world. Ffyona, who comes from Devon, began her extraordinary walk on 24th August 1983 and ended it on 14th October 1994. The walk, which was done in six stages, was 31,337 kilometres long.

a In this questionnaire, the questions are jumbled up. Read the answer and then unscramble the question.

1 you the got old you idea first How were when?

I was 14 when I got the idea to walk around the world, but I didn't know how big it is.

2 ambition of your What family did your think?

They thought it was very amusing until I started walking. Then they kept their fears to themselves and were very supportive.

3 charity is raised name of the you money for What the?

Raleigh International – it is a youth development charity. They take young people on expeditions abroad to develop their confidence and understanding of the real world beyond the search for material wealth.

4 the you place was Which most beautiful visited?

The most beautiful places were in areas of Africa where missionaries, aid agencies and commerce had not contaminated the beauty of the people.

5 give would young advice people What you to?

Hold your head up, look at what's really there and question the decisions of Western mentality. Some cultures have a different code of morals: they share, they give back to the land what they have taken. Yet they are not the ones who dictate the rights and wrongs of the world. The young people of today will be the guardians of the world tomorrow. If you learn the ways of native people, you find the answers to the great moral dilemmas of our time and far greater riches than the treadmill of the capitalist system.

b What do you think about Ffyona's ideas, especially her advice to young people?

c Would you like to follow in Ffyona's footsteps? Whether the answer is 'yes' or 'no', give your reasons.

→ 🗨 ☞ ✉ ✍ ↩ " ✓ ✏ ✱ → 🗨 ☞ ✉ ✍ ↩ " ✓ ✏ ✱ → 🗨 ☞ ✉

FOCUS ON YOUR COUNTRY

12

Find out about the world's highest mountains, longest rivers and biggest lakes. How do the mountains, rivers and lakes in your country compare? Produce a booklet advertising your country's natural features. Think about: the flora (plants) and fauna (animals), especially any which are rare, the climate and any spectacular natural attractions (NOT man-made).

Shooting Stars

LANGUAGE AREA

Explaining unusual

events

MAIN STRUCTURE

so/such, so ... that

VOCABULARY

Astronomy and astrology

PRONUNCIATION

/ʃ/ as in *shooting*

1 STARTER

Do you know anything about the following? Discuss them with another student and make notes. Use a dictionary to help you.

meteors   meteorites   meteoroids   comets
shooting stars   solar eclipses   lunar eclipses
northern lights (aurora borealis)   southern lights
(aurora australis)

**NB: We call all these 'phenomena' – when we see
something and are not sure why it happens. The
singular is 'phenomenon'.**

Has anyone in your class ever seen the phenomena mentioned above? What did they see?

2 LISTENING

a) Listen to the conversation on the cassette. Which of the phenomena from Activity 1 are mentioned?

b) Listen again and decide if the following statements are true or false.

1 A meteor is the same as a shooting star.

2 A million meteoroids enter the Earth's atmosphere every day.

3 When they enter the Earth's atmosphere, they are travelling at a top speed of 72 kilometres per minute.

4 Meteors get so hot that they always burn up.

5 Several tons of meteorites land on the Earth every day.

6 Comets consist mainly of gases.

7 They are like large, dirty snowballs.

8 Comets can be 130,000 kilometres in diameter.

9 Comets are much heavier than planet Earth.

10 The tail of a comet can be 160 million kilometres long.

3 READING

a) Read this text about the northern and southern lights. There is one misspelt word in each sentence.

One of the most magnificent natural phenomena that the skys can produce is aurora borealis, or northern lights (aurora australis is the name for the southern lights which are in the southern hemisphere). Aurora borealis and australis are luminous displays of moving lites in the night sky. They can be seen most clerely from within the Arctic or Antarctic Circles, although it is also possible to see them in non-polar regions, notably in Sweden or Canada.

Northern or southern lights are thought to be caused by high-speed particles from the sun, wich collide with air molecules. The result is a series of differant effects; patches of white light, laser beams pointing to the sky, or rainbow-shaped arcs. Sometimes they look like coloured curtains mooving across the night sky.

The effect is quiet breath-taking.

b) 'Sometimes they look like coloured curtains in the sky'. Think of an image to describe one of the following:

EXAMPLE: *A thunderstorm: The rain was like a huge waterfall outside my window.*

1 A rainbow
2 Lightning
3 A sunset you have seen
4 Dark clouds

c) Read the following extracts from letters. Which phenomena are the people describing?

> I was driving along the coast road, and suddenly I saw this amazing sight. There were white lights pointing to the stars. It was so beautiful!

> Our neighbours came round in a panic. Something from the sky went through their roof and landed in their bedroom. We went to look. It was such a strange object, like a piece of hot coal.

> I have such wonderful memories of that holiday. One night, I went for a walk on the cliffs. It was a cloudless night. I looked up at the sky and suddenly there was this white thing speeding across the sky. And then another, and another! They were so amazing!

a) **You can use *so* and *such* to express excitement, surprise or other strong emotions.**

It was *so* beautiful!
It was *such* a strange object.
They were *so* amazing!
They were *such* ugly animals!

b) **You can use *so ... that* to indicate effect.**

Meteors are *so* hot *that* most of them burn up immediately.
Some of them are *so* small *that* you can hardly see them.
It is *such* a good album *that* I decided to buy the CD.
It was *such* a funny film *that* I cried with laughter.

c) **You can also use *so/such ... that* to say more about something.**

It was *so* beautiful *that* I decided to buy it.
It was *such* a strange object *that* no one wanted to touch it.

5 **PRACTICE**

a) **Complete these sentences choosing the best ending a)–e).**

1 It was such a cold day that ...
2 It was such an impressive view that ...
3 She was such an interesting woman that ...
4 It was such a bad traffic jam that ...
5 I could hear such strange noises that ...

a) ... I decided to call the police.
b) ... I talked to her for hours.
c) ... we had to abandon the car and walk.
d) ... I could hardly move my fingers.
e) ... we stayed there all day.

b) **Using the prompts below, write sentences using *so ... that*.**

EXAMPLE: *... missed/flight.*
*The train was **so** late **that** I missed my flight.*
... jacket/cheap ...
*The jacket was **so** cheap **that** I decided to buy two.*

1 ... decided to leave.
2 ... missed the train.
3 ... felt tired all day.
4 ... raining/hard ...
5 ... film/long/went to sleep.

6 **WRITE YOUR OWN RULES**

You now know that you use *so* and *such* for emphasis. But when do you use *so* and when do you use *such*?

Look at all the examples in this Unit and make notes about how the words are used. Think about nouns and adjectives.

EXAMPLE: *You use **so** with ...*

7 **WRITING (1)**

Look at the following list of adjectives. Write sentences to express amazement, shock, annoyance or anger.

dangerous   impressive   exciting
unhelpful   irritating   loud
delightful   cruel   violent   colourful
terrible   racist

EXAMPLE: *The singer was so **exciting** that I almost screamed.*
*It was such **dangerous** driving that I reported him to the police.*

8 WRITING (2)

You are on holiday in the north of Sweden. Imagine that you have seen one of the phenomena in Activity 1. Write a postcard to a friend describing where you are, what you have been doing, what you saw and how you felt.

Try to use the images that you discussed with other students in Activity 3b).

9 PRON SPOT: /ʃ/ AS IN *SHOOTING*

a) The most obvious spelling of the /ʃ/ sound is *sh*.

she   show   shall   sh!   fish
push

The past tense of regular verbs ending in *sh* is pronounced /ʃt/.

fished   pushed   rushed   washed
wished

b) The *-tion* and *-sion* ending is usually pronounced /ʃ/.

demonstration   discussion   emotion
passionate   pollution

c) Some occupation words ending in *-cian* use this sound too.

electrician   magician   mortician (US)
physician   politician

d) These loan words from other languages (usually French) contain the /ʃ/ sound:

chandelier   chateau   chiffon   chic
chaperone   Charlotte   charade
chicane   chalet

Listen to all the words on the cassette. Use a dictionary to look up any words you do not know.

e) Try this tongue twister:

She sells sea shells on the seashore.

10 SPEAKING

In groups, talk about what you think of astrology. Do you read your 'stars' (your horoscope) every day in the newspaper? Do you think your life can be influenced by the position of the planets? What other ways do people use to try to look into the future? Do you want to know what will happen to you in the future or not?

STAR PRON SPOT NAME

Cher
/ʃeə/
American singer and actress

FOCUS ON YOUR COUNTRY 11

How popular are horoscopes in your country? Do people believe they are reliable? Are there any famous astrologers or astronomers in your country?

DANGER SIGNALS

LANGUAGE AREA

Talking about the past

MAIN STRUCTURE

Time expressions

VOCABULARY

Animal and marine life

PRONUNCIATION

/dʒ/ as in *danger*

1 STARTER

What do you know about life in your country in the past? Share the information that everyone in the class has, using these time expressions as starters.

Twenty years ago ...
A hundred years ago ...
Five hundred years ago ...

EXAMPLES: *Twenty years ago, there were no motorways in this country.*
A hundred years ago, only eighty thousand people lived in the capital.
Five hundred years ago, this country was part of ...

2 READING

a) In groups, discuss how much you know about the Earth. How old do you think planet Earth is? When was the ice age? When did dinosaurs live? When do you think humans appeared?

b) Now read this text. Does any of the information surprise you?

PLANET EARTH is believed by many scientists to be approximately 4,600,000,000 (four thousand, six hundred million) years old. If we condense this time-span into an understandable concept, we can compare the Earth to a person of 46 years of age.

Nothing is known about the first seven years of this person's life. Only a little is known about the middle years. We do know that Earth began to flower only at the age of 42.

Dinosaurs and the great reptiles did not appear until *one year ago*, when the planet was 45. Mammals arrived only *eight months ago*. The theory of evolution states that human-like apes evolved into ape-like humans in *the middle of last week*, and last weekend, the last ice age covered the Earth.

Modern humans have been around for four hours. *During the last hour*, we have discovered agriculture. The industrial revolution began a minute ago. During those sixty seconds, humans have made a rubbish tip of paradise.

c) **How do you say these numbers in English?**

4,600   46,000   1,000,000
100,000,000   4,600,000,000

NB: In British English a billion is a million million, but in American English a billion is a thousand million!

Earth seen from Apollo

d) **Discuss these questions with another student.**

1 What's the difference between human-like apes and ape-like humans?

2 What do you think the last sentence in the text means?

3 What is the value of comparing planet Earth to a 46-year-old person?

e) **Look at the text again. Write other sentences using the expressions in italics.**

EXAMPLE: *During the last hour, I have read three sentences of this text.*

3 ▶ LISTENING

a) Look at the three photographs below. Do you know the names of the animals?

b) Listen to some information about the animals. Make notes about the animals and compare them with another student.

c) Why do you think some species die out ('become extinct')? Do you think we should help protect them? What can we do?

F **FOCUS** **ON GRAMMAR** **4**
TIME EXPRESSIONS

a) **You can use these expressions when talking about the past.**

Thirty years *ago*, there were more than 5,000 white rhinos.
During the last twenty years, whales of this length and size have completely disappeared.
Between 1700 and 1800, hunting reduced their numbers by 50 per cent.
By the year 1900, they had almost completely disappeared.

b) **You can use these expressions to talk about the past in more general terms.**

In the past, people paid less attention to the environment.
All this happened *a long time ago*.
Recently, a new species of mammal was discovered in the Amazon rain forest.
Once, there were buffalo and bison wandering freely around the entire continent of North America.

5 PRACTICE

Using the time expressions from Focus on Grammar, write sentences about yourself, your family and your friends.

EXAMPLE: *Once, when I was on holiday, I saw a famous film star on the beach! During the last 5 years, we have lived in three different apartments.*

6 SPEAKING (1)

a) **In pairs, discuss the problems facing our wildlife today. Share your thoughts with other students. Think about some of the following:**

1 Destruction of natural habitat.
2 Pollution of rivers and seas.
3 Hunting for food, experimentation or for fur.
4 Reduction in food supply.

Some creatures benefit from damage to the environment. Do you know any examples of this?

b) **In groups of four, debate the following motion: "We believe that the world is becoming a better place for wildlife."**

NB: Don't forget that the purpose of a debate is to present an opinion, which is not necessarily a personal one. Your aim is to persuade others to vote for you.

c) **Half the groups should make notes to show that the world is becoming a better place for wildlife and the environment in general. The other half should try to collect information to show that things are getting worse.**

d) **When you have collected enough information, choose one person to speak on behalf of each group.**

e) **At the end, when all the speakers have put over their points of view, vote for or against the motion. If more people vote for the motion than against, we say that "the motion is passed."**

PRON SPOT: /dʒ/ AS IN *DANGER*

7

a) *j*, *g* and *dg* are the most common spellings of the /dʒ/ sound.

Japan   just   Germany   giant
bri**dg**e

b) A lot of English names contain the /dʒ/ sound.

Angela   Bridget   Jack   James
Jane   Joe (Joseph)   Joy   Geoffrey
George   Gerald   Giles   Jeremy
Gillian   Nigel   Roger

Listen to all these names on the cassette.

c) Find out if these words contain the /dʒ/ sound:

give   gin   gigantic   gig (concert)

d) Practise this poem.

Jeremy, Gerald, Roger and Jane
Met Jack and Jill on a German train
Jack suggested playing a game
Just close your eyes and shout a name
Jeremy, Gerald and Roger played
But Jane jumped off the train and said
'The problem is just how hungry I am,
I'd rather have some toast and jam!'

STAR **PRON SPOT** NAME

John Major
/dʒɒn meɪdʒə/
**Prime Minister of Great Britain
in the 1990s**

---

8 SPEAKING (2)

a) In groups, choose an endangered species. You can find information about endangered species in magazines or encyclopaedias.

b) Find some information about the problems faced by this species.

c) Try to recommend some changes that could be made to help this species.

d) Using photographs from magazines, present the information you have found to the other students in the class.

→ ❞ ☞ ✗ ⊠ ❝ ✎ → ❞ ☞ ✗

THE FASTLANE INTERVIEW

9 Emma Wilson is an environmentalist who works for Friends of the Earth in Japan. In this interview she talks about the difficulties of living and working in another country.

● Listen to the interview.

● Don't worry if you don't understand everything.

● Make a note of things she thinks are most difficult about moving to another country.

● You can read the text of the interview on page 134.

FOCUS ON YOUR COUNTRY   **10**

What wildlife species are in danger in your country? What is being done to help them? Is there a policy to protect them? Does this have much support?

Future perfect?

LANGUAGE AREA

Talking about the future

MAIN STRUCTURE

will/won't be able to

will/won't have to

VOCABULARY

Technology

PRONUNCIATION

/tʃ/ as in *future*

1 **STARTER**

a) **What do you think about these predictions for the year 2025? Do you think they will come true?**

In the year 2025 ...

1 ... we won't have to do any work at all. Machines will be able to do everything.

2 ... there will be too many cars, so ordinary people won't be able to drive unless they have a very good reason. Only the emergency services and politicians will be able to drive when and where they want.

3 ... we'll be able to visit other planets.

4 ... the population of the world will be so large that many people will have to live in a much smaller space.

5 ... we'll be able to learn everything from computers, so there won't be any teachers!

6 ... we won't be able to swim in the sea because it will be too polluted.

b) **Make some predictions of your own using *will, won't* and *will be able to*. (Look back at Unit 12 if you need more help with talking about future possibility.)**

EXAMPLE: *People **won't** go shopping any more. They **will** buy everything they need on their personal computer from home. People **will be able to** ask their computer how much things cost and what sizes are available.*

Singapore

2 READING

a) **You are going to read a text about future technological plans in Singapore. What do you think these might be?**

> EXAMPLE: *They will improve the transport system in Singapore by getting rid of all cars.*

b) **Read the text below quickly and make notes on the plans for the future in Singapore.**

> EXAMPLE: *Pupils – stay at home*
> *Children – homework on a computer*
> *Library – tell students when new book arrives*

c) **Read the text again and write down some of the things people will or won't have to do.**

IS THIS THE FUTURE?

SCHOOLS

In the future, pupils in Singapore probably won't have to go to school. They will be able to stay at home and study subjects on their personal computers.

Children will be able to do their homework on their computer and send it to school through a modem (telephone line). The computer will mark the homework and make comments. Pupils will have to do the homework again until it meets the necessary standards.

College students will be able to call up the contents of libraries on their computer screens. The library will tell them when, for example, a new book arrives about their specialist subject. They will be able to see lectures at overseas universities 'live', and communicate with their tutors electronically.

MONEY

In Singapore, you can already pay for your bus ticket by inserting a plastic 'smart' card into a machine on the bus. The machine deducts the money from your bank account. If your savings account is empty, it will deduct it from a deposit account. Soon, you will be able to pay for anything using a smart card.

ENTERTAINMENT

All over Singapore, there will be SingaTOUCH multi-media public information kiosks with a computerised screen. If you want to go to the cinema, the computer will show you (1) the best combination of buses and trains to get there (2) a seating plan for the cinema and (3) a video preview of the film. You won't have to make a phone call to book the seats. You will simply have to touch the seats you want on the screen and then pay for them by inserting your smart card into the machine.

The Colony Strikes Back by Victor Keegan.

3 PRACTICE

a) Complete these sentences using *will have to* or *won't be able to*.

1 If I don't finish this homework, I ... go to the party.

2 The bus has already left. If I walk I ... to get to the station on time. I ... take a taxi.

3 We ... see you next week because our grandparents are visiting us and we ... stay at home.

4 This radio is useless. We ... get another one or we ... listen to the Chart Show.

5 You ... queue all night if you want a ticket for the Cup Final.

b) Look at the predictions you wrote in Activity 1b). Compare them with life in the present.

EXAMPLE: *People can already buy things using a personal computer but most people still go out to the shops. In the future, they will be able to buy everything they need on their computer and won't bother to go out.*

c) Look at the text again. Try to write one or two sentences comparing life in the present with life in the future.

EXAMPLE: *You can already see a video preview of a film at the cinema. Soon you will be able to see one in the street.*

4 LISTENING

a) Listen to three people talking about future technology. What are they talking about? Choose from this list.

Personal transport   Health
Accommodation   Schools
Public transport   Office buildings
Family relationships

b) Now listen to the first speaker again. Is she for or against the technology she's describing?

c) Listen to the second speaker again. Which of the following words do you hear?

raise   arise   less   east   finds
unless   least   rays   series
serious   rise   fines

d) Listen to the third speaker again and read the following text. Make a note of any extra words you read.

> I think schools and businesses in my country will benefit from the new technology. I'm worried that families in my town won't be able to. I can foresee a time when people in my street won't have to spend any time together. Each person in the family in the apartment upstairs will eat, study and relax entirely alone, in their own rooms. They will be able to do this because they will have their own personal technology for education, entertainment and even for eating in the same room.

5 SPEAKING

a) What do we do with *old* technology (telephones, typewriters etc.)? We can't put them all in museums, so what *can* we do with them? Talk about it with other students and then discuss your ideas with the rest of the class.

b) Decide who has the best ideas for using old technology.

6 PRON SPOT: /tʃ/ AS IN *FUTURE*

a) *ch* and *t* are the most common spellings of the /tʃ/ sound.

challenge   **ch**ange   **ch**urch   **ch**oose
chin   fu**t**ure   crea**t**ure   cul**t**ure
mix**t**ure   na**t**ure

Now listen to the words on the cassette.

b) In the following words, the letters *tu* are pronounced /tʃ/ by some English speaking people:

Tuesday   **t**ube   for**t**une   **t**ulip
tuna   **T**unisia   **t**utor

c) These expressions can also be pronounced either way (/tju:/ or /tʃu:/).

aren't you?   don't you?   won't you?
haven't you?   didn't you?
wouldn't you?

Now listen to expressions containing these phrases on the cassette.

d) In Unit 27, we talked about words in which *ch* is pronounced /ʃ/. Here is a list of some common words in which *ch* is pronounced *k*.

chaos   character   Christmas   choir
chorus   chemist   chemical
technology

e) Practise these sentences.

It's a challenge to change the furniture in the church.

Why do people confuse chicken and kitchen?

Children born on Tuesdays are natural creatures.

Charlie Chaplin challenged chess champions.

Now listen to the cassette and check your pronunciation.

f) Find out the meaning of these expressions.

a chain smoker
chalk and cheese
a culture vulture

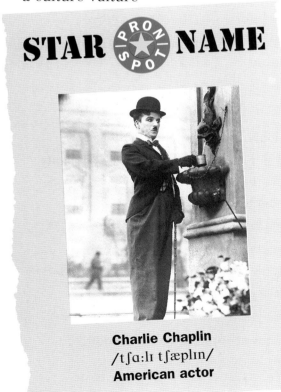

STAR PRONI SPOT NAME

Charlie Chaplin
/tʃɑːlɪ tʃæplɪn/
American actor

---

7 WRITING

Many famous novelists have written about life in the future. Imagine it is the year 2150 (halfway through the twenty-second century). Write a short story. Choose one of the following opening sentences if you want to.

After solving the main environmental problems of the twentieth century, Earth had become a paradise again. ...

Only a small group of rebel fighters had survived the invasion of the aliens in the year 1999. ...

Since the total flooding of Earth in 2050, man had learned to survive on the water. ...

→ 🙿 ☞ ✗ ✉ 🙾 ✐ → 🙿 ☞

THE FASTLANE INTERVIEW

8 Mary Windrush is a fortune-teller. I interviewed her about her work, but she wanted to tell me about my future!

- Listen to the interview.

- Don't worry if you don't understand everything.

- Which ambition does Mary think I'll be able to fulfil in the next twelve months? What won't I be able to do?

- What message does Mary have for the users of *Fastlane*?

- You can read the text of the interview on page 135.

F FOCUS ON YOUR COUNTRY **9**

What wildlife species are in danger in your country? What is being done to help them? Is there a policy to protect them? Does this have much support?

A LANGUAGE REVIEW

1 GRAMMAR EXTRA (1)

Non-defining clauses can be used to give more information about the noun. Two simple sentences can be formed into a longer one using *who* or *which*. *So* and *such* are used for emphasis.

The director is resigning. She's a lovely woman.
The director, *who* is *so* lovely, is resigning.
The director, *who* is *such* a lovely woman, is resigning.
The Tower of Pisa is being repaired. It leans at a very strange angle.
The Tower of Pisa, *which* leans at *such* a strange angle, is being repaired.

2 PRACTICE

Make one sentence from these pairs of sentences.

a) My Italian cousins are coming to stay. They are very good cooks.

b) The old laundry is being demolished. It's a very beautiful building.

c) These batteries don't last very long. They're very expensive.

d) The singer in the band is getting married. He's a very good-looking man.

3 GRAMMAR EXTRA (2)

Non-defining clauses + *so ... that*.

Vince Savage is advertising for a secretary. He gets a lot of fan letters. He never has time to answer them.

Vince Savage, *who* gets *so* many fan letters *that* he never has time to answer them, is advertising for a secretary.

London Heathrow is getting a new Terminal Building. It's a very busy airport. It's open 24 hours a day.

Heathrow Airport, *which* is *such* a busy airport *that* it's open 24 hours a day, is getting a new Terminal Building.

4 PRACTICE

Make one sentence from the three below, using *so ... that*.

a) Personal computers now use 10 per cent of the nation's electricity.
They're becoming very cheap.
Everyone can afford one.

b) My cousin is coming to see us for a few days next week.
She works very hard.
She rarely has time to go out.

c) São Paulo is the noisiest city in Brazil.
It covers a very large area.
No one knows where it ends.

d) The weather in Scotland is a frequent topic of conversation.
It's very unpredictable.
People often have to carry umbrellas.

B SKILLS REVIEW

1 **READING**

a) **Which of the world's languages are the most widely spoken? Why do you think English has developed as a major world language?**

b) **Read the following text about the growth of English and answer the questions below.**

  1 What is the first thing on the tape on Voyager One?

  2 How many people spoke the version of English that was spoken 1500 years ago?

  3 When did Shakespeare live, more or less?

  4 How many people now speak English as a second language?

  5 If you include scientific and technical words, how many words are there in English?

The English language

On 5th September 1977, the American spacecraft Voyager One blasted off on its historic mission to Jupiter and beyond. On board, scientists installed a recorded greeting from the people of planet Earth. Preceding a brief message in 55 different languages for the people of outer space, there is a statement from the Secretary General of the United Nations on behalf of 147 member states, in English.

The rise of English is a remarkable success story. When Julius Caesar landed in Britain over 2,000 years ago, English did not exist. Five hundred years later, Englisc, which is incomprehensible now, was probably spoken by as many people as currently speak Cherokee, and with as little influence. Nearly a thousand years later, when William Shakespeare was alive, English was the language of between five and seven million English people and was not spoken anywhere beyond the British Isles.

Four hundred years later, the contrast is extraordinary. Today, English is used by at least 750 million people, and barely half of those speak it as a mother tongue. It has become the language of the planet, the first truly global language.

The Oxford English Dictionary lists about 500,000 words. Another half million technical and scientific words are not included. In comparison, German has a vocabulary of an estimated 185,000 words and French has fewer than 100,000, including Franglais expressions such as *le snacque-bar* and *le hit-parade*. About 350 million people use the English language as a mother tongue, a linguistic population scattered across every continent.

Adapted from The Story of English by McCrum, Cran and McNeil.

2 WRITING

Choose one of the following subjects. Write no more than 180 words. You can use information from other parts of the book.

a) Imagine you are writing a tour guide for a country of your choice. Write an account of some of the natural features.

b) You are a member of an environmental group. Write a leaflet describing some of the main problems facing the world today and encouraging people to get involved.

c) What are the advantages and disadvantages of international sporting events?

d) Computers can be very dangerous. Do you agree?

3 LISTENING

a) Look at this timetable for trains from London to Edinburgh.

LONDON - EDINBURGH SERVICE			
DEPART			
London Kings Cross	09.00	12.00	16.00
Peterborough	10.00	13.00	
Leeds	11.00		18.45
York	11.35	14.30	
Durham	12.05		19.30
Newcastle	12.30	15.45	20.05
ARRIVE			
Edinburgh	13.00	16.45	21.05

b) Listen to the telephone information about changes in the timetable. Don't write anything until the message finishes, then make notes of the changes.

c) Now listen to the announcement again to check your answers.

4 SPEAKING

Prepare a two-minute talk on one of the following subjects. Practise your talk with a partner, and then tell it to the whole class.

a) A place that I would like to visit.

b) A famous person that I admire.

c) Good and bad things about watching television.

d) What I think about space travel.

C ACROSS CULTURES

a) The Battle of Hastings in 1066 was a key moment in British history. All British school children learn about it. What are the key events in the history of your country? In groups, talk about them.

In the past, people used comets to predict what was going to happen. Edmund Halley was an English astronomer (1656 – 1742) who predicted in 1705 that a bright comet seen in 1531, 1607 and 1682 would appear again in 1758. It was widely believed that this comet was a sign of bad times.

The same comet was also seen in 1066 when William, Duke of Normandy first landed in Britain. He was victorious at the Battle of Hastings against King Harold and was crowned King William 1 of England, the same year. The comet was believed to be a sign of bad luck for Harold. The Bayeux tapestry, which shows the story of the Norman conquest of Britain, includes the comet in one of the scenes.

After the Norman conquest, Latin became the language of Government and Norman French the literary language.

b) Make a note of things that you have learnt about other cultures from this book. Look through the book to find examples. What interested you most? What would you like to find out more about?

D COMPARATIVE PRON

/ʃ/ as in *shooting* and /tʃ/ as in *future.*

1

Charlie Sheen
/tʃɑːlɪ ʃiːn/
American actor

How many examples of each sound can you find in these sentences?

It's a shame to change the champagne, don't you think?

Should we challenge the school chess team or shouldn't we?

Practise the sentences and then listen to them on the cassette.

2

STAR NAMES

ZSA ZSA GABOR
/ʒɑː ʒɑː gæbɔː/
American actress
/ʒ/ as in *explosions.*

JOHN LENNON
/dʒɒn lenən/
Singer and songwriter
/dʒ/ as in *danger.*

a) Practise these expressions which contain both sounds.

major decision   dangerous collision
German precision   Japanese television

b) Write a story using one of the expressions from above as the title.

E COUNTDOWN TO THE END OF THE BOOK

1 In Block Six, you have practised the following language:

Non-defining relative clauses.

Ffyona Campbell, *who* comes from Devon, is the first woman to walk around the world.

Ecuador, *which* means *equator* in Spanish, is one of the most beautiful countries in South America.

so/such, so/such … that.

It was *so* beautiful!

They're *such* ugly animals!

My cousin, who works *so* hard *that* she rarely has time to go out, is coming to see us next week.

São Paulo, which covers *such* a large area *that* no one knows where it ends, is the noisiest city in Brazil.

Time expressions – talking about the past.

About twenty years ago, my family moved to La Spezia.

During the last six months, the value of the dollar has fallen dramatically.

Between 1990 and 1995, my favourite football team won the championship three times.

Recently, I met a film star.

Once, there was a huge island in the middle of the Atlantic called Atlantis.

Talking about the future.

Children *will be able to* do their homework on a computer.

They *won't* have to go to school.

They *will* have to do it again until it meets the necessary standards.

2 Have you written all the new words you have learnt in the Words section of your Workbook? Check your list now.

3 Have you added new information to your **ACROSS CULTURES** scrapbook?

CONGRATULATIONS! You have completed *Fastlane 1.* You are now ready to start *Fastlane 2!*

Keys and Communication Task

UNIT 5 ACTIVITY 4

False: Sinéad O'Connor is an Irish singer. She sings sad love songs.

False: Elvis Presley *was* born in 1935 in Nashville, Tennessee. He had lots of hit records and appeared in numerous films.

False: Crowded House are an Australian band. Some of them *were* in a band called Split Enz.

True: Prince *is* one of the richest pop stars in the world and owns a massive recording studio called Paisley Park.

False: Sting was the singer in a band called The Police. He *is* an important campaigner for environmental issues.

False: Björk is the first ever pop star from her native country Iceland. She was in a band called the Sugar Cubes.

UNIT 7 ACTIVITY 2B

1 Volvo means *I roll* in Latin.

2 Henry Ford who built the first Ford motor car was the grandfather of the Henry Ford who retired in 1980.

3 Rolls-Royce made car engines first.

UNIT 16 ACTIVITY 9

Communication Task

UNIT 17 ACTIVITY 6

The *Fastlane* Questionnaire:

If you scored 13 to 15 points:
You eat too much sugar and fatty food and should really think about giving up some of the things you like: for example, if you eat chips every day, you should try to cut down. Try to eat chocolate no more than once a week.

If you scored 10 to 12 points:
You could do better! Cut down on the item that you scored most points on. Then you will be on course for a fit and active life.

If you scored 7 to 9 points:
You are eating a small amount of things that are not good for you, but not enough to worry about. You don't need to change your diet, but make sure you don't increase the amount of sugar or fat that you eat.

If you scored up to 6 points:
Well done! You have shown that you can avoid the things that are not good for you. Keep up the good work!

Fastlane Tapescript

UNIT 1

Activity 8

INTERVIEWER: What kind of training did you have and how long did it last?

MAGGIE: My training lasted for seventeen months, and I only had about four weeks off in that time. It involved a lot of studying as well as flying. It was very intensive and hard work, but it was good fun. The course gave me my commercial pilot's licence, which I got in 1990.

INTERVIEWER: How long did it take you to get a job after your training finished?

MAGGIE: British Airways more or less guaranteed me a job, because they had sponsored me. After I left college, I was offered a place on the Boeing 757 straight away. I started learning to fly the 757 just a few weeks after leaving flying college at Prestwick.

INTERVIEWER: Is the job everything you expected it to be?

MAGGIE: In most ways it is, although I hadn't thought about how tiring it could be, especially flying overnight.

INTERVIEWER: What's your working ambition for the future?

MAGGIE: To become a captain after I've gained a few years more experience.

Activity 9

PRON SPOT: /ɪ/ as in think

a) city   million   British   sister   fifty   system   busy   women   minute

b) Maggie Risley is a British Airways pilot.
Fifty million Brazilian Indians live near the Amazon River.
I think I saw sixty busy women drinking quickly in Liverpool.

STAR NAME *Bill and Hillary Clinton*

UNIT 2

Activity 6

MAN: Is there anything you would like to ask me about the training scheme?

MONICA: Yes, I've got a list of questions, actually.

MAN: Oh. Very interesting!

MONICA: Er ... yes. How old do you have to be to do the training scheme?

MAN: Well, you're 22, that's old enough.

MONICA: Well, I was thinking about my brother.

MAN: How old is he?

MONICA: Sixteen.

MAN: That's too young, but if he's interested, he should write and find out about our junior awareness scheme.

MONICA: OK, I'll tell him. Er ... can you tell me something about the training itself?

MAN: That's a big question. Most of what you need to know will be in the training manual. You'll get that if you're accepted on the course.

MONICA: I see. Well, there is something very important that I have to ask.

MAN: What's that?

MONICA: Is there any discrimination against women in the Fire Brigade?

MAN: Absolutely none.

MONICA: Women are treated exactly the same as men?

MAN: Yes. I can assure you of that.

MONICA: What about driving the fire engines?

MAN: What about it?

MONICA: Are women allowed to drive them?

MAN: Yes, they are. In fact, there are a number of women fire officers who are training to do that this week.

MONICA: That's good. I'd really like to drive a fire engine.

MAN: That's what everyone says!

Activity 7

PRON SPOT: /iː/ as in me

a) we   deal   green   scene   chief   receive   meal   wheel

b) people   grand prix   machine   pizza   mosquito   Tina

c) greengrocer   street   cleaner   priest   teacher   police officer   newsreader

d) team   received   Stevens   scheme   read

e) Tina is a cleaner from Parsons Green
She dreams of being in a grand prix team
She wants to make the scene with her green machine
She wants to be a racing queen!

STAR NAME *Steve McQueen*

Activity 12

BARBARA: My name is Barbara Vincent and I'm a police officer with the Metropolitan Police in London.

INTERVIEWER: What kind of work do you do?

BARBARA: Well, at the moment I work as an instructor at the Public Order Training Centre in West London, and my main job is teaching police officers how to use crowd control equipment.

INTERVIEWER: What do you mean by crowd control equipment?

BARBARA: Well, riot shields, things like that. The main thing is that all police officers have to be acquainted with the equipment, even if they never use it.

INTERVIEWER: How do you teach people to use crowd control equipment if there isn't actually a crowd to control?

BARBARA: Well, while we're training police officers, we organise a public order incident at the centre.

INTERVIEWER: What do you mean by a public order incident?

BARBARA: Well, we have to simulate a ... we have to organise a kind of riot.

INTERVIEWER: You organise riots?

BARBARA: Well, half of the police officers who are training act as the crowd, while the other half are learning how to control them.

INTERVIEWER: It all sounds a bit dangerous.

BARBARA: Yes, but we have to do it. Apart from everything else, it's for the horses ... there are horses involved ... the horses have to get used to the sounds of a riot. It's usually quite safe.

INTERVIEWER: How often do you do that?

BARBARA: Well, we have groups of officers for two days, and we organise an incident for every group ... so every two days.

INTERVIEWER: So ... three riots a week?

BARBARA: Two. Two public order incidents.

INTERVIEWER: It must be a very exciting job.

BARBARA: Yes, it is. It's very interesting, but quite difficult as well.

UNIT 3

Activity 1

a) Dublin   Madrid   Athens   Berlin   Ankara   Moscow

b) The Acropolis is in Athens. Attaturk's tomb is in Ankara. The Kremlin is in Moscow.

Activity 10

ANGELA: What do you think about this job in Malawi?

GARRY: At the field hospital?

ANGELA: Yes.

GARRY: Well, it sounds very exciting.

ANGELA: I agree.

GARRY: But I don't think I want to do it.

ANGELA: Why not?

GARRY: I don't want to work in Africa. It's too hot!

ANGELA: Oh, Garry! Honestly!

GARRY: It's true! I hate very hot weather. What do you think about the other job?

ANGELA: Working in a casino on a cruise ship?

GARRY: Yes.

ANGELA: Terrible.

GARRY: Terrible?

ANGELA: Yes.

GARRY: What do you mean, terrible?

ANGELA: Well, for a start, working in a casino sounds like hell.

GARRY: You don't like the idea of working in a casino?

ANGELA: No, I hate the idea of working in a casino, and especially on a boat.

GARRY: So ... which of these jobs are you going to apply for?

ANGELA: The job in Malawi.

GARRY: At the field hospital?

ANGELA: Yes.

GARRY: Why?

ANGELA: Because I want to do something useful.

GARRY: Oh.

ANGELA: What about you?

GARRY: I think I'll apply for the job on the cruise ship.

ANGELA: Working in a casino?

GARRY: Yes.

ANGELA: Why?

GARRY: I need the money.

Activity 12

PRON SPOT: /e/ as in west

a) spell   tense   well   best   ever

b) said   read   lead   dead   unpleasant

c) cassette   expensive   better   Thames   Edinburgh
treasure

STAR NAMES *Elvis Presley   Nelson Mandela
Mandela can also be pronounced Mandela
/mændeɪlə/.*

UNIT 4

Activity 3 I'll be There

I'm leaving tomorrow on the morning train
I'm leaving, I may not come back again
If you want to see me, give me a call
I'll meet you anywhere
If you want to see me, I'll be there
If you want to see me, I'll be there
Because I want to see you too
I haven't got much time
But all the time I've got is for you
If you want to see me, I'll do what I can
But if you don't want to see me, I'll understand
If you want me to go away without saying goodbye
I think I'll understand the reason why.

Activity 9

PRON SPOT: /eə/ as in there

a) bear   square   hair   there   their

b) mayor   Mary

c)
bear	square	hair	there
pear	care	pair	where
tear	bare	air	their
wear	stare	chair	heir
	rare	stair	
	fare	fair	

tear /eə/   tear/ɪə/

STAR NAME *Mary Pierce*

Activity 10

MICHAEL: My name is Michael Klein and I'm a musician and record producer. I have my own recording studio in Central London and I specialise in making albums with unknown artists.

INTERVIEWER: What I want you to tell us, Michael, is what do you have to do if you want to make a hit record?

MICHAEL: If I knew that, I'd be a millionaire!

INTERVIEWER: But you've been very successful with artists who

were completely unknown before they came to you, so there must be, I don't know, there must be some advice you can give to people who want to make it in the music business.

MICHAEL: OK, well, let me say first of all that there isn't one successful formula.

INTERVIEWER: No ...

MICHAEL: But there are certainly one or two things you should think about if you're a songwriter or if you have a band and you want to record something.

INTERVIEWER: Right ...

MICHAEL: First of all, make sure that you play any new material in front of a live audience ... get on stage and make sure people like what you're doing.

INTERVIEWER: Why?

MICHAEL: Well, if the people don't like it, they won't buy your records.

INTERVIEWER: But surely you can make an average band sound much better in the studio. I mean ... you can do lots of things in a recording studio that you can't do in front of an audience.

MICHAEL: That's absolutely right. You can definitely improve material in the studio, but only if the song is good in the first place.

INTERVIEWER: I see.

MICHAEL: My second piece of advice is this: if you're a songwriter and you want to sing your own songs, be honest with yourself about your singing ability, about how good you actually are as a singer. It may be that your songs will sound better if they're sung by someone else.

INTERVIEWER: Yeah ...

MICHAEL: And thirdly, think about the basic instrumentation of the track.

INTERVIEWER: What do you mean?

MICHAEL: Well, if the song is successful, you'll probably have to play it on TV. Now you can have backing tracks on TV of course, but the fans want to see you perform the song.

INTERVIEWER: Of course ...

MICHAEL: So ... if there's a guitar solo, make sure the guitarist is a member of the band, not just a session musician. If there's a strong keyboard track, make sure there's a keyboard player in the band.

INTERVIEWER: Right ...

MICHAEL: There was a classic example of this a few years ago. A band called Curiosity Killed The Cat recorded an excellent song, I can't actually remember the name of it. Anyway, this song had a fabulous saxophone solo in the middle.

INTERVIEWER: Yeah?

MICHAEL: Well, the saxophone player wasn't a member of the band, he was a session musician. He didn't appear with the band on stage. The song became a hit and the band appeared on TV. When they reached the saxophone solo, which was about 45 seconds long, the singer just sort of stood there and listened to this absolutely wonderful sax solo. It was really bad TV and I think the fans were really disappointed.

INTERVIEWER: Why didn't they just put the saxophone player on TV with them?

MICHAEL: I don't know. I don't think they offered him enough money!

UNIT 5

B2

Steve McQueen appeared in *The Magnificent Seven*, which was made in 1960, *The Great Escape*, which was made in 1963 and *Bullitt*, which was made in 1969. Steven Spielberg directed or produced the following films: *Jaws*, 1975, *Close Encounters of the Third Kind*, 1977, *Raiders of the Lost Ark*, 1981, *ET*, 1982, *Schindler's List*, 1993 and *Jurassic Park*, 1994.

D COMPARATIVE PRON

/ɪ/ as in think and /iː/ as in me.

STAR NAME *Jim Reeves*

/e/ as in west and /eə/ as in there.

STAR NAME *Fred Astaire*

a)
eat and drink	meat and fish
listen and speak	cheese and biscuits

d)   Leicester Square   fresh air   hairdresser
red hair   Belfast airport

UNIT 6

Activity 2a) and b)

INTERVIEWER: Jane, have you got a computer?
JANE: Yes.
INTERVIEWER: What do you use it for?
JANE: Games.
INTERVIEWER: Computer games?
JANE: Yes.
INTERVIEWER: How many have you got?
JANE: About twenty.
INTERVIEWER: And how much time do you spend playing games on your computer?
JANE: About three hours a day.
INTERVIEWER: Phil, what about you? Have you got a computer?
PHIL: No, I haven't, but my mother's got one. I use hers.
INTERVIEWER: And have you got any computer games?
PHIL: Yes, one or two. But I'm not really interested in computer games. I prefer using the computer to get information.
INTERVIEWER: Information?
PHIL: Yes.
INTERVIEWER: About what?
PHIL: Anything. You can get information about anything.
INTERVIEWER: How much time do you spend in front of the screen?
PHIL: About six hours a day.
INTERVIEWER: Six hours a day?
PHIL: Yes. From the time I get home from school to the time I go to bed.
INTERVIEWER: What about your dinner?
PHIL: I have my dinner in front of the computer.
INTERVIEWER: What does your mother think about that?
PHIL: She doesn't mind. She only uses it during the day.

Activity 8 PRON SPOT: /æ/ as in magic

a)
cat	parrot	hamster	are all animals or birds
taxi	van	ambulance	are all means of transport
Sam	Pat	Stan	are all names
carry	catch	hang	are all verbs

STAR NAME *Batman!*

UNIT 7

Activity 3

Charles Stewart Rolls, who was born in 1863, was a sportsman and engineer. He bought his first car in 1896 and won a prize as a driver for the first time in 1900. He was also the first person to fly across the English Channel and back. Sir Henry Royce was born in 1877 and was a pioneer of electric street lighting. At the age of 19, he was chief engineer for the lighting of streets in Liverpool. He designed and built his first car in 1904. In 1906, he went into partnership with Rolls. Royce designed the cars and Rolls sold them. Rolls Royce cars are now among the most expensive cars in the world.

Activity 7

PRON SPOT: (1) The past tense of regular verbs

He filled my cup with very hot coffee.	filled
She kissed her mother and left the room.	kissed
I waited two hours for a bus.	waited

a) longed   remained   embarked   reached   ended

b) First type: climbed   cleaned   dreamed
   Second type: stopped   missed
   Third type: wanted   needed   started

Activity 8

PRON SPOT: (2) /ɑ:/ as in fast cars

a) bath   castle   darling   heart   laugh

b) He who laughs last laughs longest

STAR NAME *Arsenal Football Club*

Activity 10

WENDY: My name is Wendy Parkin, and I own a classic car, a 1963 convertible Triumph Herald.
INTERVIEWER: Convertible means ...
WENDY: Oh, it means it's got a soft top. The roof isn't made of metal.
INTERVIEWER: So your car is more than 30 years old.
WENDY: Yes.
INTERVIEWER: Why have you got such an old car?
WENDY: It's beautiful and it's the car I've always wanted. You see, an old Triumph Herald is the nearest thing you can get to driving a Cadillac ...
INTERVIEWER: It's a bit smaller than a Cadillac!
WENDY: I know it's smaller, but it's got fins at the back like a Cadillac.
INTERVIEWER: Where did you buy it?
WENDY: Well, I live in London, but I bought it in Somerset, which is in the west of England. My mother saw it advertised in a local newspaper so I jumped on a train and went down to see it right away. It was in perfect condition and I fell in love with it immediately.
INTERVIEWER: How much did you pay for it?
WENDY: One thousand six hundred pounds.
INTERVIEWER: Is that good value for such an old car?
WENDY: Stop calling it old! It's a classic car. Sixteen hundred pounds was excellent value for it. It was, and still is, in superb condition.
INTERVIEWER: Do you have any problems with it?
WENDY: Not really.
INTERVIEWER: What about when you have to buy new parts?
WENDY: No, that's not a problem at all.
INTERVIEWER: So no problems.
WENDY: Well, yes, there are some things that I get a bit annoyed about. It's not very fast, so it gets a bit boring on long motorway trips ... and it isn't always very comfortable, the suspension isn't too good ... and the heater isn't very good ... and there's no radio ... oh yes, and there is one big problem.
INTERVIEWER: What's that?
WENDY: The rain comes in through the roof. So I get really wet.

UNIT 8

Activity 8

PASSENGER: Excuse me?
AIRLINE EMPLOYEE: Yes?
PASSENGER: Can you give me some information about flights to Budapest?
AIRLINE EMPLOYEE: To where?
PASSENGER: Budapest.
AIRLINE EMPLOYEE: Certainly. What would you like to know?
PASSENGER: Well, when can I fly there?
AIRLINE EMPLOYEE: Well, there's a daily morning flight that leaves at ten o'clock.
PASSENGER: Is it non-stop?
AIRLINE EMPLOYEE: Yes, it is.
PASSENGER: How long does the flight take?
AIRLINE EMPLOYEE: About two and a half hours. There's an hour's time difference at this time of year, so the plane arrives in Budapest at half past two in the afternoon.
PASSENGER: Right ...
AIRLINE EMPLOYEE: There's also an earlier flight on Sundays. That leaves at half past nine.
PASSENGER: Is that non-stop as well?
AIRLINE EMPLOYEE: Yes.
PASSENGER: Is there an afternoon flight?
AIRLINE EMPLOYEE: Er ... not really, there's an early evening flight which leaves at 6 o'clock.
PASSENGER: Every day?
AIRLINE EMPLOYEE: Yes, er, no. It leaves at 6 o'clock on ... er ... let me see ... it leaves at 6 o'clock on Saturday and Sunday. That arrives at 9.30pm local time.
PASSENGER: What about the other days of the week?
AIRLINE EMPLOYEE: Er ... let me have a look ... we have a flight that leaves at half past eight Monday to Friday. That one arrives at just after midnight.
PASSENGER: Thank you.
AIRLINE EMPLOYEE: You're welcome.

Activity 9

PRON SPOT: /ɒ/ as in off

a) rob   doctor   body   off   fog   doll
   Tom   long   stop   boss   pot

b) oh   or   love   power
   work   move   lower

c) hop/hope   rob/robe   rod/rode

d) post   comb   only   old
   gone   Roger   one

STAR NAME *Doc Holliday*

Activity 12

BARRY: My name is Barry Anderson and I'm a pilot with British Airways.

INTERVIEWER: How long have you been working as a pilot?

BARRY: About twenty years.

INTERVIEWER: So you must have seen quite a few changes during your time as a pilot.

BARRY: Oh, absolutely. Planes are now much more reliable than they used to be and equipment is much more sophisticated. I mean, when I first started flying, there used to be three people in the cockpit, a pilot, a flight engineer and a navigator. Nowadays, there are two, a pilot and a co-pilot.

INTERVIEWER: What happened to the flight engineer and the navigator?

BARRY: Well, the pilot and the co-pilot do the work that the flight engineer used to do, and nowadays, we don't need a navigator.

INTERVIEWER: What about in the old days, the ... the early days of commercial aviation. I mean, in the 1920s and 30s ... what was it like being a pilot?

BARRY: Well, I imagine it was very exciting. But the planes they flew were under-powered and overweight. I mean, in order to have radio contact, they used to have heavy cables on board. And even then, the only contact they had was Morse code.

INTERVIEWER: Morse code?

BARRY: Yes. If you wanted any contact at all with the ground, you used to have to use Morse code. And the planes were very heavy and they used to fly very slowly. And they used to break down quite frequently, too.

INTERVIEWER: And what kind of navigational equipment did the pilots use to have?

BARRY: Their eyes. I mean, can you imagine what it was like to fly, say, from London to Paris without the navigational aids we have now? They used to take off from Croydon and follow the railway lines to Dover.

INTERVIEWER: You're not serious.

BARRY: I am! They used to follow the railway lines to Dover, cross the Channel and then follow the railway lines from Calais to Paris.

INTERVIEWER: What if it was cloudy?

BARRY: If it was cloudy, they flew lower. There are stories of planes flying so low over villages in the south of England that people standing in their gardens could see the pilot.

INTERVIEWER: You said that you don't need a navigator now.

BARRY: That's right. That all started with the Apollo moon shot. They had to develop some very clever navigational systems before they could think about anything like that. And they came up with a system called inertial navigation.

INTERVIEWER: Inertial navigation ...

BARRY: Yes, which meant you could find out where you were in relation to the earth. But even that is old-fashioned now.

INTERVIEWER: So how do you know where you are now?

BARRY: By sending a signal to a satellite.

INTERVIEWER: And the satellite can tell you where you are?

BARRY: Yes. And it's very accurate. It can tell you where you are anywhere on earth to within a metre of your position. That's close enough for me.

UNIT 9

Activity 3

GARRY: You know, I used to have a cat ...

ANGELA: Yes?

GARRY: And I'm sure that it understood everything I said.

ANGELA: That's ridiculous.

GARRY: What?

ANGELA: Ridiculous. Animals can't understand people.

GARRY: Listen – my cat could understand everything I said.

ANGELA: Give me an example.

GARRY: Well, in the morning, I used to say: Good morning Fifi.

ANGELA: Fifi?

GARRY: Yes, Fifi, that was the cat's name. I used to say: Good

morning, Fifi, would you like some breakfast?

ANGELA: And what did Fifi say?

GARRY: Well, she didn't actually say anything, but I could see that she knew what I was talking about.

ANGELA: Well of course she did, you were probably holding a tin of cat food in front of her!

GARRY: I think you're being very unfair. I think that animals can understand a lot of what we say.

ANGELA: Yes?

GARRY: Yes. And I think we could learn a lot about animal language. I'm sure they talk to each other and it would be very interesting if we tried to learn more about it. And if we could communicate with animals, we could learn a lot.

ANGELA: Well, I don't agree. I think most animals are pretty stupid and don't communicate very much with each other. I don't think we would learn much from them if they could talk.

GARRY: Well, I think you're wrong. If animals could speak to us, they would tell us a lot of things that we wouldn't like to hear.

Activity 10

PRON SPOT: /ɔː/ as in talk

a) caught   bought   horse   war   saw   water   fall   autumn

b) These words contain the /ɔː/ sound: taught   thought   law   tall   Paul
   These words don't contain the /ɔː/ sound: worse   far   later

c) I caught a ball that Paul thought he saw in the hall.
   What sort of storms fall in autumn? They're awful!
   I bought a horse and taught it to haul water.
   George Orwell was the author of *1984*.

STAR NAME *George Orwell*

Activity 11

PATRICIA: My name is Patricia Mason and I'm an animal psychologist. I trained as a veterinary surgeon and then took an extra qualification in animal psychology. I now try to help animals with their psychological problems.

INTERVIEWER: Patricia, I think that some people may think that it sounds a bit funny to help animals with psychological problems.

PATRICIA: Well, there are serious problems, particularly for animals who live in zoos.

INTERVIEWER: What kind of help can you give to zoo animals?

PATRICIA: In fact, I deal with zoo owners and zoo designers as much as the animals themselves. And of course the zoo employees who feed and work with the animals.

INTERVIEWER: What kind of thing do you do with them?

PATRICIA: Well, these days, zoos consult me when they are re-designing part of the zoo. I advise them on where to put the animals, and how close the general public can get to them. I'm not really in favour of zoos, but I realise that they are not going to go away, so I've decided that the best thing that I can do is try to prevent the animals suffering from stress because of the unsuitable accommodation that they have. I always make sure that they have plenty of space away from people, but not away from the light. Animals need to be alone but in natural light.

INTERVIEWER: Do you work with domestic animals, pets?

PATRICIA: Yes, I do. The main problem again is stress. Some animals, even quite common dogs and cats, are living in conditions that cause them a great deal of stress. A lot of dogs find it very difficult to live on a street that is constantly full of traffic, for example.

INTERVIEWER: How can you help a dog like that?

PATRICIA: Well, you have to try to persuade a dog to watch the traffic through a window, whilst keeping it calm by talking to it. It's important to do this for just a few minutes every day.

INTERVIEWER: I see. I understand that you work with people as well.

PATRICIA: I work with people who have an irrational fear of animals, especially people who are afraid of dogs or cats. I give them the opportunity to look at the animals they are afraid of from a safe place. I have a special room where people can watch dogs and cats through a one-way mirror. Then there are a series of other activities, leading up to actually sitting with the animal, or taking it for a walk. It's a bit like curing people of their fear of flying.

INTERVIEWER: Does it work?

PATRICIA: Yes, but not with everybody. There are some people who will never stop being afraid of animals, which is a pity.

UNIT 10

B2

George Orwell was born in 1903 in India. His family moved to England in 1907. In 1921, he joined the Imperial Police in Burma. His first novel, *Burmese Days*, showed how much he disliked colonial rule. For several years, he lived with the poor of two capital cities, London and Paris. He then worked as a teacher, but had to stop because of ill health. In the late 1930s, he went to Spain and fought in the Civil War, where he was wounded. Later, he wrote *Homage to Catalonia* about his experiences there. His two most famous novels are *Animal Farm*, which he wrote in 1945, and *1984*, which is a pessimistic view of the future. He chose the title *1984* by reversing the numbers of the year that he wrote the book, 1948.

D COMPARATIVE PRON

1 /æ/ as in magic and /a:/ as in car.

STAR NAME *Jack Charlton*

a) jam jar   last lap   fat chance!   bad marks

b) fat /æ/   chance /æ/   last /æ/   lap /æ/

2 /ɒ/ as in off and /ɔ:/ as in talk.

STAR NAME *Roger Moore*

a) The words and expressions which contain the /ɒ/ and /ɔ:/ sounds are: hot water   top drawer   lost cause

UNIT 11

Activity 2

ANGELA: Wow! Thank goodness we're out of the underground. It was really crowded. Are you all right, Stefan?
STEFAN: Yes, I'm fine, but you're right, there were a lot of people on that train. Hm ... and there are a lot of people here as well. What is the name of this street?
ANGELA: Oxford Street. This is the main shopping street of London.
STEFAN: It's so crowded!
GARRY: Yeah, it's very busy on Saturdays.
ANGELA: Do you have all these shops in your country?
STEFAN: Some of them, yes. Of course, we have McDonalds. But I don't recognise some of the others. Benetton, what kind of company is that?
GARRY: They make clothes. It's an Italian company, I think.
ANGELA: Yes, it is.
STEFAN: Pizza Hut. I've heard of that, but we don't have them in my country.
GARRY: It's a restaurant. They sell pizzas.
ANGELA: Obviously.
STEFAN: What does that sign say? Doctor ...
GARRY: Doctor Martens. Actually, that's not the name of the shop, it's a kind of shoe.
STEFAN: A kind of shoe?
ANGELA: Yes, Doc Martens shoes are great. They're made in Holland.
STEFAN: And what about Nike?
GARRY: Nike. They're trainers.
ANGELA: Sports shoes.
STEFAN: And Reebok?
GARRY: They're also trainers. I think Reeboks are made in Britain and Nike are made in the United States.
STEFAN: And Levi's ...
ANGELA: They're jeans. They're made in America.
STEFAN: I know that. Levi jeans are everywhere. Just like Coca-Cola. In my country, we call it Coke.
GARRY: Yes. So do we.

Activity 3c)

He packed a large quantity of denim and went to Genoa, a small port which is on the Italian coast near the French border.

Denim is really a short form of *de Nîmes*, which means from Nîmes.

But this still doesn't explain why jeans are called jeans, does it?

Even when he was rich and famous, Strauss continued to use the Italian port to import denim.

And that's why we wear jeans, and don't go camping in them!

Activity 6

PRON SPOT: /ʊ/ as in good

a) good   wood   could   would   should

b) put   pull   push   bush   bully

c) Don't push, don't push, pushing isn't good
You want me to move and I would if I could
You're putting me out with your pushing and pulling
You shouldn't be such a great big bully!

STAR NAME *George Bush*

UNIT 12

Activity 10

PRON SPOT: /ʌ/ as in love

a) bus   butter   club   fun   gum   rugby   run   Sunday
come   company   compass   done   honey   London

b) enough   rough   tough   young

c) Hey there, son, come to the rugby club
Sunday lunch-time up in London
If you're young and you can run
You can have fun, rain or sun
It's rough, it's tough, it's rugby
It's rough, it's tough – that's enough!

STAR NAME *Jeremy Guscott*

Activity 12

SUE: My name is Sue Stevens and I'm an autocue operator. Autocue is the system which enables TV presenters to read what they have to say without notes. What happens is that when they look at the camera, what they see is a kind of rolling script, they can see what they have to say. It's mainly used by newsreaders and people who present documentaries or chat shows, but it's also used in music programmes, game shows ... almost any time you see someone facing the camera and talking to you for more than about 30 seconds, you can be pretty sure that they're using an autocue.
INTERVIEWER: So what do you actually do?
SUE: Well, I have to take their script and type it onto a computer, which then plays it back slowly for them to read. Really, I should let them have a look at it before they start in case they want to change something, or say something a different way, but usually there isn't time.
INTERVIEWER: Why not?
SUE: Well, I work on a lot of live programmes. I have to work at a hundred miles an hour, as it is. There just isn't time to show them.
INTERVIEWER: Have you ever made any mistakes.
SUE: Not many, actually. But I did the evening news one day with this really excellent woman, really professional, reading the news. The first thing she was supposed to say was 'Good evening.'
INTERVIEWER: And what did she say?
SUE: Well, she said 'Good evening', but the autocue said 'God evening'. The problem was that she laughed, and the first item on the news was quite serious.
INTERVIEWER: Who do you work for?
SUE: I'm a freelance. I work for anybody.
INTERVIEWER: So you must be quite pleased about the increase in the number of TV channels.
SUE: What do you mean?
INTERVIEWER: Well, if there are more TV channels, that must mean more work for you.
SUE: I'm afraid that isn't true. Most of the new satellite and cable channels just show films or imported game shows or comedies. There's very little live material on them. So ... no work for autocue operators.
INTERVIEWER: Oh.
SUE: No, I think things will be very much harder for a lot of people in the TV business. There will simply be too much entertainment, less news, fewer documentaries. I don't think things will get better at all.

UNIT 13

Activity 1

Hugh Grant was the star of *Four Weddings and a Funeral*. Eddie Murphy appeared in *Beverly Hills Cop*. Gérard Depardieu, the French actor, was in *Green Card*. Buster Keaton directed and starred in the film *The General*. Ingrid Bergman appeared in the black and white film *Casablanca*. Isabella Rossellini was in *Cousins*, and Tina Turner was the star of *Mad Max 3*. Michelle Pfeiffer appeared as Catwoman in *Batman* and Jack Nicholson was the star of *Wolf*.

Activity 8

PRON SPOT: /ə/ as in the

a) horror action thriller Tina Turner
theatre funeral syllable American
Iceland Nicholson Pfeiffer

b) at to of was can have for were

I've been at the cinema.
I want to tell you something.
London is the capital of the United Kingdom.
He was here yesterday.
She can swim well, can't she?
Where have you been?
I'm waiting for a friend.
Were you here yesterday?

Activity 9

I closed the door and turned round. He was standing there, next to the picture of his father, the movie actor. 'Where have you been?' he asked. 'At the cinema,' I answered. He wasn't listening. He was thinking about something else. 'Was it raining at the cinema?' he asked suddenly. 'What do you mean?' I replied. 'Your coat is rather wet.' 'I walked back,' I said. 'I couldn't get a taxi.' The smile disappeared from his face. 'You haven't been anywhere near a cinema,' he said. 'Perhaps you'd better leave now.'

Activity 11

STUART: My name is Stuart Nurse and I'm an actor. I've been an actor for about 10 years now. I've worked for about six different theatre companies and I've also appeared in three or four television shows.
INTERVIEWER: What's the biggest show you've appeared in?
STUART: Return to the Forbidden Planet, which is a rock musical based on a Shakespeare play. I played the lead in that and I toured Britain for two years. I'm also a member of the English Teaching Theatre, which is a theatre company which travels round the world performing shows for learners of English.
INTERVIEWER: Where have you been with the English Teaching Theatre?
STUART: I've been to France, Italy, Spain, Switzerland, Belgium, Holland, Scandinavia, all sorts of places, and I've also been to the island of La Réunion in the Indian Ocean.
INTERVIEWER: And what's your ambition?
STUART: Well, I love working in the theatre and I want to do lots more stage work, but I really want to get into films.
INTERVIEWER: What kind of films?
STUART: Any kind of films! No, I think I know what I'd like to do, I want to play the villain in an action movie.
INTERVIEWER: The villain.
STUART: Yes, the bad guy. Have you noticed? In Hollywood films, the bad guy is very often English.
INTERVIEWER: Yes, I've noticed that. What about Shakespeare?
STUART: Well, I love playing Shakespeare on stage, but in films? I don't know ... maybe it would be nice to play a comedy role in the film of a Shakespeare play.

UNIT 14

Activity 2

The first soccer World Cup took place in 1930. The winners were Uruguay, who beat Argentina 4-2 in the final. In 1934, Italy were the winners, beating Czechoslovakia 2-1 in the final. Italy won again in 1938, winning 4-2 against Hungary. Uruguay won again in 1950, beating Brazil 2-1 in the last match. In 1954, West Germany beat Hungary 3-2 in the final. The 1958 and 1962 finals were both won by Brazil. They beat Sweden 5-2 in 1958 and Czechoslovakia 3-1 in 1962. England beat West Germany 4-2 in 1966, and Brazil won again in 1970, beating Italy 4-1. In 1974, West Germany beat the Netherlands 2-1, and the Netherlands also lost the 1978 final, 3-1 to Argentina. In 1982, Italy beat West Germany and in 1986, Argentina also beat West Germany. In the 1990 World Cup, West Germany beat Argentina. Brazil won the World Cup for the fourth time in 1994, beating Italy on penalties.

Activity 8

PRON SPOT: /ɜː/ as in earth

a) /ɜː/

b) bird person heard word burn
third serve earth worm hurt
first alert learn world turn

These words begin with the letters wor but are pronounced differently: wore worn worry

c) pear wear bear tear
near fear hear dear

d) First come, first served.
The early bird catches the worm.

STAR NAME *Spurs*

UNIT 15

B3

There is now a small car on the road that will give you everything you could want in a big car, the Newton Carnival. It's as spacious, quiet, reliable and fast as a Ford Mondeo, and about half the price.

It's new! It's fun! It's Funky! Funky is the new biscuit from National Chocolate. Children love Funky, and they'll love you if you buy it for them!

Christine gets into her car and drives into her worst nightmare. *Drive*, the new film from Walter Fitzpatrick, is the most terrifying thing you are likely to see in your life. See *Drive* at a cinema near you. Don't go if you don't want to feel nervous.

Are your clothes clean, or are they Dosh clean? Dosh is the powder you want to make your clothes look bright and extra clean. Try Dosh today!

Try Wondercola, it's fresh, it's exciting, it's got a taste that will make you say, mmm! Wondercola!

D COMPARATIVE PRON

1 /ʊ/ as in good and /ʌ/ as in love.
STAR NAME *Nutbush City Limits*

2 /ə/ as in the and /ɜː/ as in earth.
STAR NAME *Uma Thurman*

a) good wood put push bush bull bully
up butter fun rugby London money

b) good fun wonderful running bulls
cut wood put up

c) How much wood could a woodchuck chuck if a woodchuck could chuck wood?

d) the first the birds
the third the words

UNIT 16

Activity 5

GARRY: Angela! What's the matter?
ANGELA: I'm soaked to the skin!
GARRY: I can see that! But it isn't raining.
ANGELA: I know!
GARRY: So what happened?
ANGELA: I was standing at the front door when an idiotic man poured a bucket of water on my head. I'm absolutely furious!
GARRY: The front door? Of this house?

ANGELA: Yes. There was a man in the upstairs bedroom.
GARRY: Oh, that's Mr Evans. He's a window cleaner. He's a pleasant man.
ANGELA: Really?
GARRY: Yes. Where are you going?
ANGELA: I'm going to have a few words with Mr Evans ...

Activity 10

PRON SPOT: /eɪ/ as in make

a) label   place   made   age   cake   male
   same   lane   tape   late   wave   lazy

b) gain   mail   wait   sailor   available   day   lay   may
   play   stay   way   eight   weigh   weight   straight

STAR NAME *Doris Day*

Activity 11

She looks quite old, she's got white hair and she's wearing glasses. She looks like a really interesting person.

He's young, he's got curly dark hair and he's quite good-looking.

She's got very nice eyes, long dark hair and a really nice smile.

He's got a moustache and he's wearing something on his head. He looks as if he spends a lot of time in the desert.

UNIT 17

Activity 10

MAN: What advice would you give to people who are worrying about their diet?
WOMAN: Well, I think most people should stop worrying and eat what they want. But they should be careful about how much fat they eat.
MAN: How can they do that?
WOMAN: Well, hamburgers and other meat products like sausages contain a lot of fat.
MAN: So we should stop eating meat.
WOMAN: Oh no, not at all! Just be careful, cut down a bit.
MAN: Is there anything else we should do?
WOMAN: Yes. Sugar and salt can be quite dangerous if you eat too much. So I would recommend eating less of them. Butter, as well.
MAN: Anything else?
WOMAN: Yes. Young people especially need a lot of Vitamin C, so they should eat lots of fruit and vegetables.
MAN: What about dairy products?
WOMAN: Well, that's interesting. As I said, it's better to reduce the amount of butter you eat, but you do need some milk or yoghurt in your diet. They're rich in calcium and iron.
MAN: Finally, is it true that vegetarians don't get enough protein?
WOMAN: Oh no. But if you don't eat meat, you have to make sure that you get your protein and iron from other sources. Cheese and eggs, for example.

Activity 11

PRON SPOT: /aɪ/ as in life

a) dine   fine   line   mine   nine   pine   wine
   lime   time   bike   like   life   wife

b) die   lie   tie

c) apply   by   cry   fly   July   rhyme   sky   try

d) delighted   high   light   might   night   sight   tight
   tonight

Simon said to Michael and Michael told his wife
I have never been so excited in all my life
I'm delighted to say that I'm going to dine
With the Prime Minister, tonight at nine
I think this means he's going to resign
I must go out and buy some wine.

STAR NAME *Michael Stipe*

Activity 13

LAUREN: My name is Lauren Brewer and I'm a holistic therapist.
INTERVIEWER: What exactly is a holistic therapist?

LAUREN: Well, a therapist is someone who tries to help people with some kind of illness or infirmity using methods beyond what a medical doctor would use, by talking about the patient's life problems, for example. And holistic therapists look at everything about a person, a person's whole being, to try to solve the problem. If you developed a stomach pain for example, a traditional doctor would probably diagnose the problem and recommend a series of drugs or other medicaments. That kind of doctor might ask you about what you eat, but really wouldn't look into your lifestyle or where you are in your life at the moment. A holistic therapist would ask you about what you eat, but would also ask you a series of questions to find out more about your whole person, everything about you.
INTERVIEWER: What kind of questions?
LAUREN: That really depends on the patient. Someone who clearly is in distress often simply needs advice and counselling about their life. But if the patient looks pretty healthy and seems to lead a normal lifestyle, but still exhibits behaviour abnormality, then you have to look more deeply to find the causes of the problem.
INTERVIEWER: Your special interest, I understand, is teenagers and eating disorders.
LAUREN: That's right. I have a theory that most teenage illness centres around problems related to what they eat.
INTERVIEWER: They eat badly ...
LAUREN: No, not necessarily. I think teenagers are always being advised to eat well, and that advice may be putting pressure on them.
INTERVIEWER: So parents should stop telling their children what to eat and what not to eat.
LAUREN: Actually, more of this pressure comes from school. Health education is terribly important, and school is the best place for it, but some of it is unnecessary. It's my belief that there is absolutely nothing wrong with teenagers eating whatever they want.
INTERVIEWER: Isn't that a bit dangerous?
LAUREN: No. Eating isn't dangerous. Not eating at all is dangerous. I believe that teenagers will find their own way to healthy eating, as long as people stop trying to influence what they eat. I had a patient, a boy of 14, who was sent to me because he seemed to be having terrible difficulties, at home, at school, with people in general. And he wasn't eating. It only took me a few minutes to discover what the problem was.
INTERVIEWER: And what was the problem?
LAUREN: He wanted to eat chocolate biscuits and bananas, and he wanted to drink milk.
INTERVIEWER: Is that all?
LAUREN: Yes.
INTERVIEWER: Did his parents know about this?
LAUREN: Well, he lived with his father, who was trying very hard to feed him a balanced diet. The father refused to let him have the chocolate biscuits, so he didn't eat anything.
INTERVIEWER: So what happened?
LAUREN: I asked the father to let the boy do what he wanted. The father wasn't happy but he agreed to try. I persuaded him to do this for a month before we thought about alternative strategies.
INTERVIEWER: A month? What happened?
LAUREN: Within two weeks, the boy was so fed up with chocolate biscuits that he never wanted to eat another one in his life. And he started eating normal food.

UNIT 18

Activity 2b)

I've had this dream about five times. I'm standing in front of a crowd of about 400 people, I think I'm making a speech, but it's not clear. But just as I begin to speak, my teeth fall out, all of them, one by one. They fall on the floor and make an incredible noise. I work as a radio announcer, so you can imagine how this makes me feel!

I had a really complicated dream once, and I can't imagine why I dreamt about any of it. It started off at a railway station. There were about ten people, all men, waiting for me to give them instructions. I explained that we had to find a man called Mr Biscuit, yes, Mr Biscuit! – who probably lived on an island in Scotland. We travelled by train to Scotland and then we took a helicopter to the island. There were hundreds of other planes and helicopters flying in all directions, but no one seemed very worried about it. On the island, we asked about Mr Biscuit, but no one knew him. Eventually, we decided to take a boat to another island. I started talking to the captain. 'I know Mr Biscuit,' he said. 'He's there.' And we looked over the side of the boat and there was a man swimming alongside the boat and smiling. And then I woke up. I was really annoyed! I wanted to go back and find out more!

My grandfather died about five years ago but I dreamt about him last week. It's the first time that's happened. He was sitting in the kitchen talking to me. He told me that we had made a mistake, and he wasn't really dead. I woke up the next morning feeling very strange and I telephoned my grandmother. She seemed to be OK, but I decided to make sure that I talk to her every week from now on.

I often dream about my hair. I'm only 22 and my hair is all right, but in my dream, my hair is really beautiful! The sun shines on it and everyone smiles and tells me how lucky I am. The strange thing is that I can see it so clearly, as if my eyes are above my head. I usually wake up feeling really depressed.

I had a nightmare once. It was so awful I don't like talking about it. I was in the street. I knew it was the street where I live, but it looked nothing like it. A bomb had destroyed most of the buildings. There were wild animals, horrible grey things, and people who looked like animals. Everyone looked wild and angry and kept shouting at me. I was really frightened.

Activity 6

(Series of Sounds)

Activity 7

PRON SPOT: /əʊ/ as in most

a) grocer   rode   joke   home
   alone   hope   note

b) love   move   whose   lose
   gold   sold   hole
   gold   sold   hole

c) wore   store   more   bore   core

d) only   no   go   so   don't   most   folk   toast

e) Joe's the only one who saw *Home Alone*.
   Grocers don't close until everything's sold.
   Don't you like folk music? No! Only rock and roll!

STAR NAMES   *The Rolling Stones   Home Alone*

Activity 10

EDWARD: My name is Edward Wayne, and I'm a psychologist. My special area of interest is dreams, and I'm conducting research into the dreams of children and young people. It's my belief that dreams and nightmares have a profound effect on young people, and that they should be encouraged to talk about them. In fact, children benefit from regularly writing down the details of dreams that affect them.
INTERVIEWER: Are you thinking especially of nightmares?
EDWARD: Nightmares certainly have a serious effect on young people, especially children of course, but my research suggests that most young people are able to deal with nightmares quite easily.
INTERVIEWER: How do you mean?
EDWARD: Well, children sometimes wake up crying during a nightmare, and someone usually comes to see if they are all right. By the morning, they have usually forgotten what the dream was about. I think there are other kinds of dreams that are more important, and can have quite a strong impact on children.
INTERVIEWER: What kind of dreams?
EDWARD: Well, there are three types of dream that particularly interest me. The first, of course, are guilt dreams.
INTERVIEWER: Guilt dreams ...
EDWARD: Yes, we all have dreams that make us feel guilty about something, and adults tend to forget about them in the morning. Some children, on the other hand, wake up feeling guilty and spend days, even weeks, carrying the burden of guilt when they have nothing to feel guilty about.
INTERVIEWER: I see.
EDWARD: The second kind of dream that I have been researching are the dreams that reflect your inner anxiety. We all feel anxious about something, and this is often reflected in our dreams. Again, with children, if they don't talk about their dreams, these feelings of anxiety can affect their performance at school and even their health.
INTERVIEWER: Right ...
EDWARD: But for me the most important dreams that children should be encouraged to talk about are dreams that make them feel depressed when they wake up. Emptiness dreams, when life seems absolutely pointless. It is very important that children and young people should be encouraged to write down what they dream about and talk about them. And any parent who notices that their child is seriously affected by what they dream should spend a lot of time talking them through what they remember. When the child sees that the parent isn't shocked or angry or surprised, the child soon realises that there's nothing wrong with the dream.
INTERVIEWER: I see.
EDWARD: And a beneficial side effect of this is that children actually start to enjoy their dreams, even the scary ones!

UNIT 19

Activity 1b)

Queen Victoria is Prince Charles's great-great-great grandmother.
Princess Diana is Barbara Cartland's step-granddaughter.
Winston Churchill is Jenny Jerome's son.
Barbara Cartland is Princess Diana's step-grandmother.
Prince Charles is Queen Victoria's great-great-great grandson.

Activity 2

My name is Diana Spencer, which of course was Princess Diana's name before she married Prince Charles. You can't imagine how difficult life is. No one believes me when I say my name, and it can be really embarrassing in banks and post offices. I have to take my passport everywhere to prove it's my real name. And I can't even try to book theatre tickets by telephone. People think I'm trying to get free tickets!

My name is Paul McCartney, and I quite enjoy it when people say: Are you the Paul McCartney? I'm about 30 years younger than Paul McCartney, but no one seems to think about that. The funny thing is that my girlfriend's name is Linda, which is Paul's wife's name.

My name is Julie Roberts, not Julia Roberts, but people always think I say Julia Roberts. No, Julie, I say. Really? they say ... what's it like having the same name as a famous film star? It gets quite boring, actually.

My name is Alan Shakespeare. As far as I know, I am no relation at all to William Shakespeare, but you have to agree that it's an unusual name. I don't mind when people ask me if I'm related to him. Sometimes I say yes, he's a very nice man. But I nearly got into trouble once when a policeman stopped me in the street and asked me my name. He nearly arrested me. Fortunately, I had some identification with me.

My name is Michael Jackson. It always makes people laugh when I say it. For a start, I'm white and I'm nearly bald. Secondly, I can't sing and thirdly, I'm a terrible dancer. I actually know three other people called Michael Jackson. But then, it's not a very unusual name, is it?

Activity 3c)

The Office of Population Censuses and Surveys (OPCS), is responsible for finding out how many people live in Britain. But it is also open to any member of the public who wishes to trace his or her ancestry. The Public Search Room is always full of people who are trying to find out about their family history. The Public Search Room has records relating to births, marriages and deaths in England and Wales since 1st July 1837 (including births and deaths at sea). The records used to be kept in alphabetical order in yearly quarters (that is one for every three months). In 1984, they began to arrange the indexes in alphabetical order for the whole year. You can compile a family tree at St Catherine's House. If you want to trace the record of your father's birth (but you don't know when he was born), you can first of all look for the record of your parent's marriage. A certificate of marriage should give you your father's name (and the name of his father) and provide a starting point for tracing his date of birth. What happens when you reach 1837? Before 1837, churches kept records of births, marriages and deaths. Unfortunately, not all churches were very careful about these records and many have none at all. In this case, you can employ a professional genealogist (you will hear an interview with one later in this Unit), who may be able to find out about your family from other sources.

Activity 8

PRON SPOT: /u:/ **as in who**

a) blue   clue   glue   true   blew
crew   flew   grew   Jewish
moon   zoo   too   June   rule

pool   fool

b) do   two   who   you   usual   suit   route

STAR NAME *Lulu*

Activity 10

FRANK: My name is Frank Kincade and I'm a genealogist. I help people trace their ancestry, find out more about their ancestors. Now you can find out a lot about your ancestors without the help of a genealogist, by going to the Office of Public Records at St Catherine's House, for example, in London. Records there go back to the middle of the nineteenth century. If you want to find out about your ancestors before that, you have to employ a professional, like me!

INTERVIEWER: You can help people find out about their ancestors before records began?

FRANK: Yes.

INTERVIEWER: How do you do that?

FRANK: Well, the records at St Catherine's House are national records, there are also local records, usually church records of baptisms. You start by going to the church in the area where you think the people were born. Some churches have absolutely marvellous records going back before that. But there are also other ways. It may be possible to find out about people if you know what their occupation was. Records were kept by guilds and trade unions. And then of course, there are people who emigrated. Often we have to try to find out about people who went to live in America nearly 200 years ago.

INTERVIEWER: How do you do that?

FRANK: Well, you go to the United States Information Service. There's one at every United States embassy. In fact, the most interesting thing about this job is trying to find out about ancestors who finished up all over the world.

INTERVIEWER: What's the most unusual thing you found out?

FRANK: Well, I was asked by a family to try to find some information about the brother of their great-grandfather. They knew that he had worked in Burma in the 1930s, but after that, there was no record of him at all. My first thought was that he had probably died there. I therefore checked the colonial records, and indeed there were a great many British people who died in Burma in those years, but his name wasn't in the records.

INTERVIEWER: So what did you do?

FRANK: Well, I noticed that there was a hand-written note next to one name which said: Possibly killed in air crash, so I started searching through records of air disasters in the area. I discovered that a British military plane had left Burma and crashed in China. I made more enquiries, and I discovered that records of the dead had been kept in Hong Kong. And I found the man's name in the list of those who had been killed.

INTERVIEWER: Were the family pleased?

FRANK: No, in fact, they seemed extremely upset. I think they would have preferred not to know. But in fact, I think that most people are rather unhappy about what they discover. Sometimes I think they wish they'd never started trying to find out.

UNIT 20

B3

My name is Sandra, I'm 14 years old and I live in Leeds, in the north of England. What makes me smile? Well, I have to say that the funniest person I know is my grandmother. She just sits there and tells funny stories about when she was a girl. She's very funny. What makes me want to stay in bed in the morning? Well, nothing really, I'm quite a positive sort of person, and I like

getting up, but I must say I'm not very happy if it's raining. What makes me angry? People who sit around all day and don't do anything, like my brother Paul. He should get out of the house and do something.

Hello, my name is Ravi Raman. I'm 15 years old and I live in West London. What makes me smile? Well, I like watching cartoons on TV. I sometimes get up at seven o'clock in the morning on Sundays, so I can watch about three hours of them. What makes me want to stay in bed in the morning? Mathematics lessons. What makes me angry? I get angry when my local football team, Queens Park Rangers, lose.

My name is Gina Baptiste. I'm 15 and I live in Birmingham. The one person who can really make me smile is my sister, who is a nurse in a hospital. She always comes home with the most incredibly funny stories that patients in the hospital have told her. I always want to stay in bed in the morning for another half hour because I always feel tired when I wake up. And people who drop litter in the street make me very very angry.

D COMPARATIVE PRON

/eɪ/ as in make and /aɪ/ as in life.

STAR NAME *David Icke*

/əʊ/ as in most and /u:/ as in who.

STAR NAME *Peter O'Toole*

a) eighty-nine
at the same time
seatbelts save lives
break time
five past eight
take your time

d) So do I
No through road
Oh no! Not you!
Opening soon

f) Though, slow and robot contain the /əʊ/ sound. The other words are cough and allow.

g) Through, shoe and blue contain the /u:/ sound. The other words are enough and does.

UNIT 21

Activity 2

PASSENGER: Excuse me.

RAIL EMPLOYEE: Good morning, can I help you?

PASSENGER: Yes. I want a ticket.

RAIL EMPLOYEE: You want a ticket.

PASSENGER: Yes. I want a ticket to Birmingham

RAIL EMPLOYEE: You want a ticket to Birmingham?

PASSENGER: Yes.

RAIL EMPLOYEE: Why?

PASSENGER: What did you say?

RAIL EMPLOYEE: Why do you want a ticket to Birmingham?

PASSENGER: I live there.

RAIL EMPLOYEE: Birmingham's a terrible place.

PASSENGER: I live there.

RAIL EMPLOYEE: Why don't you go to Oxford?

PASSENGER: I live there!

RAIL EMPLOYEE: What? In Oxford?

PASSENGER: No, in Birmingham.

RAIL EMPLOYEE: Oh.

PASSENGER: I live in Birmingham, I work in Birmingham, I was born in Birmingham ...

RAIL EMPLOYEE: ... and you'll probably die in Birmingham.

b)

PASSENGER: I live in Birmingham, I work in Birmingham, I was born in Birmingham ...

RAIL EMPLOYEE: ... and you'll probably die in Birmingham.

PASSENGER: Ye ... no! I want to go to Birmingham. Today.

RAIL EMPLOYEE: Today?

PASSENGER: Yes.

RAIL EMPLOYEE: Impossible.

d)

PASSENGER: Give me a second class single ticket to Birmingham, please.

RAIL EMPLOYEE: Pardon?
PASSENGER: Can you give me a second class single ticket to
    Birmingham, please?
RAIL EMPLOYEE: No, I can't.
PASSENGER: Well, why not?
RAIL EMPLOYEE: Well, this is not the ticket office.
PASSENGER: What?
RAIL EMPLOYEE: No. The ticket office is next door.
PASSENGER: Oh no!
RAIL EMPLOYEE: What's the matter?
PASSENGER: I'm going to miss my train!
RAIL EMPLOYEE: No, no, you've got plenty of time.
PASSENGER: Plenty of time? You said the train was leaving any
    minute now!
RAIL EMPLOYEE: Yes, but there's no hurry.
PASSENGER: Why not?
RAIL EMPLOYEE: Because I'm the driver.
PASSENGER: You're the driver.
RAIL EMPLOYEE: Yes. The train can't leave without me, can it?
PASSENGER: No, I suppose not.
RAIL EMPLOYEE: So ... you come with me.
PASSENGER: Platform 2?
RAIL EMPLOYEE: No, Dave's café. We'll have a nice cup of tea and
    a sandwich before we go.

Activity 3c)

An Englishman went to stay at a hotel in Paris. On the first
morning, he went to have breakfast. There were no tables free,
so he sat at the same table as a Frenchman.
When the Englishman's breakfast arrived, the Frenchman said:
'*Bon appetit.*' The Englishman thought that it was his name.
He replied by saying his own name: 'Sidebottom.' This happened
every day for a week.
At the end of the week, an English friend of Sidebottom's arrived
at the hotel. 'I want you to meet my friend, Mr Bon Appetit,' said
Sidebottom.
'That isn't his name,' said Sidebottom's friend. 'That's what
French people say before they eat something.'

Activity 4b)

CUSTOMER: Excuse me?
WAITRESS: Yes?
CUSTOMER: What's this fly doing in my soup?
WAITRESS: I think it's swimming.

WOMAN: What's the matter?
MAN: I've lost my dog.
WOMAN: Why don't you put an advertisement in the newspaper?
MAN: I can't do that. My dog can't read.

Activity 6b)

carried   played   arrived   died   stopped   hoped   cut
rented   looked   watched

Activity 9b)

A Spanish man goes into a clothes shop to buy some clothes. He
can't speak English and he isn't very good at describing things
with gestures. The woman in the clothes shop is very helpful. She
shows him a pair of trousers. He shakes his head. She shows him
a suit. He shakes his head. She shows him overcoats, scarves,
shirts, pullovers, underwear, ties, suits and he keeps shaking his
head. Finally, she shows him a pair of shoes. He looks at them,
and points inside the shoe. She nods and takes out a pair of
socks.
'*Eso si que es*!' says the Spanish man, looking very pleased. ('*Eso
si que es*' is a Spanish expression which means 'That's it!'). The
woman looks puzzled. 'If you knew how to spell it, why didn't you
tell me when you came in?'

Eso si que es is the spelling of socks. S O C K S.

Activity 10

PRON SPOT: /ɔɪ/ **as in boy**

a) boy   joy   Roy   toy   destroy   loyal   oyster   royal
    boil   coil   foil   soil   toil   avoid

b) A boy called Roy destroyed my toys.
    I boiled the oysters in oil and covered them with foil.

   Jersey /dʒɜːzɪ/   Jersey /dʒɔɪzɪ/

STAR NAME *Paul Gascoigne*

Activity 12

a What is improvised comedy?
   Comedy without a script. We create the scenes and sketches
   as we perform them. At the Comedy Store, people in the
   audience suggest the characters and locations.

b Do people from other countries visit the Comedy Store?
   Yes. Many tourists in Central London go to theatres and clubs
   to see shows. Sometimes they're amused, sometimes they're
   confused!

c Who's your favourite comedian?
   I haven't got a single favourite comedian. My favourite British
   comedians are Spike Milligan and John Cleese. My favourite
   American comedians are Groucho Marx and Garry Shandling.

d Have you ever tried to tell a joke in a foreign language?
   Yes, I know a joke in German. The problem is that when I tell
   it to German people, they think I can speak German really
   well and they start telling me other jokes that I can't
   understand at all.

UNIT 22

Activity 8

The Autolock is very simple to use. You attach it to the steering
wheel of your car and you can be certain that the car will not be
stolen in your absence.

Premier Securities offer a reliable and inexpensive security
service for your factory, office or home. Trained guards with dogs
provide a 24-hour service.

The Safescreen offers total protection for your possessions by
recording on film anyone who passes anywhere near your home.

The Red Alert alarm is clearly visible on the side of your house
and starts ringing as soon as anyone attempts to enter the house
by force.

Protect your bicycle with the new improved Bluebelt locking
system. It makes it impossible to move your bike or remove the
wheels.

Activity 10

PRON SPOT: /aʊ/ **as in allowed**

a) allow   brown   cow   how   now   wow!
    about   plough   house   loud   mouse   out

b) bow /aʊ/   bow /əʊ/   row /aʊ/   row /əʊ/

c) follow   know   low   mow   tow

STAR NAME *Crowded House*

Activity 11

HAZEL: My name is Hazel Garvey and I'm a designer. I design
   furniture, tables, chairs, either made of wood or metal. I also
   design my own jewellery, which a friend makes for me. Which
   is why it was such a shock when I discovered that it had all
   been stolen.
INTERVIEWER: What exactly happened?
HAZEL: Well, I had a party at my flat on a Friday evening and the
   next day, I went away. I went to an art exhibition in Paris,
   actually. It was something I had been looking forward to for
   months. I didn't get back until Monday afternoon. I had a
   meeting that I had to go to early the next morning, so I started
   to get ready for that. I started to think about what to wear. It
   was only then, when I opened the box where I keep all my
   jewellery, that I realised that it had gone. Nothing else had
   been disturbed at all.
INTERVIEWER: What did you do?
HAZEL: Well, I panicked for a minute. I was scared that the thief
   might still be in the flat. But I calmed down and searched the
   place and there was obviously no one there. Then I called the
   police. To their credit, they sent two people very quickly, a
   young constable, who was wonderful, and a woman, who
   seemed to know a lot about burglary. She was a bit surprised
   that there was no sign of a break-in. It was then that I realised
   that someone at the party might have stolen it. And then I got
   really angry. I couldn't imagine who could have done such a
   thing. Anyway, fortunately, I had some very good photos of the
   stuff and the police were able to circulate them.

INTERVIEWER: Was the jewellery worth a lot of money?

HAZEL: I think it's worth a fortune. It's all my own stuff and I think it's very valuable. But that's not really the point. I wanted it back, but I also wanted to know who it was who stole it.

INTERVIEWER: Yes, of course.

HAZEL: Anyway, they rang me a couple of weeks later and said that they had found some of it on a market stall. The poor bloke who was selling it had bought it from someone. It was obvious that he hadn't stolen it.

INTERVIEWER: So you got it all back.

HAZEL: Not all of it. About half.

INTERVIEWER: And do you know who stole it?

HAZEL: No, I don't. I really haven't a clue. But I'm not going to have another party in a hurry.

UNIT 23

Activity 1

ANGELA: Guess what Garry! You won't believe this!

GARRY: What?

ANGELA: Vince Savage has been arrested!

GARRY: Who?

ANGELA: Vince Savage, the lead singer of that new band.

GARRY: No! You're joking. Has he really?

ANGELA: Yes!

GARRY: Why?

ANGELA: Apparently he didn't pay his hotel bill.

GARRY: No!

ANGELA: Yes! It says here: Vince Savage was arrested last night at the Empire Hotel, Liverpool after refusing to pay for a meal he had eaten at the hotel. Savage (41) said that the meal was rubbish ...

GARRY: No!

ANGELA: Yes! Savage was arrested and taken to Liverpool Central Police Station.

GARRY: Wow!

Activity 3a)

And now some other news. Many of Britain's top fashion designers have been at a fashion show in Manchester and today a new prize for young fashion designers has been awarded for the first time. It's called The Montana Prize, and it has been won by 19-year old Paul Kennedy, a student at Epping Forest Art College. Paul's revolutionary casual wear was considered to be the most inventive of the 1,200 items that were examined by the judges. What is very surprising about the award is that Paul is not studying fashion design. He's at Epping Forest Art College to study theatre design.

And now some sports news. England manager Lee Sharpe has been sacked after England's 5-3 defeat by Albania at Wembley last night. England, who scored three goals in the first half, played very badly in the second half and will probably lose their chance of playing in the World Cup Finals in Japan. Sharpe said it was the most embarrassing night of his professional life.

And now some news from outer space. According to a report in the *National Reporter*, buildings have been seen on the moon. Space experts at the Kennedy Space Centre in California are convinced that the buildings were built by creatures from another planet.

Bobbie Sharon, twenty-something star of TV series The People Next Door was in London last night to promote her new record, *All the Poor People*. At a party, she was introduced to Sam Parrish, who is 6 feet 5 inches tall (1 metre 95).

Susan Morgan (18) and her friend Angela Costello (19) claim that they saw the Loch Ness monster while they were walking around the Loch last Saturday. The monster, which hasn't been 'seen' for several years, looked very healthy, they said.

Last night soap star Bobbie Sharon was delighted when she got the chance to meet Sam Parrish, who describes himself as her biggest fan. You can see why he says that, Sam is an incredible 1 metre 95 tall. He was introduced to Bobbie at her record company's party to advertise Bobbie's latest song, *All the Poor People*. Bobbie was interviewed by Bill Bright for Rock Sound Radio.

'I'm just so pleased to be here. English people are so wonderful!'

You can hear the complete interview on David Wayne's What's New? programme tonight at ten thirty.

And yet another story about the Loch Ness Monster! Nessie has been seen by two Scottish teenagers during a walk round Loch Ness. 18-year old Susan Morgan talked to Rock Sound Radio.

'We just turned the corner and there she was! She looked very nice and healthy.'

Susan and her friend, Angela Costello, were interviewed by reporters when they returned to their homes in Aberdeen.

Activity 7

PRON SPOT: /ɪə/ as in here

a) ear   clear   dear   fear   gear   hear   near   tear   year
   beer   career   cheers!   deer   steer

   bear   pear   tear   wear

   tear /ɪə/ and tear /eə/

b) here   mere   pier   tier   we're (we are)

c) auctioneer   engineer   mountaineer   pioneer

d) Andalusia   Korea   Kampuchea   Nicosia   Aramathea

e) We're here, we're here
   Can you hear? Can you hear?
   Oh dear, no one here
   Are they near? Are they near?
   Never fear, have a beer, cheers!

STAR NAME *Richard Gere*

Activity 9

GILLIAN: My name is Gillian Dickinson and I'm a freelance journalist. I live in Norfolk, which is in East Anglia, in the east of England, and I specialise in writing stories about local news in towns and villages near where I live.

INTERVIEWER: What kind of stories?

GILLIAN: Well, I started work as a cub reporter on a local newspaper in the town where I was born, Kings Lynn, which is in the north of Norfolk, near the coast. It's really amazing that so many local papers survive in this country. But they do survive and it's because people like reading about themselves or people they know. I was sent to all sorts of odd things, weddings, funerals, charity events, and the only thing I was told was to get as many names as possible in my article, and to get a photograph of as many people as possible.

INTERVIEWER: What, at funerals?

GILLIAN: Well, we don't take photographs at funerals, of course, but we often make a list of the people who attended it. You know, the funeral was attended by Joe's wife Mary, his three children Tom, Dick and Harry, that sort of thing.

INTERVIEWER: So do you still write stories like that?

GILLIAN: Oh no! Goodness me no! The national newspapers don't buy stories like that.

INTERVIEWER: What sort of things do they buy?

GILLIAN: Well, the stories that I sell are mainly from the local courts, strange stories of local disagreements about property, or people in court because their dogs make too much noise, things like that. I mean, there aren't any murder trials in local courts, of course, they would be dealt with in a city court. But some pretty strange things happen, I can tell you.

INTERVIEWER: Give us an example.

GILLIAN: Well, the most famous story that I sold was about a man and his wife who wanted to get a divorce. Well, she wanted a divorce, but he didn't. Anyway, in the middle of divorce proceedings, he took all her clothes and hung them in trees around the village where she lived. Everything, dresses, underwear, the lot.

INTERVIEWER: I think I remember reading about that. It was quite funny.

GILLIAN: Well, it wasn't very funny for the woman, actually. And also, it was the most dangerous story I ever covered.

INTERVIEWER: Why?

GILLIAN: Well, I went to the man's house to talk to him. I got there a few hours before the national newspaper crowd arrived, and I was talking to him through his letter box.

INTERVIEWER: Yes?

GILLIAN: Well, suddenly, he opened the door and he was standing there with a gun!

INTERVIEWER: Wow!

GILLIAN: I was scared stiff, I can tell you.

INTERVIEWER: How do you actually sell stories?

GILLIAN: I have contacts on all the big national newspapers. I just ring them up and tell them when a story is breaking.

INTERVIEWER: And they buy it from you.

GILLIAN: Usually.

INTERVIEWER: Wouldn't it be cheaper if they sent one of their own reporters?

GILLIAN: Well, they do if it's a very big story. If it's just a human interest story, they trust me to get it right and buy it from me.

UNIT 24

Activity 2b)

INTERVIEWER: I'm talking to Professor Flora Macdonald about the Loch Ness monster.

PROFESSOR MACDONALD: Hello.

INTERVIEWER: Tell me, Professor Macdonald, why do you think Loch Ness has this special legend of the monster?

PROFESSOR MACDONALD: Well, Loch Ness is an enormous lake, I mean, it's the biggest lake in Britain.

INTERVIEWER: Really? I didn't know that.

PROFESSOR MACDONALD: And it's extremely deep, it's so deep that you could comfortably hide the world's tallest buildings in it ...

INTERVIEWER: Wow!

PROFESSOR MACDONALD: And even using modern equipment, it has always been impossible to search the Loch completely, so there is reason to believe that there could be some large monster at the bottom of the lake ...

INTERVIEWER: Incredible ... and what kind of creature is the monster, if it exists?

PROFESSOR MACDONALD: Well, there are all kinds of theories, some people think that it could be a huge mammal of some kind ...

INTERVIEWER: A mammal, right.

PROFESSOR MACDONALD: But there are other people who think that it could be a member of the plesiosaur family ...

INTERVIEWER: Plesiosaur? You mean from the dinosaur period?

PROFESSOR MACDONALD: Yes. They've been extinct for 70 million years.

INTERVIEWER: Astonishing! So how did the monster get there?

PROFESSOR MACDONALD: Well, the theory is that a family of plesiosaurs were stranded in what is now Loch Ness at the end of the ice age.

INTERVIEWER: Really amazing. When did all these stories about the Loch Ness monster begin?

PROFESSOR MACDONALD: Well, the first ones were in the Middle Ages ...

INTERVIEWER: Is that right?

PROFESSOR MACDONALD: Yes, but the first real interest in the 20th century came when that very famous photograph was taken by a London surgeon in 1933.

INTERVIEWER: Oh yes, that famous photograph. How long did he have to wait to take it?

PROFESSOR MACDONALD: Well, he said that he was just incredibly lucky and it was a complete accident ...

INTERVIEWER: No! Really?

PROFESSOR MACDONALD: He said that he was passing the Loch in his car ...

INTERVIEWER: Amazing!

PROFESSOR MACDONALD: That's what he said. I'm afraid I don't believe him.

INTERVIEWER: Why not?

PROFESSOR MACDONALD: Because in 1994, just before he died, he admitted that it was all a practical joke.

INTERVIEWER: Oh no! You mean there's no Loch Ness monster!

PROFESSOR MACDONALD: That's not what I said. All I'm saying is that photograph is a forgery.

INTERVIEWER: Oh. Well, what a pity.

Activity 11

PRON SPOT: /aʊə/ as in flower

a) bower   cower   flower   power   tower   flour   hour   sour

b) grower   lower   lawnmower   rower

c) Flowers grow bigger in lower fields.
   A rower rowed with power past the tower.
   Our flour will be ready in an hour.

STAR NAME *Tyrone Power*

Activity 12

JOHN: 1995 was the year I saved the country. I'll always remember it, it was Christmas Eve and I had a ticket to see *Phantom of the Opera* and I decided to go for a walk until it started. Anyway, suddenly, a car pulled up and two men jumped out. They said they were special police officers and they needed me to help them with a matter of national emergency. They needed me to replace the Queen. Apparently, she'd just filmed her message to the nation and then she'd gone to the corner shop for a bottle of milk and a bag of potatoes. Anyway, while she was out, one of her dogs had got the video ... the video of her Christmas message .... and had chewed the tape. Somebody ran out to tell the Queen and, surprise, surprise – a meteorite had hit the Queen – right on the crown! She wasn't badly hurt but she was in no condition to do any more filming that day. Now the Queen's Christmas message is a national tradition. Something had to be done. Now, as you can see from the photo, I look a little bit like the Queen. This took place when my hair was curlier. I was taken to Buckingham Palace and the make-up people did a very good job. They gave me one of the Queen's silver and gold dresses, I remember the skirt was a bit tight, but that didn't matter because they only filmed the top half of me. I must have been very good because at one point Prince Charles walked in and said 'Mum, do you know where my bicycle is?' And Prince Philip, the Queen's husband, came in and asked if I was making chips for tea. I suppose she was planning to make chips, that's why she went to the corner shop for the bag of potatoes. Anyway, the recording of the Christmas message went well, and I remember that the only ones who were suspicious were the dogs, and I got a bit frightened because one of them came towards me growling. In fact, if you watch the recording, you can clearly hear one of the Queen's bodyguards saying: Rover! Sit! They were very pleased with my work and they let me keep the crown, I keep it in the bathroom. Yes, I'll never forget the day I was the Queen. It was the day before something similar happened to Luciano Pavarotti. And that was really funny, because what happened was this ...

UNIT 25

B3

Motorists have had some very bad weather on the motorways today, with heavy rain and winds. Several cars were involved in a serious accident on the M2 motorway near Canterbury.

Tom Morland, a fireman from Manchester, has won this week's lottery prize. He was given the prize by TV personality Des Moyne. Tom said that the prize wouldn't change his life, and he was still planning to have a holiday in Brighton next month.

Film star Stuart McShane flew into London today for the premiere of his new film *All My Love*. Mr McShane was annoyed when reporters started asking him questions about his marriage to rock singer Lucy Lester.

D COMPARATIVE PRON

/aʊ/ as in allowed and /ɔɪ/ as in boy.

STAR NAMES *Chairman Mao and President Moi*

/aʊə/ as in flower and /ɪə/ as in here.

STAR NAMES *Dwight D. Eisenhower and Mia Farrow*

a) brown   mouse   town

b) soil   boil   destroy

c) dear   ear   here   hear   year

d) shower   tower   hour   flour

UNIT 26

Activity 6

One of the most dangerous natural forces on planet Earth are fault lines, places where different parts of the earth's crust are in conflict with each other.

The San Andreas Fault, which is in California, is probably the most famous fault in the world, but it isn't the only major fault. It

conflict with each other.

The San Andreas Fault, which is in California, is probably the most famous fault in the world, but it isn't the only major fault. It isn't even the only major fault in California. There are three other major faults, the Zayante Fault, the Sargent Fault and the Calaveras Fault.

The San Andreas fault, which is 1,500 kilometres long, is the place where the Pacific Plate and the North American plate, meet.

For the past 30 million years, the Pacific Plate has been passing the North American plate at the rate of 6 centimetres a year. Unfortunately, most of this movement occurs suddenly, after the two plates have become locked. This is what causes earthquakes.

The most famous earthquake in American history occurred in 1906, but there was also a very serious one on the 17th October 1989. Scientists believe that an even worse earthquake is almost certain to occur, but they don't know when.

Activity 10

PRON SPOT: /ʒ/ as in explosion

a) pleasure   television   usually

b) leisure   measure   treasure
   disclosure   enclosure   exposure

c) collision   decision   precision   revision   vision

STAR NAME *Jean-Michel Jarre*

UNIT 27

Activity 2

INTERVIEWER: What exactly is the difference between meteors and meteorites?
EXPERT: Well, let's start with meteoroids. Outside the Earth's atmosphere, there are millions and millions of flying objects, huge pieces of rock and metal and they are called meteoroids.
INTERVIEWER: I see.
EXPERT: Now ... when a meteoroid enters the Earth's atmosphere, it becomes a meteor. It becomes extremely hot, so hot in fact that it usually burns up very quickly.
INTERVIEWER: So, it's like a shooting star.
EXPERT: Well, a shooting star is a meteor.
INTERVIEWER: Really?
EXPERT: Yes. Shooting star is simply a popular, but unscientific name for a meteor. Meteors are not stars, of course.
INTERVIEWER: No, of course.
EXPERT: Now, most meteors are so small that they burn up quite quickly. But some of them are big enough to reach the Earth. The ones that reach the Earth are called meteorites.
INTERVIEWER: I see.
EXPERT: Some of these are so small that you can hardly see them.
INTERVIEWER: So they aren't dangerous.
EXPERT: Oh yes they are! They can be very dangerous. The fact is that one billion meteoroids enter the Earth's atmosphere every day!
INTERVIEWER: Wow! A million!
EXPERT: Not a million, a billion! And they are travelling at speeds of up to 72 kilometres a second.
INTERVIEWER: Gosh!
EXPERT: And several tons of this stuff actually reaches the ground.
INTERVIEWER: Where do all these meteoroids come from?
EXPERT: Well, that's a question that scientists are still asking themselves. But there's no doubt that most of them come from comets.
INTERVIEWER: And what are comets?
EXPERT: Well, a comet is a celestial body ... er ... something that flies through the sky ...
INTERVIEWER: A planet?
EXPERT: No, it's nothing like a planet. A comet consists mainly of gas and ice, but with lots of particles of rock attached to it.
INTERVIEWER: And how big are comets?
EXPERT: Absolutely enormous. They can have a diameter of 130,000 kilometres.
INTERVIEWER: They must be very heavy.
EXPERT: No, they aren't. They're mostly gas and ice, so enormous comets weigh much less than planets which are smaller than they are, like Earth. They're ugly things, like big, dirty

snowballs.
INTERVIEWER: And meteors?
EXPERT: Yes, well, parts of the rock fall off the comet and form a tail. And occasionally, parts of the tail drop off. These pieces that drop off become meteors.
INTERVIEWER: How long is the tail of the comet?
EXPERT: The tail of a comet can be 160 million kilometres long.
INTERVIEWER: Good heavens!
EXPERT: Exactly.

Activity 9

PRON SPOT: /ʃ/ as in shooting

a) she   show   shall   sh!   fish   push
   fished   pushed   rushed   washed   wished

b) demonstration   discussion   emotion   passionate   pollution

c) electrician   magician   mortician   physician   politician

d) chandelier   chateau   chiffon   chic   chaperone
   Charlotte   charade   chicane   chalet

e) She sells sea shells on the seashore.

STAR NAME *Cher*

UNIT 28

Activity 3

The white rhino is the largest of all rhinos. A large male may be two metres tall and weigh four tonnes. Rhinos are placid and gentle by nature but extremely nervous, which makes them panic when they think they are in danger. Thirty years ago, there were more than 5,000 white rhinos in Africa. Now there are fewer than 300 left.

Fifty years ago, it was common for a blue whale to reach thirty metres in length and to weigh as much as the combined weight of 1,500 people, or 24 elephants. During the last twenty years, whales of this length and size have completely disappeared. Even a 24-metre blue whale is now very rare.

At the time of the early colonisation of North America by Europeans, the passenger pigeon was easily the most common bird on the continent. There were probably 9 billion of these birds in existence. In the middle of the seventeenth century, someone noted that a passing flock or group of passenger pigeons was more than a kilometre wide, and nearly 300 kilometres long. Between 1700 and 1800, hunting reduced their numbers by 50 per cent. By 1900, they had almost completely disappeared. The last one died in a zoo on the 14th September 1914.

Activity 7

PRON SPOT: /dʒ/ as in danger

a) Japan   just   Germany   giant   bridge

b) Angela   Bridget   Jack   James   Jane   Joe (Joseph)
   Joy   Geoffrey   George   Gerald   Giles   Jeremy   Gillian
   Nigel   Roger

c) Gin and gigantic contain the /dʒ/ sound.

d) Jeremy, Gerald, Roger and Jane
   Met Jack and Jill on a German train
   Jack suggested playing a game
   Just close your eyes and shout a name
   Jeremy, Gerald and Roger played
   But Jane jumped off the train and said
   'The problem is just how hungry I am,
   I'd rather have some toast and jam!'

STAR NAME *John Major*

Activity 9

INTERVIEWER: Can you tell me something about your studies?
EMMA: Yes, I studied German and Russian at Cambridge University. I studied mostly literature, but I also studied quite a lot of the language. Why did you choose Russian?
EMMA: I chose Russian because ... well, it was a chance to start a new language at university and it seemed to be a very exciting language and quite a challenge. And I found Russian literature

EMMA: Yes, I did. I didn't want to go straight to Russia, to Moscow. I wanted to see some other country beforehand or I wanted to travel and get a broader view on the whole world. And also most people in England have a very European perspective on Russia and so I thought I would like to see the Asian perspective and so I decided to go to Asia, to Japan.

INTERVIEWER: And you've spent two years in Japan. What things were different from what you expected?

EMMA: Well, when I went over there, I didn't really have any expectations. I maybe had an image of a lot of very hard-working people and the neon lights of Tokyo and a very busy, busy lifestyle. When I arrived there, I guess Tokyo was as busy as I expected. One thing that did surprise me was how crazy the Japanese people could be in their spare time. I noticed this particularly while watching television. Television is quite bizarre. Other things, the food, I found, I found at first quite difficult, difficult to eat. I was quite ill the first time I had raw fish. But gradually I got to love the food. It's very, very good food. And the people are very, very generous and warm. I made some very good friends among the Japanese people.

UNIT 29

Activity 4

I think the most important changes will take place not in the field of business technology, but in the way we build and design homes. At the moment, there are a number of things that our houses can do ... they can turn on the heating, for example, and we can also put machines in our home that can take telephone messages. But the technology of all this is so old-fashioned! Very soon, we will be able to telephone our houses and tell them to start cooking dinner. And if the right ingredients for the food aren't in the kitchen, the house will be able to contact the food store and order the food, and then cook it when it arrives! Now that is real technology.

In order to raise money to finance public transport, we'll have to pay a lot more for the right to drive our own cars. And this means a number of things. First of all, the situation may soon arise when we won't be able to drive a car unless there are at least two passengers in it. Secondly, we will be in serious trouble if we drive too fast, not from the police but from a series of cameras and computers that are situated all along the road. They'll be able to photograph us and even to take money from our accounts to pay the fines! Now that's all wrong.

I think schools and businesses will benefit from the new technology. I'm worried that families won't be able to. I can foresee a time when people won't have to spend any time together. Each person in the family will eat, study, and relax entirely alone, in their own rooms. They will be able to do this because they will have their own personal technology for education, entertainment and even for eating.

Activity 6

PRON SPOT: /tʃ/ as in future

a) challenge change church choose chin future creature culture mixture nature

b) Tuesday tube fortune tulip tuna Tunisia tutor

c) aren't you? don't you? won't you? haven't you? didn't you? wouldn't you?

You're Italian, aren't you?
You live in Manchester, don't you?
You'll be here tomorrow, won't you?
You've received my letter, haven't you?
You did your homework, didn't you?
You'd like a cup of coffee, wouldn't you?

d) chaos character Christmas choir chorus chemist chemical technology

e) It's a challenge to change the furniture in the church.
Why do people confuse chicken and kitchen?
Children born on Tuesdays are natural creatures.
Charlie Chaplin challenged chess champions.

STAR NAME *Charlie Chaplin*

Activity 8

MARY: My name is Mary Windrush and I'm a fortune-teller.

INTERVIEWER: What do you have to do to become a fortune-teller?

MARY: You don't become a fortune-teller. You are a fortune-teller.

INTERVIEWER: Yes, but don't you have to study something? I don't know, the position of the planets, something like that?

MARY: A fortune-teller knows when he or she is a fortune-teller. You are born with the skills you need.

INTERVIEWER: I see. Now ...

MARY: I'd like to tell your fortune now, if I may.

INTERVIEWER: Well, that would be nice, but actually I'd like to find out more about your work.

MARY: Are you planning to visit a foreign country in the near future?

INTERVIEWER: No.

MARY: Hm. Have you got a secret ambition that involves travel?

INTERVIEWER: Well, it's not a secret, but yes I have.

MARY: What is this ambition?

INTERVIEWER: I want to go to travel through the rainforests.

MARY: I see. Well, I think you'll be able to do this quite soon.

INTERVIEWER: Really?

MARY: Yes, I can see you walking through the Amazon rainforests, in the next twelve months, probably.

INTERVIEWER: That's very nice. But actually, I want to visit the rainforests in Africa.

MARY: Hm. You won't be able to do that this year. You'll have to wait until next year.

INTERVIEWER: Have you got any predictions for the users of *Fastlane*?

MARY: Yes, I can foresee a very exciting future for all people who are involved in education, particularly young people who are learning English.

INTERVIEWER: Well, thank you very much, Mary, this has been very interesting.

MARY: Thank you. Enjoy your trip to Latin America.

INTERVIEWER: Africa.

MARY: No, Latin America. That's where you'll be going.

INTERVIEWER: Oh, right. OK, thank you.

UNIT 30

B3

This is the London and Scotland Railway information service. Due to engineering works, the following changes will take place on the London-Edinburgh line tomorrow, the 11th July.
The 9 o'clock train from London Kings Cross will not stop at Peterborough, and will arrive at Leeds at 10.50, departing at 10.55. From Leeds, the train will proceed directly to Durham, without stopping at intervening stations. It will arrive at Durham at midday, leaving at 12.05. From Durham, the train will proceed non-stop to Edinburgh, arriving at 12.45. The midday train from Kings Cross will stop at Peterborough, departing at the normal time, and will also stop at Leeds at 2 o'clock, departing at 2.05. The train will make all other scheduled stops, arriving 15 minutes later than advertised. The four o'clock train will leave 45 minutes later than scheduled. It will make all scheduled stops, with departure times 45 minutes later than advertised.

D COMPARATIVE PRON

1 /ʃ/ as in shooting, and /tʃ/ as in future.

STAR NAME *Charlie Sheen*

a) It's a shame to change the champagne, don't you think?
shame and champagne contain the /ʃ/ sound
change and don't you contain the /tʃ/ sound

Should we challenge the school chess team or shouldn't we?

should and shouldn't; challenge and chess

2 /ʒ/ as in explosion and /dʒ/ as in danger.

STAR NAMES *Zsa Zsa Gabor and John Lennon*

major decision	German precision
dangerous collision	Japanese television

Grammar Check

1 Answer these questions using *I'd prefer* or *I'd rather*.

a) Would you like some coffee?
b) Would you like to meet a famous politician?
c) Would you like to visit England?
d) Would you like to play chess?

2 Make these sentences negative.

a) You must finish your homework before you go home.
b) He had to apologise to the teacher after the accident.
c) You must finish that essay tonight.
d) You must say you're sorry, it was your fault.

3 *Mustn't* or *don't/doesn't have to*?

a) You ___ do this exercise if you don't want to.
b) It's free. You ___ pay.
c) You ___ say such terrible things about your grandmother.
d) She's having an operation later. She ___ eat or drink anything.
e) The office manager ___ arrive as early as everyone else.

4 *Should* or *shouldn't*?

a) People who have made mistakes ___ criticise others.
b) People ___ be cruel to animals.
c) It's hard to meet English people. They ___ try to meet more foreigners.
d) Young children ___ cross busy roads by themselves.

5 Complete these sentences using a comparative or superlative.

a) She's one of ___ opera singers of all time.
b) That test was ___ than the one we had last week.
c) He's 91. He's probably ___ person in the street.
d) There are three people who live ___ to the school than me.
e) That dress must be ___ one I've seen.
f) My aunt gave me £100 for my birthday. She's ___ person I know.
g) We're really late. Can you go a bit ___
h) Scottish people are ___ to understand than English people.

6 Suggest alternatives.

EXAMPLE: *If it's sunny, we'll play tennis.*
If it isn't sunny, we'll play cards.

a) If we arrive early, we'll go to the museum.
b) If Alan passes the exam, he'll go to university.
c) If they win, they'll be champions.

d) If she phones him, he'll apologise.
e) If I have time, I'll come and see you.
f) If she catches the first plane, she'll be home by midnight.
g) Wendy will be very angry if you forget her birthday.

1 Answer the questions below using the present simple. No short answers!

EXAMPLE: *Why does she leave the house so early?*
Because she starts work at 7am.

a) What does she do for a living?
b) Does she live in that house by herself?
c) Does he work?
d) What do they usually do at the weekends?
e) Where do her parents live?
f) Why doesn't she save money and live with them?
g) What's her ambition?

2 Put this story in the past, using the past simple or *used to*.

Every day, Sarah gets up at five o'clock, as she has to be at work by seven. She tries to make as little noise as possible because she doesn't want to wake up her brother Cyril. He stays in bed until midday and then goes to work as an engineer at a radio station. Sarah makes a cup of coffee and has something to eat when she arrives at the hospital. Cyril, on the other hand, eats some toast and honey. He also has a chocolate croissant when he arrives at work.

3 Write a second sentence using *used to*.

EXAMPLE: *He's a professional actor.*
He used to be a priest.

a) These apples are £3 a kilo! They ___
b) It only takes three hours to get to Paris these days. It ___
c) She lives in a small apartment in the centre of town. She ___
d) French soldiers do 12 months military service these days. They ___
e) The capital of Germany is Berlin. It ___
f) My uncle was a famous soccer star. He ___
g) These days, we always have fruit for breakfast. We ___

4 Make conditional sentences.

EXAMPLE: *We've got a dog, We can't spend the weekend with you.*
If we didn't have a dog, we could spend the weekend with you.

a) I haven't got any money. I can't afford a ticket for the concert.

b) She's over 16. She has to pay full fare on the bus.

c) Andrea doesn't speak English. She can't apply for the job.

d) Ben eats chocolate. He's putting on a lot of weight.

e) I have to do my homework. I can't go to the party.

f) My parents won't buy me a saxophone. They're too expensive.

g) I haven't got a screwdriver. I can't mend the door handle.

BLOCK THREE

1 Add *who*, *that* or *which* to the sentences below if necessary.

a) He's the man ___ told me about the job.

b) That's the computer ___ I learnt to type on.

c) The teacher ___ we had last year has resigned.

d) Is it your car ___ is making the funny noise?

e) The dog ___ my mother bought is a real nuisance.

f) The students ___ come in the afternoon are from a different school.

g) We mustn't use the plates ___ are in the cupboard on the left.

2 Answer these questions about yourself.

a) When will you be 50?

b) When will your next holiday start?

c) What time will you get home?

d) Who will you be with on Friday evening?

e) When will you finish these exercises?

f) What time will you start school tomorrow?

g) What lessons will you have?

3 Answer these questions using *I've never*.

a) What do you think of Shakespeare?

b) Do you like Korean food?

c) When did you last climb a mountain?

d) Is Mr Potts a nice man?

4 a) Apologise using the present perfect with *already*.

EXAMPLE: *Can I have my cake, please?*
*Sorry, I've **already** eaten it.*

1 Where's the rest of my money?

2 Can I do the crossword?

3 Can we open our presents now?

4 Can I have the last can of cola?

b) Ask questions using *yet*.

EXAMPLE: *Have you made your bed **yet**?*
Yes, I made it this morning.

1 Yes, I wrote to her last night.

2 Yes, I paid for it yesterday.

3 No, but I'm going to wash them this evening.

4 I don't get homework today.

c) Answer these questions using *still*.

EXAMPLE: *Where's Tom?*
*He's **still** in the shower.*

1 Did you get that new job?

2 Are you going out with Paul tonight?

3 How are you feeling?

4 Why are you walking? Where's your car?

BLOCK FOUR

1 Add *absolutely* to these sentences, if appropriate. If not, add a different modifier.

EXAMPLE: *She's **absolutely** brilliant at tennis.*

a) The football match was ___ fantastic.

b) She's 19, which is ___ young for a teacher.

c) I'm ___ delighted with my exam results, but my sister is ___ unhappy with hers.

d) Did you see that ___ amazing programme about dolphins?

e) I'm ___ certain that he is not responsible for the mistake.

f) The people who bought that yacht must be ___ rich. I'm ___ envious.

2 Complete these sentences with a suitable multi-word verb.

a) look: He spends three hours a day ___ his daughter.

b) catch: He was running so fast it was impossible to ___ him.

c) get: It's not unusual if you don't ___ your neighbours.

d) put: He asked if we could ___ three of his friends who had nowhere to stay.

e) end: We got completely lost and ___ in Wales.

3 Find a place in these sentences for a frequency adverb.

EXAMPLE: *I liked his girlfriend.*
*I **never** liked his girlfriend.*

a) I can understand why people think he's good-looking.

b) Do you have an evening meal with your family?

c) She's visited the Great Wall of China.

d) We must be careful when we're making accusations like that.

e) I wonder why we spend so much time watching TV.

4 a) What do you think the machine below is? Give more than one answer.

EXAMPLE: *It could be a boat, or ...*

b) Answer these questions using _might be_.

1 Who do you think that man is?
2 What do you think the time is?
3 Have you any idea where I put my glasses?
4 What does the author of this book do?

c) Make predictions using _may_.

1 How do you think United will do in the European Cup?
2 What are you and your family going to do in the summer?
3 How long will you stay at school?
4 What are you going to do on Sunday?

BLOCK FIVE

1 Complete the new sentences using the past simple or _used to_.

a) She works for an oil company. ___ last year.
b) We live in Paris. ___ in London.
c) The woman next door always goes skiing. ___ sailing last year.
d) Why do the people next door make so much noise? ___ last night?
e) Do you smoke? No I ___ a lot.

2 Make sentences using the past continuous.

EXAMPLE: _spaghetti/friend_
I **was cooking** spaghetti when my friend arrived.

a) book/telephone
b) letter/door
c) dog/friend
d) homework/noise
e) television/sister

3 a) Answer these questions, using the present perfect passive.

EXAMPLE: _What's happened to Alan? (arrest)_
He's **been arrested**.

1 Where's your bicycle? (steal)
2 Where are the Goya paintings? (sell)
3 What happened to Joan and Carol? (injure)
4 Where's my hat? (eat)
5 Is there any news about your wallet? (find)
6 What have they done to those old buildings in Ham Street? (demolish)

b) Now give more information, using the past passive.

EXAMPLE: _Alan **was arrested** by the police at his office yesterday._

4 Reported speech. What did the people actually say?

EXAMPLE: _She said she was very pleased to meet me._
'**I'm very pleased to meet you.**'

a) She said she didn't remember my name.
b) He told me he was Italian.
c) He said he was sure he'd met me before.

d) She asked me if I'd ever been to Spain.

BLOCK SIX

1 Add a non-defining clause for extra information.

EXAMPLE: _My uncle, **who lives in Liverpool**, is an engineer._

a) Her father works in a chocolate factory.
b) Rio de Janeiro has incredible natural beauty.
c) Our history teacher is called Mr Jordan.
d) Charles Dickens never finished the last novel he wrote.

2 a) Rewrite the sentences.

EXAMPLE: _The day was so beautiful._
**It was such a beautiful day.**

1) Those people were so nice.
2) That building used to be so ugly.
3) These flowers are so colourful.
4) That man is so annoying.

b) Now add more information to the sentences above.

EXAMPLE: _It was such a beautiful day **that we decided to have a picnic.**_

3 Make these sentences more realistic.

EXAMPLE: _We came to live in London nine hours ago._
We came to live in London **nine weeks ago**.

a) In the last few days, computers have revolutionised our lives.
b) Man first walked on the moon recently.
c) The first transatlantic flight took place a few days ago.
d) English has been spoken for the last few months.

4 Rewrite these sentences using _will_ or _won't be able to_, if appropriate.

a) I can't see you tomorrow.
b) I can visit Eurodisney when I'm in France.
c) I can't swim.
d) We can't stay until Monday.
e) She can speak three languages.

5 Make suggestions using _will have to_.

EXAMPLE: _I haven't finished my homework._
You'll **have to finish** it this afternoon.

a) She hasn't got enough money for the bus fare.
b) He needs to see the doctor, but there's a long queue.
c) I'm trying to ring my girlfriend but the line is busy.
d) They want to get a job in London.

The answers to the Grammar Check are in the Teacher's Book.

Word List

(be) afraid (of) (verb) *unit 1*

abandon (verb) *unit 27*

abroad (adverb) *unit 26*

absolutely (adverb) *unit 16*

absurd (adjective) *unit 25*

accelerate (verb) *unit 7*

accent (noun) *unit 20*

achieve (verb) *unit 1*

acoustic (adjective) *unit 4*

action (adjective) *unit 13*

active (adjective) *unit 26*

actor (noun) *unit 13*

actress (noun) *unit 8*

actually (adverb) *unit 1*

addict (noun) *unit 13*

addictive (adjective) *unit 6*

admiral (noun) *unit 20*

advertise (verb) *unit 12*

advertiser (noun) *unit 12*

advertising (adjective) *unit 2*

aero-engine (noun) *unit 7*

aerodrome (noun) *unit 8*

aeronautical (adjective) *unit 8*

afraid (adjective) *unit 7*

age (noun) *unit 2*

agriculture (noun) *unit 28*

aide (noun) *unit 24*

air (noun) *unit 1*

aircraft (noun) *unit 20*

airline (noun) *unit 1*

alarm (noun) *unit 25*

alert (adjective) *unit 14*

alien (noun) *unit 23*

alive (adjective) *unit 13*

almost (adverb) *unit 15*

alone (adjective) *unit 18*

alphabetical (adjective) *unit 19*

amazed (adjective) *unit 25*

amazement (noun) *unit 24*

amazing (adjective) *unit 16*

ambition (noun) *unit 1*

ambulance (noun) *unit 6*

amnesia (noun) *unit 12*

ancestor (noun) *unit 19*

ancestry (noun) *unit 19*

angle (noun) *unit 30*

angry (adjective) *unit 4*

animal (noun) *unit 11*

annoyed (adjective) *unit 25*

Antarctic Circle (noun) *unit 27*

anxiety (noun) *unit 18*

anxious (adjective) *unit 16*

apologise (verb) *unit 14*

appear (verb) *unit 4*

appoint (verb) *unit 5*

approximate (adjective) *unit 4*

Arctic (noun) *unit 27*

area (noun) *unit 4*

aristocrat (noun) *unit 10*

armed (adjective) *unit 10*

arrange (verb) *unit 8*

arrest (verb) *unit 23*

arrested (adjective) *unit 19*

art (noun) *unit 3*

artist (noun) *unit 4*

ash (noun) *unit 14*

assault (noun) *unit 22*

astonished (adjective) *unit 25*

astonishment (noun) *unit 24*

astronomer (noun) *unit 30*

athlete (noun) *unit 8*

atmosphere (noun) *unit 27*

attach to (verb) *unit 12*

attack (verb) *unit 25*

attempt (noun) *unit 7*

attend (verb) *unit 5*

attractive (adjective) *unit 3*

auctioneer (noun) *unit 23*

audience (noun) *unit 4*

autocue (noun) *unit 12*

available (adjective) *unit 12*

average (adjective) *unit 2*

avoid (verb) *unit 19*

award-winning (adjective) *unit 12*

awareness (noun) *unit 2*

awful (adjective) *unit 16*

bad-tempered (adjective) *unit 17*

balaclava (noun) *unit 22*

bank account (noun) *unit 29*

bare (adjective) *unit 4*

based (adjective) *unit 11*

battery (noun) *unit 30*

Bayeux tapestry (noun) *unit 30*

bear (noun) *unit 4*

beard (noun) *unit 20*

believable (adjective) *unit 10*

believe (verb) *unit 1*

benefit (verb) *unit 26*

best-selling (adjective) *unit 6*

beyond (preposition) *unit 30*

biscuit (noun) *unit 14*

bisect (verb) *unit 9*

bison (noun) *unit 28*

bite (verb) *unit 21*

blast off (verb) *unit 30*

blow up (verb) *unit 7*

blues (noun) *unit 16*

boil (verb) *unit 25*

border (noun) *unit 11*

bore (noun) *unit 18*

bored (adjective) *unit 25*

boring (adjective) *unit 12*

bottom (adjective) *unit 4*

brake (verb) *unit 2*

brand (noun) *unit 11*

break a record (verb) *unit 7*

break up (verb) *unit 17*

breathtaking (adjective) *unit 27*

bright (adjective) *unit 15*

broadcast (verb) *unit 4*

bucket (noun) *unit 2*

buffalo (noun) *unit 28*

bullring (noun) *unit 20*

bully (noun) *unit 11*

burger (noun) *unit 11*

burglary (noun) *unit 22*

burn (verb) *unit 14*

burn up (verb) *unit 27*

bury (verb) *unit 26*

bush (noun) *unit 15*

cable (noun) *unit 5*

calcium (noun) *unit 17*

call up (verb) *unit 29*

calory (noun) *unit 17*

campaign (noun) *unit 2*

camping (noun) *unit 11*

capitalist (adjective) *unit 26*

capture (adjective) *unit 6*

car (noun) *unit 14*

carbohydrate (noun) *unit 17*

care (noun) *unit 4*

career (noun) *unit 7*

carry on (verb) *unit 17*

cartoon (noun) *unit 11*

casino (noun) *unit 3*

castle (noun) *unit 7*

casual wear (adjective) *unit 23*

catch up with (verb) *unit 20*

cause (noun) *unit 10*

census (noun) *unit 19*

century (noun) *unit 5*

chain-smoker (noun) *unit 29*

chalet (noun) *unit 27*

chance (noun) *unit 4*

chandelier (noun) *unit 27*

channel (noun) *unit 4*

chaos (noun) *unit 29*

chaperone (noun) *unit 27*

character (noun) *unit 13*

charade (noun) *unit 27*

charismatic (adjective) *unit 10*

charity (noun) *unit 26*

chase (verb) *unit 18*

chateau (noun) *unit 27*

cheap (adjective) *unit 27*

check (verb) *unit 7*

check-in (noun) *unit 1*

chemical (adjective) *unit 29*

chemist (noun) *unit 29*

chic (adjective) *unit 27*

chicane (noun) *unit 27*

chief (noun) *unit 2*

chiffon (noun) *unit 27*

chip (noun) *unit 6*

chocolate (noun) *unit 24*

chorus (noun) *unit 29*

christen (verb) *unit 15*

cinema (noun) *unit 13*

classic (adjective) *unit 12*

clerk (noun) *unit 1*

climate (noun) *unit 3*

climb (verb) *unit 15*

cloth (noun) *unit 11*

clothing (noun) *unit 11*

clue (noun) *unit 19*

coast (noun) *unit 11*

code (noun) *unit 26*

coffin (noun) *unit 24*

college (noun) *unit 1*

collision (noun) *unit 26*

colonial (adjective) *unit 10*

colony (noun) *unit 9*

colourful (adjective) *unit 18*

coma (noun) *unit 14*

comb (noun) *unit 8*

comedian (noun) *unit 21*

comedy (noun) *unit 4*

comet (noun) *unit 27*

comfortable (adjective) *unit 3*

commerce (noun) *unit 26*

commercial (adjective) *unit 8*

commit (a crime) (verb) *unit 25*

common (adjective) *unit 1*

commonly (adjective) *unit 11*

company (noun) *unit 4*

compare to (verb) *unit 9*

compass (noun) *unit 12*

compile (verb) *unit 19*

complain (verb) *unit 1*

complaint (noun) *unit 14*

complex (adjective) *unit 9*

complicated (adjective) *unit 9*

computer (noun) *unit 1*

computerised (adjective) *unit 29*

concert (noun) *unit 4*

condense (verb) *unit 28*

confident (adjective) *unit 16*

confuse (with) (verb) *unit 19*

considerable (adjective) unit 9

constitute (verb) unit 9

contaminate (verb) unit 26

contestant (noun) unit 12

continue (verb) unit 11

convert (verb) unit 6

convict (verb) unit 22

convincingly (adverb) unit 10

cooker (noun) unit 17

core (noun) unit 18

cottage (noun) unit 25

cough (verb) unit 20

creature (noun) unit 9

crew (noun) unit 19

crime (noun) unit 22

criminal (noun) unit 21

cruel (adjective) unit 11

cruise (verb) unit 3

Cup Final (noun) unit 21

curly (adjective) unit 16

currently (adverb) unit 4

cycling (noun) unit 19

dairy (adjective) unit 17

damaged (adjective) unit 18

dampen down (verb) unit 2

danger (noun) unit 2

dark (adjective) unit 18

darling (adjective) unit 7

dashboard (noun) unit 22

database (noun) unit 12

date of birth (noun) unit 19

daughter-in-law (noun) unit 10

deal (noun) unit 2

deal with (verb) unit 2

decade (noun) unit 26

decision (noun) unit 26

dedicated (adjective) unit 4

deduct (verb) unit 29

defeat (verb) unit 6

degree (noun) unit 1

delay (noun) unit 1

delighted (adjective) unit 7

Democrat (adjective) unit 5

demolish (verb) unit 30

demonstrate (verb) unit 9

demonstration (noun) unit 27

denim (noun) unit 11

dense (adjective) unit 26

deposit account (noun) unit 29

depressed (adjective) unit 3

depressing (adjective) unit 18

descendant (noun) unit 5

describe (verb) unit 21

desert (noun) unit 9

design (verb) unit 11

destroy (verb) unit 24

destroyed (adjective) unit 18

destruction (noun) unit 18

detect (verb) unit 22

detective (noun) unit 22

diabetic (adjective) unit 14

die (verb) unit 5

dig (verb) unit 2

digital (adjective) unit 6

dilemma (noun) unit 26

dine (verb) unit 17

dinosaur (noun) unit 28

diplomat (noun) unit 2

disappointed (adjective) unit 25

disappointing (adjective) unit 25

disbelief (noun) unit 24

disc jockey (noun) unit 4

disclosure (noun) unit 26

discover (verb) unit 9

discrimination (noun) unit 2

discussion (noun) unit 27

disgusting (adjective) unit 3

display (noun) unit 14

display (verb) unit 6

distinguish (verb) unit 2

documentary (noun) unit 12

dolphin (noun) unit 20

dominate (verb) unit 14

dramatic (adjective) unit 3

dramatically (adjective) unit 30

drawer (noun) unit 10

dream (noun) unit 18

dream (verb) unit 7

dry (verb) unit 25

dull (adjective) unit 3

dusty (adjective) unit 20

duty (noun) unit 3

earthquake (noun) unit 26

effect (noun) unit 6

effective (adjective) unit 12

elect (verb) unit 5

electric (adjective) unit 5

electrician (noun) unit 27

electronically (adverb) unit 29

embark on (verb) unit 7

embarrassing (adjective) unit 23

emergency (noun) unit 2

emergency service (noun) unit 29

emotion (noun) unit 27

employ (verb) unit 2

emptiness (noun) unit 18

enclosure (noun) unit 26

encourage (verb) unit 7

end up (verb) unit 17

enemy (noun) unit 23

engineer (noun) unit 23

engineering (noun) unit 1

enthusiastic (adjective) unit 1

entrance (noun) unit 9

envious (adjective) unit 10

environmentalist (noun) unit 28

equipment (noun) unit 2

erupt (verb) unit 25

eruption (noun) unit 26

escalator (noun) unit 21

escape (verb) unit 6

especially (adverb) unit 1

essential (adjective) unit 3

estimate (verb) unit 30

estimated (adjective) unit 4

eventually (adverb) unit 11

evidence (noun) unit 22

evil (adjective) unit 6

evolution (noun) unit 28

examine (verb) unit 12

exceptional (adjective) unit 26

excited (adjective) unit 1

exciting (adjective) unit 3

exercise (noun) unit 17

exhausted (adjective) unit 24

exist (verb) unit 14

existence (noun) unit 26

expand (verb) unit 4

expect (verb) unit 1

expedition (noun) unit 26

expensive (adjective) unit 3

experience (noun) unit 14

expert (noun) unit 12

exploded unit 1

explosive (noun) unit 2

exposure (noun) unit 26

express (verb) unit 1

extinct (adjective) unit 24

extraordinary (adjective) unit 16

extrovert (adjective) unit 16

facial (adjective) unit 9

facility (noun) unit 2

failure (noun) unit 14

fair (adjective) unit 6

false (adjective) unit 17

family tree (noun) unit 19

famous (adjective) unit 7

fan (noun) unit 14

fan letter (noun) unit 30

fantastic (adjective) unit 3

fare (noun) unit 4

fast food (noun) unit 11

fat (adjective) unit 10

fault (noun) unit 26

favourite (adjective) unit 6

fear (noun) unit 23

fence (noun) unit 2

fertile (adjective) unit 26

fiasco (noun) unit 23

film (noun) unit 13

finance (verb) unit 7

fingerprint (noun) unit 22

firefighter (noun) unit 2

fix (verb) unit 6

flame (noun) unit 2

flash (verb) unit 25

flight (noun) unit 3

flight of stairs (noun) unit 21

flood (noun) unit 24

fluently (adverb) unit 16

fog (noun) unit 8

folk music (noun) unit 18

food (noun) unit 17

footwear (noun) unit 11

forest (noun) unit 9

forever (adverb) unit 12

forgery (noun) unit 24

fortunately (adverb) unit 6

fortune-teller (noun) unit 29

franglais (adjective) unit 30

fraud (noun) unit 22

free (adjective) unit 4

freelance journalist (noun) unit 23

freezer (noun) unit 17

fridge (noun) unit 17

fried (adjective) unit 17

friendship (noun) unit 10

frightened (adjective) unit 18

fuel (noun) unit 8

funeral (noun) unit 13

funny (adjective) unit 21

fur (noun) unit 28

furious (adjective) unit 16

furthest (superlative) unit 3

fuse (noun) unit 2

future (noun) unit 1

gain (verb) unit 16

game show (noun) unit 12

gardener (noun) unit 2

gear (noun) unit 23

geese (noun) unit 25

genealogist (noun) unit 19

General strike (noun) unit 12

generation (noun) unit 9

generous (adjective) unit 20

gesture (noun) unit 21

get away with (verb) unit 20

get on with (verb) unit 20

get rid of (verb) unit 12

giant (adjective) unit 28

gig (noun) unit 28

gigantic (adjective) unit 28

give up (verb) unit 17

glamorous (adjective) unit 13

glove (noun) unit 25

glue (noun) unit 19

goal (noun) unit 1

gold (adjective) unit 20

Gold Rush (noun) unit 11

good (noun) unit 11

go on (verb) 17

gorgeous (adjective) unit 16

government minister (noun) *unit 24*

governor (noun) *unit 5*

graffiti (noun) *unit 24*

grammar (noun) *unit 20*

grandparent (noun) *unit 6*

grand prix (noun) *unit 2*

graphic (noun) *unit 6*

greasy (adjective) *unit 17*

great-aunt (noun) *unit 19*

great-granddaughter (noun) *unit 19*

great-grandfather (noun) *unit 19*

great-grandmother (noun) *unit 19*

great-grandson (noun) *unit 19*

great-neice (noun) *unit 19*

great-nephew (noun) *unit 19*

great-uncle (noun) *unit 19*

greengrocer (noun) *unit 2*

guard (noun) *unit 10*

guardian (noun) *unit 26*

guess (noun) *unit 14*

guilt (noun) *unit 18*

guilty (adjective) *unit 18*

gum (noun) *unit 12*

gunfight (noun) *unit 10*

gunfighter (noun) *unit 10*

habitat (noun) *unit 9*

haircut (noun) *unit 24*

hairdresser (noun) *unit 5*

half-naked (adjective) *unit 25*

halfway (adjective) *unit 10*

hamster (noun) *unit 6*

handbag (noun) *unit 2*

handful (noun) *unit 13*

handy (adjective) *unit 2*

hang (verb) *unit 6*

hanged (adjective) *unit 10*

harpoon (noun) *unit 24*

headquarters (noun) *unit 4*

health (noun) *unit 5*

healthy (adjective) *unit 23*

height (noun) *unit 1*

heir (noun) *unit 4*

helpful (adjective) *unit 21*

hero (noun) *unit 6*

hijack (verb) *unit 22*

high energy (adjective) *unit 6*

highly (adverb) *unit 24*

historic (adjective) *unit 30*

hitchhike (verb) *unit 3*

hive (noun) *unit 9*

holistic (adjective) *unit 17*

homesick (adjective) *unit 3*

hope (verb) *unit 18*

horoscope (noun) *unit 27*

horror (adjective) *unit 13*

hosepipe (noun) *unit 2*

hospital (noun) *unit 15*

however (adverb) *unit 1*

huge (adjective) *unit 18*

hunt (verb) *unit 28*

hunter (noun) *unit 12*

hurry (verb) *unit 21*

hurt (verb) *unit 14*

ice age (noun) *unit 24*

ideal (adjective) *unit 26*

identify (verb) *unit 9*

illegal (adjective) *unit 5*

imagine (verb) *unit 18*

immediate (adjective) *unit 4*

immigration (noun) *unit 4*

impatient (adjective) *unit 1*

impressed (adjective) *unit 25*

impressive (adjective) *unit 27*

imprisonment (noun) *unit 5*

improvised (adjective) *unit 21*

incomprehensible (adjective) *unit 30*

incredible (adjective) *unit 3*

incredibly (adverb) *unit 4*

independent (adjective) *unit 4*

indicate (verb) *unit 9*

individual (noun) *unit 11*

individuality (noun) *unit 11*

in excess of *unit 2*

inform (verb) *unit 9*

in power (adjective) *unit 5*

insist (verb) *unit 15*

instant (adjective) *unit 4*

instantly (adverb) *unit 7*

instead (adverb) *unit 26*

instruction (noun) *unit 2*

intellectual (noun) *unit 12*

intelligent (adjective) *unit 9*

inter (verb) *unit 24*

interest (noun) *unit 1*

interview (noun) *unit 1*

invade (verb) *unit 6*

invasion (noun) *unit 19*

inventive (adjective) *unit 23*

involve (verb) *unit 6*

involve in (verb) *unit 10*

iron (noun) *unit 17*

iron (verb) *unit 15*

irritating (adjective) *unit 27*

jazz (noun) *unit 16*

jet lag (adjective) *unit 1*

jewellery (noun) *unit 22*

Jewish (noun) *unit 19*

joke (noun) *unit 18*

journey (noun) *unit 6*

judge (noun) *unit 22*

judo (noun) *unit 17*

jug (noun) *unit 7*

jungle (noun) *unit 9*

jury (noun) *unit 22*

keep (verb) *unit 20*

key (noun) *unit 14*

kidnap (verb) *unit 22*

kill (verb) *unit 13*

kiosk (noun) *unit 22*

knowledge (noun) *unit 2*

label (noun) *unit 4*

lane (noun) *unit 16*

lap (noun) *unit 10*

laser beam (noun) *unit 27*

last (adjective) *unit 10*

laugh (verb) *unit 21*

laundry (noun) *unit 30*

lava (noun) *unit 26*

lawyer (noun) *unit 5*

lazy (adjective) *unit 12*

leather jacket (noun) *unit 24*

legend (noun) *unit 24*

leisure (noun) *unit 26*

level (noun) *unit 6*

lie (noun) *unit 5*

life (noun) *unit 5*

lifeblood (noun) *unit 26*

lifestyle (noun) *unit 13*

lift (noun) *unit 1*

lightning (noun) *unit 27*

lime (noun) *unit 17*

limit (noun) *unit 2*

limousine (noun) *unit 8*

lion (noun) *unit 21*

literary (adjective) *unit 30*

literature (noun) *unit 15*

litter (noun) *unit 20*

live (adjective) *unit 4*

lively (adjective) *unit 12*

local (adjective) *unit 1*

located (adjective) *unit 20*

location (noun) *unit 10*

long for (verb) *unit 7*

look for (verb) *unit 17*

look forward to (verb) *unit 20*

lost (adjective) *unit 10*

lunar eclipse (noun) *unit 27*

luxury (adjective) *unit 8*

machinery (noun) *unit 1*

madness (noun) *unit 12*

magic (adjective) *unit 6*

magician (noun) *unit 27*

magma (noun) *unit 26*

magnificent (adjective) *unit 9*

mail (noun) *unit 16*

mail train (noun) *unit 25*

major (adjective) *unit 4*

male (noun) *unit 16*

mammal (noun) *unit 9*

manufacture (verb) *unit 11*

manufacturer (noun) *unit 7*

mark homework (verb) *unit 29*

material (adjective) *unit 26*

material (noun) *unit 4*

mausoleum (noun) *unit 24*

maximum (adjective) *unit 12*

meander (verb) *unit 20*

meaning (noun) *unit 10*

means (noun) *unit 4*

measure (verb) *unit 26*

medal (noun) *unit 20*

medium (adjective) *unit 16*

member (noun) *unit 1*

memorable (adjective) *unit 14*

mentality (noun) *unit 26*

mere (adjective) *unit 23*

mess (noun) *unit 15*

message (noun) *unit 9*

meteor (noun) *unit 27*

meteorite (noun) *unit 27*

meteoroid (noun) *unit 27*

method (noun) *unit 12*

miaow (verb) *unit 10*

Middle Ages (noun) *unit 24*

military (adjective) *unit 23*

mineral (noun) *unit 17*

miss (verb) *unit 3*

mission (noun) *unit 30*

missionary (noun) *unit 26*

misspelt (adjective) *unit 18*

mixture (noun) *unit 4*

model (adjective) *unit 20*

modem (noun) *unit 29*

monster (noun) *unit 13*

mood (noun) *unit 16*

moody (adjective) *unit 16*

moral (noun adjective) *unit 26*

mortician (noun) *unit 27*

mother tongue (noun) *unit 30*

motorway (noun) *unit 28*

mountaineer (noun) *unit 23*

movement (noun) *unit 6*

movie (noun) *unit 4*

multimedia (adjective) *unit 29*

multiscreen (adjective) *unit 13*

murder (noun) *unit 22*

murderer (noun) *unit 22*

muscular (adjective) *unit 16*

musician (noun) *unit 2*

naked (adjective) *unit 2*

narrative (noun) *unit 18*

nationality (noun) *unit 4*

natural (adjective) *unit 9*

nearby (adjective) *unit 25*

negative (adjective) *unit 20*

neglect (to) (verb) *unit 20*

nervous (adjective) *unit 15*

newsmaker (noun) *unit 12*

nickname (noun) *unit 15*

nightmare (noun) *unit 18*

non-polar (adjective) *unit 27*

Norman conquest (noun) *unit 30*

northern lights (noun) *unit 27*

nowadays (adjective) *unit 8*

nutrient (noun) *unit 26*

oak (noun) *unit 20*
oar (noun) *unit 24*
obstacle (noun) *unit 6*
occur (verb) *unit 13*
odd (adjective) *unit 20*
old-fashioned (adjective) *unit 16*
olive oil (noun) *unit 17*
on board (adjective) *unit 30*
open (adjective) *unit 1*
operate (verb) *unit 4*
opinion (noun) *unit 10*
opportunity (noun) *unit 3*
order (noun) *unit 19*
ordinary (adjective) *unit 10*
organise (verb) *unit 2*
originally (adverb) *unit 11*
otherwise (adjective) *unit 9*
out of work (adjective) *unit 4*
overboard (adverb) *unit 24*
overcoat (noun) *unit 21*
overpaid (adjective) *unit 14*
overseas (adjective) *unit 29*
overtake (verb) *unit 7*
pack (verb) *unit 11*
painful (adjective) *unit 25*
pair (noun) *unit 4*
paradise (noun) *unit 28*
parcel (noun) *unit 18*
parrot (noun) *unit 6*
passionate (adjective) *unit 27*
passport (noun) *unit 13*
patient (adjective) *unit 1*
peak (noun) *unit 26*
pear (noun) *unit 4*
perform (verb) *unit 6*
performance (noun) *unit 14*
personally (adverb) *unit 9*
pessimistic (adjective) *unit 10*
petrol gauge (noun) *unit 22*
phosphorus (noun) *unit 26*
physician (noun) *unit 27*
pilot (noun) *unit 1*
pine (verb) *unit 17*
pioneer (noun) *unit 7*
plain (adjective) *unit 16*

plain (noun) *unit 12*
plan (noun) *unit 5*
planet (noun) *unit 23*
playwright (noun) *unit 25*
pleasure (noun) *unit 26*
plesiosaur (noun) *unit 24*
plough (verb) *unit 22*
poet (noun) *unit 15*
politician (noun) *unit 27*
pollution (noun) *unit 27*
poor (adjective) *unit 5*
popular (adjective) *unit 1*
pornography (noun) *unit 15*
portrait (noun) *unit 10*
position (noun) *unit 5*
potassium (noun) *unit 26*
powder (noun) *unit 11*
power (noun) *unit 8*
powerful (adjective) *unit 12*
precede (verb) *unit 30*
precision (noun) *unit 26*
predict (verb) *unit 12*
prefer (verb) *unit 1*
preferably (adverb) *unit 2*
pregnant (adjective) *unit 10*
premises (noun) *unit 2*
prevention (noun) *unit 2*
priest (noun) *unit 2*
print out (verb) *unit 12*
prison (noun) *unit 5*
prize (noun) *unit 7*
process (noun) *unit 1*
produce (verb) *unit 9*
programmer (noun) *unit 6*
programme (noun) *unit 4*
protection (noun) *unit 11*
protein (noun) *unit 17*
Protestant (adjective) *unit 10*
proud (adjective) *unit 1*
prove (verb) *unit 19*
provincial (adjective) *unit 20*
provisional driving licence (noun) *unit 24*
pull into (verb) *unit 22*
pullover (noun) *unit 21*
pull someone's leg (verb) *unit 24*
punk (adjective) *unit 15*
purse (noun) *unit 20*
put out (verb) *unit 11*
put up with (verb) *unit 20*

puzzled (adjective) *unit 25*
pyjama (noun) *unit 25*
pyramid (noun) *unit 13*
qualification (noun) *unit 20*
qualify (verb) *unit 5*
quantity (noun) *unit 11*
quite (adverb) *unit 1*
race (noun) *unit 24*
racing (adjective) *unit 2*
racism (noun) *unit 4*
racist (adjective) *unit 27*
railway station (noun) *unit 21*
rainbow (noun) *unit 27*
rainbow-shaped (adjective) *unit 27*
range (noun) *unit 26*
rare (adjective) *unit 4*
rather (adverb) *unit 1*
realise (verb) *unit 10*
receive (verb) *unit 6*
receptionist (noun) *unit 2*
recognise (verb) *unit 9*
recommend (verb) *unit 10*
record-breaking (adjective) *unit 7*
recording (noun) *unit 4*
recover (verb) *unit 25*
red-haired (adjective) *unit 20*
reform (verb) *unit 5*
refuelling (noun) *unit 8*
refuse (verb) *unit 14*
regularly (adjective) *unit 26*
related (to) (adjective) *unit 19*
relationship (noun) *unit 7*
relaxed (adjective) *unit 16*
release (verb) *unit 4*
reliable (adjective) *unit 15*
relieved (adjective) *unit 7*
remark (noun) *unit 14*
remind (so) of (st) (verb) *unit 18*
rent (verb) *unit 7*
repair (noun) *unit 8*
reptile (noun) *unit 28*
request (noun) *unit 14*
research (noun) *unit 9*
resemble (verb) *unit 24*
resign (verb) *unit 17*
respond (verb) *unit 2*
responsible (for) (adjective) *unit 19*
restaurant (noun) *unit 11*

restaurateur (noun) *unit 24*
retired (adjective) *unit 7*
reverse (verb) *unit 10*
review (noun) *unit 10*
revision (noun) *unit 26*
revolutionary (adjective) *unit 23*
rhyme (noun) *unit 17*
road block (noun) *unit 22*
roar (verb) *unit 21*
robber (noun) *unit 22*
robbery (noun) *unit 22*
robot (noun) *unit 6*
rock and roll (adjective) *unit 18*
romantic (adjective) *unit 13*
rough (adjective) *unit 12*
round-up (noun) *unit 12*
route (noun) *unit 19*
rubbish tip (noun) *unit 28*
rugby (noun) *unit 12*
rule (noun) *unit 10*
run out (verb) *unit 22*
rural (adjective) *unit 25*
Russian (noun) *unit 1*
sacred (adjective) *unit 26*
sailor (noun) *unit 16*
saloon (noun) *unit 10*
salt (noun) *unit 17*
savings account (noun) *unit 29*
scandal (noun) *unit 12*
scared (adjective) *unit 15*
scarf (noun) *unit 21*
scene (noun) *unit 2*
scenery (noun) *unit 3*
scientist (noun) *unit 6*
scoring (noun) *unit 6*
scream (verb) *unit 13*
screen (noun) *unit 6*
script (noun) *unit 12*
scurry (verb) *unit 9*
search (verb) *unit 11*
seasick (adjective) *unit 3*
seatbelt (noun) *unit 20*
seating plan (noun) *unit 29*
second (adjective) *unit 10*
second-hand (adjective) *unit 11*
secret (adjective) *unit 5*
security feature (noun) *unit 22*
semi-skimmed (adjective) *unit 17*

sense of humour (noun) *unit 11*
sensitive (adjective) *unit 16*
sentence (s.o) to (verb) *unit 5*
separate (verb) *unit 26*
serious (adjective) *unit 1*
several (adjective) *unit 1*
shadow (noun) *unit 7*
shake one's head (verb) *unit 21*
shame (noun) *unit 30*
shave (verb) *unit 25*
shaving foam (noun) *unit 25*
shed (noun) *unit 2*
sherpa (noun) *unit 26*
shift (noun) *unit 2*
shipmate (noun) *unit 24*
shirt (noun) *unit 21*
shocked (adjective) *unit 25*
shooting star (noun) *unit 27*
shout (verb) *unit 22*
shower (noun) *unit 25*
signal box (noun) *unit 25*
silent (adjective) *unit 16*
skateboard (noun) *unit 1*
sketch (noun) *unit 21*
skill (noun) *unit 1*
skimmed (adjective) *unit 17*
sleepy (adjective) *unit 18*
slipper (noun) *unit 25*
slope (noun) *unit 26*
smart card (noun) *unit 29*
smell (verb) *unit 5*
snow covered (adjective) *unit 26*
snowball (noun) *unit 27*
snowstorm (noun) *unit 24*
soap opera (noun) *unit 11*
soccer (noun) *unit 14*
socks (noun) *unit 21*
soil (noun) *unit 25*
solar eclipse (noun) *unit 27*
sole (adjective) *unit 20*
solve (verb) *unit 25*
sophisticated (adjective) *unit 1*
soul (noun) *unit 25*
sound (noun) *unit 9*
sound like (verb) *unit 15*
sour (adjective) *unit 25*

source (noun) *unit 9*

southern (adjective) *unit 11*

southern lights (noun) *unit 27*

spacious (adjective) *unit 15*

specialist (adjective) *unit 29*

species (noun) *unit 9*

specific (adjective) *unit 12*

spectator (noun) *unit 14*

speculation (noun) *unit 9*

speed (verb) *unit 22*

spell (verb) *unit 3*

spiky (adjective) *unit 16*

spill (verb) *unit 13*

splendid (adjective) *unit 7*

sponsor (verb) *unit 1*

spread (verb) *unit 14*

squadron (noun) *unit 1*

square (noun) *unit 4*

screech to a halt (verb) *unit 25*

stadium (noun) *unit 14*

staff (noun) *unit 2*

stair (noun) *unit 4*

stand for (verb) *unit 4*

stare (verb) *unit 4*

state (noun) *unit 16*

statement (noun) *unit 30*

steal (verb) *unit 5*

steer (verb) *unit 23*

steward (noun) *unit 1*

stewardess (noun) *unit 1*

store (verb) *unit 6*

stove (noun) *unit 18*

straight (adjective) *unit 16*

stranded (adjective) *unit 24*

strict (adjective) *unit 10*

struggle (verb) *unit 25*

studio (noun) *unit 4*

stunning (adjective) *unit 12*

style (noun) *unit 11*

stylish (adjective) *unit 11*

subject (noun) *unit 29*

substance (noun) *unit 5*

subterranean (adjective) *unit 26*

succeed (verb) *unit 1*

success (noun) *unit 4*

success story (noun) *unit 30*

sudden (adjective) *unit 12*

suddenly (adverb) *unit 18*

suggest (verb) *unit 21*

suggestion (noun) *unit 26*

suit (noun) *unit 19*

summary (noun) *unit 10*

sunrise (noun) *unit 3*

sunset (noun) *unit 27*

supervise (verb) *unit 2*

supplement (verb) *unit 20*

support (verb) *unit 25*

supporter (noun) *unit 14*

supportive (adjective) *unit 26*

suppose (verb) *unit 10*

surgeon (noun) *unit 24*

surprised (adjective) *unit 25*

survey (noun) *unit 19*

survival (noun) *unit 9*

swallow (verb) *unit 24*

sweet (noun) *unit 5*

sword (noun) *unit 24*

system (noun) *unit 1*

tail (noun) *unit 27*

tailored (adjective) *unit 11*

take over (verb) *unit 6*

take up (verb) *unit 17*

talented (adjective) *unit 16*

tall story (noun) *unit 24*

task (noun) *unit 6*

tear (noun) *unit 23*

tear (noun verb) *unit 4*

techno (adjective) *unit 6*

technological (adverb) *unit 29*

technology (noun) *unit 1*

teenage (adjective) *unit 25*

teenager (noun) *unit 4*

teeth (noun) *unit 17*

tell (verb) *unit 5*

tell a joke (verb) *unit 21*

temple (noun) *unit 26*

temporary (adjective) *unit 16*

tense (noun) *unit 3*

tent (noun) *unit 11*

terrified (adjective) *unit 7*

terrifying (adjective) *unit 15*

theft (noun) *unit 22*

theme (noun) *unit 18*

theory (noun) *unit 20*

therapist (noun) *unit 17*

thief (noun) *unit 20*

thought (noun) *unit 10*

thriller (adjective) *unit 13*

ticket (noun) *unit 21*

ticket office (noun) *unit 21*

tie (noun) *unit 21*

tie (verb) *unit 17*

tight (adjective) *unit 17*

till (noun) *unit 22*

time-span (noun) *unit 28*

tin (noun) *unit 21*

toast (noun) *unit 18*

ton (noun) *unit 27*

top (adjective) *unit 10*

torchlight *unit 2*

tough (adjective) *unit 12*

trace (verb) *unit 19*

track (noun) *unit 9*

traffic congestion (noun) *unit 21*

traffic lights (noun) *unit 22*

train (verb) *unit 3*

trainer (noun) *unit 15*

training (noun) *unit 1*

transport (noun) *unit 4*

travelcard (noun) *unit 24*

treadmill (noun) *unit 26*

treasure (noun) *unit 3*

trial (noun) *unit 22*

trousers (noun) *unit 21*

turbulence (noun) *unit 1*

tutor (noun) *unit 29*

typhoid (noun) *unit 10*

ultrasound (noun) *unit 9*

unattended (adjective) *unit 2*

underwear (noun) *unit 21*

undoubtedly (adverb) *unit 3*

unemployed (adjective) *unit 4*

unfortunately (adverb) *unit 22*

unhelpful (adjective) *unit 27*

university (noun) *unit 1*

unknown (adjective) *unit 4*

unlikely (adjective) *unit 24*

unpleasant (adjective) *unit 3*

unsafe (adjective) *unit 14*

untidy (adjective) *unit 20*

valley (noun) *unit 20*

van (noun) *unit 6*

variety (noun) *unit 15*

vary (from) (verb) *unit 20*

vegetarian (noun) *unit 17*

victorious (adjective) *unit 30*

video (noun) *unit 4*

viewer (noun) *unit 4*

villain (noun) *unit 6*

violence (noun) *unit 15*

violent (adjective) *unit 27*

vision (noun) *unit 26*

visually (adverb) *unit 12*

vital (adjective) *unit 26*

volcano (noun) *unit 25*

volunteer (noun) *unit 3*

wander (verb) *unit 28*

warning (noun) *unit 18*

waterproof (adjective) *unit 11*

wave (noun) *unit 16*

wavy (adjective) *unit 16*

wealth (noun) *unit 26*

weapon (noun) *unit 23*

weave (verb) *unit 11*

wedding (noun) *unit 13*

wedding dress (noun) *unit 21*

weigh (verb) *unit 16*

weight (noun) *unit 16*

well-paid (adjective) *unit 3*

whale (noun) *unit 23*

whisper (verb) *unit 14*

white rhino (noun) *unit 28*

wick (noun) *unit 2*

wild (noun) *unit 9*

winding (adjective) *unit 26*

wine (noun) *unit 17*

witness (noun) *unit 22*

wolf (noun) *unit 13*

worldwide (adjective) *unit 12*

world champion (noun) *unit 14*

World Cup (noun) *unit 14*

worm (noun) *unit 14*

worry (verb) *unit 1*

wounded (adjective) *unit 10*